The First Few Minutes
of Spanish Language Films

The First Few Minutes of Spanish Language Films

Early Cues Reveal the Essence

RICHARD K. CURRY

McFarland & Company, Inc., Publishers
Jefferson, North Carolina

LIBRARY OF CONGRESS CATALOGUING-IN-PUBLICATION DATA

Names: Curry, Richard K., author.
Title: The first few minutes of Spanish language films : early cues reveal the essence / Richard K. Curry.
Description: Jefferson, N.C. : McFarland & Company, Inc., Publishers, 2017. | Includes bibliographical references and index. | Includes filmography.
Identifiers: LCCN 2016056949 | ISBN 9781476665887 (softcover : acid free paper) ∞
Subjects: LCSH: Motion pictures—Spain—History and criticism. | Motion pictures, Spanish—History and criticism.
Classification: LCC PN1993.5.S7 C85 2017 | DDC 791.430946—dc23
LC record available at https://lccn.loc.gov/2016056949

BRITISH LIBRARY CATALOGUING DATA ARE AVAILABLE

ISBN (print) 978-1-4766-6588-7
ISBN (ebook) 978-1-4766-2723-6

© 2017 Richard K. Curry. All rights reserved

No part of this book may be reproduced or transmitted in any form or by any means, electronic or mechanical, including photocopying or recording, or by any information storage and retrieval system, without permission in writing from the publisher.

Front cover images © 2017 iStock

Printed in the United States of America

McFarland & Company, Inc., Publishers
  Box 611, Jefferson, North Carolina 28640
  www.mcfarlandpub.com

For mac,
for my children,
for all the students who have heard
this over the years,
and for all the directors whose work
continues to provoke, inspire and amaze.

Table of Contents

Preface	1
Introduction: In the First Few Minutes: *An Approach to Reading Film*	3
1. Through a Child's Eyes: Víctor Erice's 1973 *El espíritu de la colmena* *(The Spirit of the Beehive)*	27
2. Reflections of Art and Life: Carlos Saura's Flamenco Trilogy: *Bodas de sangre* (1981); *Carmen* (1983); *El amor brujo* (1986) *(Blood Wedding; Carmen; Love, the Magician)*	42
3. Through a Woman's Eyes: Maria Luisa Bemberg's 1984 *Camila*	64
4. From Bystanding to Standing For: Luis Puenzo's 1985 *La historia oficial* *(The Official Story/Version)*	83
5. For the Lack of: Tomás Gutiérrez Alea's 1993 *Fresa y chocolate* *(Strawberry and Chocolate)*	102
6. Dream Story: Alejandro Amenábar's 1996 *Abre los ojos* *(Open Your Eyes)*	120
7. Sins of Our Fathers: Carlos Carrera's 2002 *El crimen del Padre Amaro* *(The Crime of Father Amaro)*	139

8. The Need to See and Be Seen:
   Icíar Bollaín's 2003 *Te doy mis ojos*
   (Take My Eyes) 159

Filmography 179
Chapter Notes 194
Bibliography 206
Index 223

Preface

The present volume brings together ideas and texts that extend over a period of many years, and they are coextensive with the larger part of my research and teaching in Hispanic film. Some of the ideas have already appeared in other frameworks; others have remained in unpublished or class discussion form until now. In organizing these texts now, I have sought to place them into wider scholarly dialogue as well as to share the special relationship that I have enjoyed with them.

The American Association of Teachers of Spanish and Portuguese dedicated the September 2015 issue of its official journal *Hispania* to "The Scholarship of Film and Film Studies," as it recognizes that "[f]ilm is a powerful vehicle for learning (about) languages and cultures at all levels of instruction; [and it] captures our student's attention and invites them to consider unique perspectives" (383); and that "what we say about film ... will determine our future relevance and success" (388). The first time I taught a Spanish film class was 1983, and for these many years I have continued to teach Hispanic film courses, with the very objectives that the AATSP would have its members target. These courses have been immersive experiences in Spanish-language filmic humanities texts for practice of linguistic, cultural, and critical thinking skills. Film study has been a training for close reading with the premise that is repeated in this book; the belief that a cogent close reading that produces a fundamental understanding of a text is the absolute requirement in order to sustain critical analysis, promote meaningful discussions of larger sociocultural issues, and engage in interdisciplinary practice. The approach herein employed is an outgrowth of a desire to create lifelong lovers of film.

This book would not have been possible were it not for a faculty development leave from Texas A & M University, and I am grateful to my university for the time and support it has afforded me. I am also grateful for all of those friends and colleagues who have read portions of this volume and have generously offered their wisdom and advice. I am grateful to professors and colleagues along the way who have contributed to my ability to analyze, appreciate, and think; and special among them are Dámaso Alonso, María José Chaves Abad, Rob Englert, Miguel J. Flys, Mercedes Junquera, Leonel Menéndez, Michel Valentin, and Emil Volek.

INTRODUCTION
In the First Few Minutes:
An Approach to Reading Film

> You never get a second chance to make a good first impression.
> —Will Rogers

Julio Cortázar opened his monumental 1963 novel *Rayuela* with a "Table of Instructions" ("Tablero de Dirección") for the reader. It reads:

> In its own way, this book consists of many books, but two books above all.
>
> The first can be read in a normal fashion and it ends with Chapter 56, at the close of which there are three garish little stars that stand for the words *The End*. Consequently, the reader may ignore what follows with a clean conscience.
>
> The second should be read by beginning with Chapter 73 and then following the sequence indicated at the end of each chapter. In case of confusion or forgetfulness, one need only consult the following list:
>
> 73–1–2–116–3–84–4–71–5–81–74–6–7–8–93–68–9–104–10–65–11–136–12–106
> 13–115–14–114–117–15–120–16–137–17–97–18–153–19–90–20–126–21–79–22
> 62–23–124–128–24–134–25–141–60–26–109–27–28–130–151–152–143–100–76
> 101–144–92–103–108–64–155–123–145–122–112–154–85–150–95–146–29–107
> 113–30–57–70–147–31–32–132–61–33–67–83–142–34–87–105–96–94–91–82
> 99–35–121–36–37–98–38–39–86–78–40–59–41–148–42–75–43–125–44–102–45
> 80–46–47–110–48–111–49–118–50–119–51–69–52–89–53–66–149–54–129–139
> 133–140–138–127–56–135–63–88–72–77–131–58–131.[1]

Far from suggesting that the current book pretends to the stature of *Rayuela*, this volume does participate in the reader-responsibility, hopscotch spirit of that stream-of-consciousness hallmark of Latin American boom literature. In its own way, this book is two books: one is a scholarly methodological exercise in the application of a particular approach to reading film, and the second is a collection of quasi-independent essays offering readings of frequently taught, often discussed, if not canonical Spanish-language films.

That is, the reader can approach this book from two directions. The first way is to read in the normal fashion, beginning with this introductory chapter and following linearly through the following chapters, and it ends in the index.

The second can be read in "hopscotch" fashion. The reader can select and read analyses of films in any order, jumping from one to another according to his or her preference for or interest in any or all of the Spanish-language films analyzed. Consequently, with a clear conscience the reader may ignore analytical readings of certain films as well as, perhaps, the following explanation and justification of the methodological approach.

The beginning of a novel, sometimes its prologue, serves to establish the narrative's themes, characters and environment, to establish its point-of-view, its narrative voice. The establishing cues orient the reader as to how he should read/interpret the novel. In the prologue to *Don Quijote*, for example, Cervantes tells the reader that "…yo, que, aunque parezco padre, soy padrastro de *Don Quijote*…" (…I, though I seem to be the father, am the stepfather of *Don Quijote*…), and he famously begins the novel thus, "En un lugar de la Mancha, de cuyo nombre no quiero acordarme…" (In a place in the Mancha, whose name I do not want to remember…). Of course there is much more readerly orientation in the opening pages of this, the first modern novel, but with these cues, one feigning narrative distance and the other hinting at parody, Cervantes prepares the reader for the authorial gambit that creates fictional and metafictional levels within the work as well as for the parody that reigns over the course of the two-part series.

The introduction to an essay serves to establish the topic, the theme [message], and the major points that the essay will treat. It quite often, too, introduces the point of view or theoretical perspective that will be adopted and applied throughout. The introduction serves to orient the reader as to how the essay is to be read. Most often the same can be said about the introduction to a film. In their first few minutes, most every film primes the viewer for the manner in which the film should be received, providing matrix-building cues for how the viewer should read the film.

The most specific premise that underlies the methodical approach to the films herein analyzed is that for most every film, the first few minutes are important, if not fundamental, to orienting the viewer as to how the film should be read. In its establishing moments, a film provides a matrix for its own analysis, which guides the viewer in terms of concretizing the film's relationship to reality, its tone, its meaning. The analytical strategy employed in this volume is the search for meaning informed by and consistent with the hermeneutic orientation provided by a film's establishing first few minutes.

This premise and its attendant strategy are rooted in notions of film grammar, a view of the filmic text as a work of art, and in notions of reception/

perception. In this second sense, the work offers itself in its double characterization as independent phenomenological structure and as a complex semiotic artistic fact. And, the critical reader/viewer tries to make sense of it, not only in terms of its parts but also as a whole. Viewing a film involves a process of intellection, a process of reasoning in which the viewer's reading of the film is a search for unity, a search for a level of meaning at which any dialectical tensions among elements are resolved and at which everything in the film makes sense.

In the chapters that follow, a number of well-known Spanish-language films will be read and analyzed from the perspective of the establishing hermeneutic[2] matrix provided by each of the films' first few minutes. It will become evident that this approach to reading film produces rich results, offering readings that are often different and more highly nuanced than existing readings of some canonical films from the world of Hispanic cinema. But, it is first incumbent to provide a solid foundation for the approach to be used.

A first basic premise that underlies this volume's approach to reading a film is that of the autonomy of the filmic text. The approach employed by this volume's readings of several Spanish-language films assumes that the films themselves offer sufficient evidence for the scholar-viewer to be able to arrive at a deep and complete understanding of them.

One of the important contributions of a significant part of 20th century formalist critical theory and practice has been to focus the analysis of texts from the texts themselves, ignoring or relegating to secondary importance their relationship with any private social, psychological or biographical information. In one way or another, at the phenomenological level, the effect of this type of approach has been to consider the artistic text as an autonomous system (or sign) made up of complexly and hierarchically ordered signs. These signs, in turn, are made up of a variety of signifiers and signifieds, and one of the jobs of the critical reader/viewer is to describe the functions and interrelationships of these signs and to analyze their particular inscription at the various levels of meaning of the text. At a nomothetic level, the effect of this type of approach has been to give the principle (if not the only) value to the analysis of the text.

The filmic work, because of its dual character as autonomous phenomenological structure and as communicative function, offers itself as an artistic semiotic artifact which is by nature very complex. As a complex sign, the filmic work integrates elements of multiple codes of varying disciplinary specificity within it as a concretized structure at a phenomenological level.

From a domain of aesthetic theory, past and future aesthetic codes intersect in the filmic text. At a more concrete level, that of the anthropological, there is an intersection of cultural codes, (for example, objects and structures that form part of the collective conscience), and of historical-social codes (for example, those dealing with political or social organization). Moving to the level of generalization of the existing, also intersecting in the text are the philological code (in other words, the historical science of language and corresponding critical activity), the linguistic code (synchronically speaking), the rhetorical code (that is to say, the repertoire of tropes, syntactical figures, etc.), cinematic codes (the historical science of the study of film techniques and their accepted meanings), and the symbolic code, which in turn adds to the multiplicity of codes intersecting as it represents psychoanalytical, mythical, and allegorical codes. Overall, this intersection of multiple codes presents itself within the framework of the semiotic code.

The multiple codes intersect at the phenomenological level to create a sign-message whose principle function is found in an orientation towards the sign-message as such [sign-message]. Thus, insofar as it is an object, the filmic text is also a system of complexly and hierarchically organized signs and composed of a variety of types of signs, having in their turn their signifiers and signifieds structured and inflected by the operant cultural and artistic codes. These various signs are subordinate to the artistic function and to the coherence of the system, which in their turn are inflected and informed by those multiple codes present and intersecting within the text.

From this conception of the text it is easier to define the critical, readerly enterprise. First, the scholar-viewer must see and describe how the multiple codes are represented in the text as an object. From there, he moves on to a description and analysis of the hierarchization of those codes represented at the phenomenological level. It is clear that this multiplicity of codes bestows on the text a rich signifying potential that perhaps no one reading can exhaust; which is not to say that the text so conceived invites any arbitrary reading that a reader or critic without objective restraint might want to offer. That potential for signification, at the same time as it may remain open to more than one interpretation because of the multiplicity of codes intersecting, is closed textually and contextually by that same network of meanings present in the work. The job of the scholar-viewer, then, is to concretize the text on its various levels of meaning in terms of its own particular meaningful structures that index elements objectively observable within its rich network of semantic potentialities.

In contrast with other communicative signs, those in which each semantic element can be verified in terms of the reality to which it refers, the work of art (a filmic text), as an autonomous sign, directs attention towards its internal organization, and it establishes a relationship with the receiver/viewer as a whole and the whole of those internal relationships. For that reason, the unity as a whole, a semantic unity is an important condition of the work of art. Distancing formalism from intentional fallacy and directing himself to this aspect of the condition of the work of art, aesthetic theorist Jan Mukařovský states that

> The unity of a work of art ... can rightly be found only in intentionality, the force operating within the work which strives toward the resolution of the contradictions and tensions among its individual parts and components, thereby giving each of them specific relation to the others and all of them together a unified meaning. Hence, intentionality in art is semantic energy.[3]

Intentionality, understood from this quote from Jan Mukařovský, is the force that gives to all its components a unity that allows the work-sign to have meaning. It is that unifying force, that semantic unity which the scholar-viewer's reading activity seeks to discover.

In order to arrive at an understanding of that intentionality, different kinds of evidence can be brought to bear, and it is necessary to consider the types of evidence that can and should be brought to bear in the analysis of a filmic text.

The first type of evidence is, of course, internal; it is the evidence that the filmic text itself provides through its semantic, syntactic, and visual components. The discovery of these elements allows the reader/viewer/critic to analyze the relationships among them and their inscription into the various levels of meaning that the text has. Clearly, this type of evidence is very public, in as much as it is available to anyone watching the film. It is also clear, as with the multiple codes alluded to above, that the availability of this evidence depends on the receiver/viewer's degree of initiation into those codes and his ability cope with them. A viewer unversed in cinematographic practices, for example, may leave untapped some of a film's signifying potential.

In a recent interview, a director of one of the films that are the object of this volume's focus, Víctor Erice, in response to a question seeking his opinion about a film he had made, stated that

> ... por mi carácter yo no hablaría nunca, nunca de mis películas ... por mi carácter ... porque si lo que uno ha pretendido no está en la película, no está en la película, está perdido para siempre. Lo que sucede es que nos obligan tanto a la hora de la promoción a los cineastas hablar y hablar y hablar de nuestras películas. Y creo que a veces engendramos una cierta retórica, ¿no?, en base de la repetición, pero por mi carácter yo no hablaría.... ¿Cómo se puede explicar que en el supuesto que uno haya hecho un poema lo que un poema es? Es que uno ... la flor debe conservar su aroma, si no, si pierde su aroma, la flor ya no es la flor. Creo que hay una pulsión muchas veces respecto a las obras donde se cultiva un arte taxidermista, taxidermista, que acaba con ... a veces no importa la obra como el acontecimiento social que suscita. Es más importante el acontecimiento social que la propia obra. Ya no se tiene ojos para la obra ...
>
> (given my personality, I would never, never talk about my movies ... given my personality ... because, if what one has tried to express is not in the movie, if it is not in the movie, it is lost forever. What happens is that they force us filmmakers so often at the time of the films' promotion to talk and talk and talk about our films. I think that sometimes we create a kind of rhetoric, you know?, on the basis of repetition,

but given my personality, I would not talk about my films.... How can you explain what a poem is on the hypothesis that one has written a poem? One just … the flower should keep its fragrance, if not, if it loses its fragrance, it is no longer a flower. I think that there is often a push with respect to works of art where what is practiced is taxidermy, taxidermy, that ends up … sometimes the work is less important than the social events it awakens. The social event is more important than the work itself. No longer are there eyes for the work of art…) [Erice 2014].

Even though much current critical analysis seems to have moved beyond, and indeed looks down on, an insistence on the immanence of the text, here in 2014, Erice emphasizes the primacy of the work of art. He recommends not losing sight of the work itself, not ignoring its aroma, its essence in favor of the work of taxidermy, stuffing the work with rhetoric from the outside. In this way, the Spanish director indexes another type of evidence frequently adduced in the analysis of works of art.

A second type of evidence that is customarily brought to bear as a guide to the analyses of texts, filmic or otherwise, is external evidence. It is external evidence in the sense that it does not belong to or come from the text as a linguistic, graphical/visual, or semiotic fact. It is evidence that is not ascertainable by viewing and re-viewing the film. One type of external evidence is characterized by its being exclusivist, and it often consists of revelations made through letters, essays, conversations, friends' and actors' testimonies, and so on. Another less exclusivist and somewhat more public evidence perhaps, yet still external to the work itself, is evidence such as interviews and a director's known biographical information. Such evidence is brought to bear in order to explain the motives, the message, and is related to the circumstances for a director making a film. While this type of information is often the stuff of movie lore, it is evidence that does not belong to the filmic text itself, and its critical application to the analysis of a text's meaning ought to awaken a certain mistrust. Though it can be of human interest to sectors of the movie-consuming public, this type of information should not serve as the basis of the analysis of a film or a body of filmic works. For the Víctor Erice of the interview quoted above, use of this kind of evidence in critically reading a film is akin to taking one's eyes off of or losing sight of the filmic work.

If a film does not manage to communicate a motive, message, or circumstance that a director reveals in an interview, for example, it is more important to analyze what it is in the filmic text that makes it fall short than it is to try to confirm any sort of biographical anecdote. If the filmic text goes beyond the expression of some exclusively revealed motive, message, or circumstance in order to communicate to the scholar-viewer a more universal meaning, then the biographical anecdote is no more than that, anecdote. Or, if, in fact, the film achieves the expression of a particular externally revealed circumstantial reference, the revelation is not only anecdotal but also wholly unnecessary to such an analytical practice.

There is another kind of intermediate, intertextual evidence that can be useful in the analysis of [filmic] texts. This type of evidence consists of internal evidence from works by the same director; from works by directors of the same school, generation, or style; it may be evidence from other antecedent work that through intertextual or intermedial relationships can shed light on semantic, syntactic, filmic, or thematic, associations of images, words, sounds, editing, rhythms in the text being analyzed. It is intermediate evidence because it is somewhat less public than the internal evidence offered by the text itself as work thing. Although it is evidence that is external to a single text itself, it is evidence that is still readily accessible to a wide audience. It is not extra-artistic; it is textually and artistically familial. This type of evidence is similar in character to the previously mentioned cinematic codes that intersect within the textual structure, and most often it is evidence that the filmic text itself activates.

As an example of this kind of intermediate evidence, it is instructive to look at a Spanish-Mexican coproduction from 2013. Diego Quemada-Díez's *La jaula de oro* relies on evidence of this type in order to situate its viewers in terms of their early hermeneutic orientation as to how to read the film.

Viewing the film, after some 20 seconds of information about production and coproduction support, the screen goes to black. On this black screen the title appears in white, lower-case letters, *la jaula de oro*. There are no credits at the beginning of this film, and no words of dialogue are spoken until the 7-minute mark of the filmic narrative. What the viewer sees in these early minutes are scenes involving three youths. The first of them walks quickly down the narrow street of a favela type slum. Then, an adolescent girl apparently from that same favela enters through a makeshift door marked "damas," where she cuts off her hair and binds her breasts before putting on a baseball cap and leaving.

The title, *La jaula de oro* (*The Cage of Gold*, translated for U.S. release as *The Golden Cage*) activates an intermedial relationship that in turn activates a series of associations with the migration genre.[4] The film *La jaula de oro* finds an antecedent genre correlate in popular music. Through its title, the film indexes a 1983 corrido or ranchera song. "La jaula de oro" is the title of a song written by Enrique Franco; it is a corrido included on an album of the same title *La jaula de oro* recorded and published by the popular Los Tigres del Norte in 1983.[5]

Composed of mainly eight-syllable assonant verses, the corrido "La jaula de oro" by Los Tigres de Norte possesses the typical characteristics of this musical genre. It has its greeting, prologue and introduction of the story's singer; it develops a story, and its moral is repeated twice in a refrain, the second time serving as the finish:

De qué me sirve el dinero?	What good is money?
si estoy como prisionero	If I am like a prisoner
dentro de esta gran nación	In this great country,
cuando me acuerdo hasta lloro	When I remember, I even cry,
y aunque la jaula sea de oro	and even though the cage is made of gold,
no deja de ser prisión.[6]	It doesn't stop being a prison.

The lyrics of the corrido tell of a Mexican immigrant in the United States, where he brought his wife and young kids. He laments that they no longer remember his dear Mexico and that he cannot return, repeating that he sees himself as a prisoner. The 2013 film title indexes this song and its immigrant story, and as it does, it actualizes for the scholar-viewer the expectations associated with the migration genre.

But the popular corrido is not the only antecedent genre correlate indexed by the title of the 2013 copro. What the title *La jaula de oro*, as well as the film's first few minutes, now also brings to the interpretive enterprise is another Mexican film with the same title, *La jaula de oro* (Sergio Véjar, 1987). Inspired by the corrido just described, this earlier film's storyline follows the one laid out by the song, but it ends with the Mexicans returning to Mexico. The focus is the successful immigrant years later, but the cultural complexities faced by immigrants get lost in a Manichean dichotomy of good versus bad. This film seems to suggest a nationalistic message of "Stay in Mexico," very different from what soon would become the critical reflection characteristic of New Mexican Cinema.

The intermedial relationship to these two texts actualizes the migration genre, which fills in the gaps left by the Quemada-Díez's filmic narrative. This narrative offers few, if any, motivations for the trip that the four adolescents undertake. But, since its title indexes the migration genre, it might be argued that such motivation is unnecessary, as it is implicit in established expectations for the genre. In actualizing all that is associated with the migration genre, 2013's *La jaula de oro* is free to concentrate primarily on the human dimension during the trip/crossing over itself. Though these two pieces of evidence, and the attendant genre expectations, are external to the film, they are indexed by evidence that comes from within the filmic text. And, they are examples of evidence that continues to be public (in the sense of having been offered as artistic texts and being widely available to listenership/viewership).

There is yet another general premise that underlies the methodological approach that ascribes importance to a film's first few minutes establishing a hermeneutic orientation to the filmic text. The approach to the films herein analyzed assumes that the scholar-viewer endeavors to interpret the signs that he perceives in order to complete the process of intellection. The scholar-viewer strives to make sense out of what he is seeing and hearing. The more that can be done to facilitate the viewer's work (such as calling his attention to the matrix-establishing value of a film's early minutes), the more resonant the cinematographic work will be for him.

Like other works of art, in order to achieve its semiotic potential, film relies on human perception and the dynamism of intellectual activity. The mind of the scholar-viewer seeks continually to find order and meaning. The film relies on the unifying quality of intellection in its reception. Films, like all works of art, cue and induce the viewer to perform a specific activity. Without some prompting from the work of art, it is difficult for the viewer to begin the interpretive process, and the work might remain artifact.

Prompts offered by the work are not random; rather they are organized, and elements or any set of elements depend on and affect others within the whole. Films have form, an overall system of relations that the viewer can perceive among and formed by the elements in the whole. In the process of intellection, the scholar-viewer actively relates elements to one another. Form is the total system that the viewer attributes to a film, where every component functions as part of the overall pattern that is perceived. In this pattern, there is no inside or outside, and the viewer relates all elements to one another dynamically. Film form guides the viewer's reception activity, and because of his need for form, the viewer's reading seeks to resolve, reason, and understand relationships between and among parts and their relationship to the whole of the artistic communication. The general process of intellection, a search motivated by a need to make sense of, manifests itself in the analytical strategies and practices that a viewer employs in that search.

A film is a continuum of meaning production, and it is composed of shots that contain as much information as the viewer wants to or can read in them. The images within these shots composing the filmic discourse have denotative meaning. The viewer does not need to work too hard to understand this meaning, since at a denotative level, the images are what they are. As Christian Metz put it, referring to this very quality, "A film is always more or less understandable. If by chance it is not at all understood, that is as a result of peculiar circumstances, and not of the semiological process proper to cinema" (72). Generally intelligible to the viewer is the film's "diegesis," that is, the events, figures and objects seen, as well as the events and actions presumed to have happened in the world of the story it narrates. But, because film is a product of culture, because it functions as a communicative sign, and because its images are edited together and combined with sound, a film's discourse creates meanings that supersede the whole of its denotations. Images and sound combine to create meanings beyond the denotative level.

The meaning of a particular shot depends not only on its denotative quality, but also on its relationships with preceding and following shots. In this sense, a shot or a sequence of shots is viewed as a syntagma, a shot or sequence of shots that forms a syntactical or constitutive element of the filmic discourse. When the meaning of a shot depends on it being compared with actual shots that precede or follow it, reading of the filmic discourse begins to involve syntagmatic connotation. Because of their quality of being/occurring first, the shots and sequences of a film's first few minutes are those to which subsequent constituent shots and sequences refer back in order to create connotative meaning. Having no antecedent shots or sequences, they are those establishing shots and sequences that prime and foreshadow readings of what syntagmatically follows.

Once a director has chosen what to shoot, two major choices remain. The director's choice of how to shoot is made vertically; from among all the possible ways to shoot, a choice is made. A specific shot, then, depends on it having been determined from a range of other possible shots; a choice has been made from the paradigm, and the choice may bring with it paradigmatic connotations that affect the viewer's reading of the film. For example, a low angle shot might be used to create a sense of powerlessness where the height of the focused object may allow it to inspire fear and insecurity within a scene; or the shot's lack of background, presenting only sky or ceiling, adds a sense of disorientation or confusion. The denotative meaning of the object focused is apparent, yet its signifying potential within the filmic discourse is fully concretized by the shot used, including the meanings suggested by paradigmatic selections, and the shot's relationship as a combined, constitutive element of the whole.

Finally, director and editor must decide how to present what has been shot, how to edit the shots. Montage or editing creates the continuum of meaning production. Through the syntagmatic placing of shots end to end [end to beginning], a filmic syntax is created. The process of the viewer's intellection involves comprehending the sequence of the syntax created by the joining of shots, but also comprehending the connotations indexed by the interrelationships of shots and sequences with and among each other.

The analogy, then, becomes reading and comprehending a simple sentence and, then, a network of sentences woven into a narrative. The sentence is realized syntagmatically over time. The placing of syntagmatic elements in proper order and including the requisite syntagmatic elements to satisfy syntactical-semantic exigencies among elements, creates a syntagmatic whole that is realized in time. The overall syntax and meaning of the sentence are established from the very beginning of the sentence, whose ultimate meaning depends upon the interrelationships of all the syntactical constituents of the sentence. The placing of sentences in syntagmatic order to satisfy the syntactical-semantic exigencies of a narrative then creates a network, a larger whole that also is realized in time. The overall syntax and meaning of the narrative rests on the interrelationships of all the sentences. Like the sentence, and the subsequent network of sentences woven into a narrative, a film is realized syntagmatically over time, and overall syntax and meaning begin to be established from the start of the film, whose ultimate reading depends upon the created network of syntagmatic interrelationships between and among shots and sequences.

In his essay "The Work of Art in the Age of Mechanical Reproduction," Walter Benjamin recognizes the syntagmatic quality of filmic discourse when he writes that directives given "to those looking at pictures ... become even more explicit and more imperative in the film where the meaning of each single picture appears to be prescribed by the sequence of all preceding ones" (226). Since a film's first few minutes precede all other sequences in the film, they take on a "prescriptive" importance for all following sequences.

The relating of a film's first few minutes to notions of film grammar[7] obviously also makes use of the well-known idea and cinematographic practice of the establishing shot. The idea is that a film's first few minutes are the establishing moments of the filmic discourse, and they are compared to an establishing shot for a scene.

In filmmaking, and also television, establishing shots set up the context for a scene. By showing the relationships between a scene's figures and objects, they establish parameters for reading the scene. Establishing shots are usually long- or extreme-long shots at the beginning of scenes, and they provide indications as to where, and sometimes when, the remainder of the scenes takes place. So, very often establishing shots function in order to indicate location, and they may use landmarks or other culture-bound locales to indicate the city or the place where the scene's action is to take place, or to indicate the place to which the action has moved. Sometimes, through the use of an establishing shot, it is possible for the viewer to be guided in his understanding of time of the filmic action. For example, in Carlos Saura's *Carmen* (see Chapter 2), an exterior shot of a building [rehearsal studio] at night followed by an interior shot of Carmen and Antonio in bed together implies that the scene is taking place at night inside his apartment in that rehearsal hall. Other times, through the use of an establishing shot, it is possible for the viewer to be guided in his understanding of the relationship between characters of the filmic action. That same exterior shot of a building at night followed by an interior shot of Carmen getting dressed and Antonio in bed smoking implies that she is leaving him alone in the middle of the night. And, on other occasions, rather than a location, an establishing shot may be used to establish a concept crucial to a scene. For example, opening with a flamenco dance rehearsal drill visually establishes the theme of flamenco. Or a shot of low hanging fog could be an establishing shot with which a filmmaker colludes with the viewer to provide a coded orientation learned through a common cinematic and/or cultural background where what is signaled is mystery.

Historically, establishing techniques can become somewhat fossilized. For example, by the 1940's, filmmaking in Hollywood had managed to create an efficient grammar for point-of-view. In point-of-view filmic grammar, the standard use of the establishing shot was the employment of a long shot. That long shot established place; often it established time, and sometimes it offered viewers other necessary information. Alfred Hitchcock's opening establishing shot in *Rear Window* is an instructive and frequently cited example of this filmic practice; and it serves as an exemplary link to this volume's notion of the importance of a film's first few minutes. In the classic Hitchcock film, the opening pan and track, some four minutes long, orients the viewers as to the where of the filmic narrative, as to why they are there, whom they are with, what is going on in the filmic, diegetic now, what has happened to that point, and who the characters in the story are. Further, *Rear Window*'s opening minutes suggest possible ways in which the filmic narrative might develop.

The experienced viewer quickly realizes, though, that modern filmic style offers greater "grammatical" latitude.[8] In classic filmic narrative, notions of filmic grammar imply beginning with an establishing shot, then narrowing down from the generalization to the specifics of the scene or sequence. The first few minutes or establishing moments of a film are to the filmic discourse as the establishing shot is to a scene. In such a comparison, if the establishing shot orients the viewer as to how he is to read a scene, a film's first few minutes orient the viewer as to how he is to read the film. But, this orientation is as much a question of general interpretive guidance as it is a specific one.

If it is possible to theoretically compare the establishing shot to the first few minutes or the establishing moments of a film, it is possible, indeed necessary, to extend the analogy to levels of praxis. As establishing shots can and have come to be categorized as to the nature of the readerly information they provide, so too, establishing moments or the first few minutes of films can be viewed from the kinds of hermeneutic guidance they can provide. Matrices provided by the first few minutes of films may offer orientation to the scholar-viewer as to a film's message, the point of view of its discourse, its style, its tone, its central motifs or tropes, or as to other interpretative cues. All or any one of these interpretation-preparing cues can be key to the internal semantic unity of the whole of the film's constitutive elements, and thus to the richness of its meanings. In addition, a film's establishing moments can provide more diegesis-specific mappings as to time, place, and character, which, of course, are fundamental to "reading" the film.

One observable case of the establishing potential for a film's first few minutes is in the orientation towards the filmic narrative's perspective and point-of-view. The opening minutes of a film frequently offer the scholar-viewer a matrix for interpreting the perspective (as well as the point of view) that structures the filmic discourse and the point of view from which it should be read.

For example, a mariachi band begins a sad melody as the voice of Lola Beltrán intones "Soy infeliz." As the soundtrack of the ranchera ballad continues, a series of twenty-one frames occupy the first 2 minutes and 50 seconds of the film's running time. Nearly all of the frames are static shots over which film credits appear. With few exceptions, any one of the backgrounds of these frames could suggest a sort of post-modern, cubist flag design. The horizontal rectangular space in broken up into usually smaller rectangular sections, distributed in each case in a singular pattern and repeating an intense color palate often associated with the film's director, where red predominates.

The fourth frame is unique in that it features movement. Large, red, block capital letters slowly move across the screen from right to left spelling M-U-J-E-R-E-S (W-O-M-E-N). Each letter is accompanied by a stylized cutout rendering of a woman posed fashion magazine style and wearing what seems like 1950's fashion. Once M-U-J-E-R-E-S completes its movement to the left, the whole frame is presented with MUJERES occupying the whole screen, and then there is a fade to the next frame, a red vertical panel left, and black vertical panel right, and in the center, half of a fashion model type woman's face. Over the frame, the words "al borde de un ataque/de" (on the verge of a) appear above, and below right, "NERVIOS" (nervous breakdown) appears.

The twenty-one frames are populated with a montage of images proper to a fashion magazine, as they feature clothing, makeup, jewelry, shoes, undergarments, hairdos, and models typically posed. The intertitles are of differing sizes, with both intertitles and images suggesting cutouts from a magazine or catalog. Among the stylized images are:

> A woman tugging on a nylon stocking;
> Two eyes, a mouth, and a naked shoulder;
> A hand with long red fingernails scratching (the hand bears five rings on four fingers);
> A reclining woman, arms back and down, dressed in a pink bustier;
> A hand and arm with a long women's glove holding a flower;
> A hand with an extended index finger upon which is balanced a green high-heeled shoe, two bracelets on the wrist; and so on.

Only four of the twenty-one frames offer the presence of a male figure.[9] In only one of these cases, do man and woman connect. In the twelfth frame, a left-side, vertical panel features a stylized drawing of a man and woman kissing opposite a right-side, vertical panel of a woman's slim legs ending in white, strapped shoes. The twentieth frame similarly splits into left and right, with a woman's facial profile in the left panel, and a man clad in formal dinner attire right. The other two frames present men as observers. In the first, frame seventeen, with the notes of a musical score, chairs, music stands, and a harp as background, an orchestra director observes a group of four fashion-dressed and posed women to the right of the frame. And, in the final frame, from a silhouetted background of a movie set with lights, microphone boom, and camera, a man's silhouette observes the foregrounded three women, posed red-white-red and again as fashion cutouts. Over this last frame, intertitles identify the film's director, Pedro Almodóvar.

At the end of the first two minutes and fifty seconds, there is a fade to black followed by a fade-in to a model of an apartment building and three cars. It is clear that the building and cars are models because in the background there is life-size foliage. The background ranchera music stops, and the first diegetic sounds are the sounds of chickens and ducks. As the camera lingers on some chickens and ducks populating an apartment balcony, a female voiceover describes the reasons for her living in the apartment and the collection of animals. The woman's voiceover ends with: "En cualquier caso, no conseguí salvar la pareja que más me interesaba: la mía." (At any rate, I didn't manage to save the relationship that was most important to me: mine.)

A cut to a close-up of a Lola Beltrán album jacket covering a fashion magazine, an unfinished drink, and an ashtray is accompanied by an male voiceover that reads the note left in green and red ink and incorporating the previously heard song title: "Pepa, cariño: no quiero oirte nunca decir 'Soy infeliz.' Tu Iván." (Pepa, I never want to hear you say "I am unhappy," Your Ivan).

An alarm clock showing 8:00 o'clock sounds unattended next to a photograph of couple. The photograph is signed "Te quiero, te necesito, te deseo. Tu Iván" (I love you, I need you, I want you. Your Ivan). After showing another alarm clock, the camera pans a woman sleeping facedown, and when the camera's focus reaches her head, there is a fade to black and white. A distinguished, suit-clad man, microphone in hand, walks from right to left. The camera follows him as thirteen times he comes across a woman moving left to right. Each time as they cross paths, the man quickly looks the female over and suavely spouts one of the many "lines" from the male rhetorical arsenal aimed at pacifying and conquering the female, phrases that the male believes the female dreams of hearing. He says, for example, "Without you my life has no meaning," "Will you marry me" (to a nun!), "I can't live without you," "I love you, I want you, I need you," "I love you just the way you are," and so on. Only the last female responds. A smoking tart retorts, "Pues, mira qué bien" (Well, good for you.). A fade back to color returns the viewer to the diegetic world of the filmic narrative. And so end the first few minutes of *Mujeres al borde de un ataque de nervios* (*Women on the Verge of a Nervous Breakdown*) (Pedro Almovodóvar, 1988), the first 4 minutes and 58 seconds to be precise.

Having viewed these first nearly five minutes of the film, the scholar-viewer now has clear orientations as to how to read the film. The perspective from which a reading of the film is to be realized is that of unhappy women. Even though, the guiding perspective is to be that of woman, given the character of the many "cutout" images, it is evident that part of that perspective includes woman as two-dimensional stereotype, and as objectified.

Like in the frames (especially in the ones with the orchestra director and the film director) and the black and white sequence, man is an observer; the male-dominant discourse is the objectifier. It is a male-dominant gaze that objectifies, that cuts out. The moving capital letters, MUJERES, emphatically calls readerly attention to the perspective on WOMEN.

The use of capital letter in film's establishing minutes intimately associates MUJERES and NERVIOS, the only two words in all capital letters. The scholar-viewer also needs to notice that "NERVIOS" is presented within quotation marks, where the placing of this key term within quotation marks is a clear indication that a reading of the term, and thus a reading of the film, needs to put things in question. Here, the quotation marks function much like "air quotes" (also referred to as "ersatz quotes") popularized in the 1990's as a means of expressing irony, sarcasm, or satire. "NERVIOS" thus used is a euphemism to mock societal or male-dominant expectations for female behaviors. The whole concept of being on the verge of a nervous breakdown is put into question from the very beginning by this key element of the establishing readerly matrix. In terms of the implications for the reading of the film, this "wink" programs the scholar-viewer for a sarcastic or ironic reading of the "cutout" image of women.

The music playing behind the opening frames and credits is a very traditional love ranchera instrumentalization, and it is sung by a lone lamenting female voice. This non-diegetic beginning of the soundtrack featuring the lone woman's voice proclaiming her unhappiness and lamenting her lost love, emphasizes the centrality of the lovelorn woman's perspective to the reading of this film, and at the same time it also serves to immediately prime the viewer to read from this perspective. The establishing exegetical programming for the viewer is clear. Because of the fashion cutout frames, the early centrality and predominance of women in them, and the music, the viewer knows that the film is to be read from women's eyes, so many of which are featured in the establishing frames.

And, it does not take the filmic narrative very long to identify which woman's point-of-view will prevail. It is Pepa. Point-of-view and perspective unite in Pepa with the establishing voiceover and the close-ups of her lying in bed facedown in the opening minutes. As the camera focuses on her head, there is a cut to the sequence in black and white, signaling her inner thoughts, imagination, or dreaming. The focal woman, her personal questioning and search are identified as central to any allegorical-symbolic or political meanings produced. With Pepa's female voiceover, it is clear also that one of the readerly missions of the scholar viewer is to ascertain why and how the narrating female was unable to "save" her relationship.

The elements of this opening make clear another of a film's first few minutes' possible orientations, which is offering to the viewer interpretive keys for reading the film. Here, in addition to the "wink" programming a sarcastic matrix, the establishing minutes include a juxtaposition foregrounding a contrast between a modern high-rise, urban apartment building and a pre-modern, rural chicken/duck coop on the balcony, which prepares the viewer for an analytical reading involving contrast. At the same time, the presence of an animal menagerie on the balcony warns the viewer not to take the story too seriously. With these cues, the scholar-viewer is programmed for a filmic narrative that is not to be read literally as a realist narrative, but rather as a post-modern popular tale, whose ultimate meanings may respond to an allegorical-symbolical level.

Temporal perspective, too, is established in the first few minutes. Because of the modern high-rise, urban apartment building, the style of the model cars, the color palate, and the dress, hairdo, and demeanor of a few of the women in the black-and-white "line-up," and so on, the scholar-viewer knows not only that the film is to be read as a post-modern urban tale with ironic implications at a level of abstraction, but that it should be read specifically in terms of its reference to "Transition" Spain.

The establishing minutes frequently supply the viewer with interpretive keys for the reading of the filmic narrative. As a further example, one might consider the opening moments of another film, one that begins with the non-diegetic sound of organ music accompanying male children's voices singing a religious hymn and a blank, black screen. For the brief period of twenty-seven seconds, the film title and six film credits appear on the black screen. As the singing continues, it overlaps and blends into the opening visual, a flashback presenting the confusion of boys at a Catholic school having just suffered a bombing. After the camera scrutinizes the dust-filled air, the boys moving about astonished and frightened, the priest helping them, the toppled furniture, and the lifeless bodies, there is a flash forward. The music of the boys' choir again overlaps in a sound bridge, as the camera pans the Barcelona harbor and moves to the hill overlooking the city. The singing overlaps some ten seconds into present-tense narrative, where the focus closes in on a hillside cemetery and two vehicles. As two men remove the skeletal remains from one of the niches, two others look on. One of the onlookers is a serious, late-forties, mostly bald and suit-clad man (José Luis López Vázquez) standing outside of his car, a black 1970 Seat 1430. The other, a very old gentleman seated in the back seat of a taxi, looks fixedly at the remains. After the first two men place the bones into a small coffin, one of them places the coffin into the trunk of the Seat. There is a quick cut to a highway splitting the dry Castilian plain. The only vehicle on the road, the black Seat approaches. The driver, the mostly bald, now casually dressed man, slows the car and pulls to the side of the road. As he exits the car, he looks to the horizon, where he ponders the profile of a small city. Walking a few meters away from his car toward the horizon, he continues to stare and to seem pensive. Then, as the man turns to his right, so does the camera to discover a black 1930's sedan with a woman and a man exiting it, both dressed in 1930's clothing. As the man impatiently smokes a cigarette, the woman approaches the late-forties-ish man, and she addresses and treats him as a young boy, as her son.

Some five minutes and fifteen seconds into the filmic narrative, the scholar-viewer is cognizant of interpretive keys for the reading of the film. When the late-forties-ish, bald man, standing in 1970, turns to be cared for by his 1930's mother, the viewer experiences a sensation of confusion, and that very confusion is established as an interpretive key for the film.

With the early insistence on flashback/flash forward, it is clear to the scholar-viewer that the use of this temporal/narrative device is to be an interpretive key for reading the film as it continues. Approximating the man's visual perception, the camera zooms quickly, though not completely, on the view of the city in the distance and retreats. As it does, adult Luis turns to find himself transported to the 1930's[10] and into the presence of his mother and father. The stimulation of the sense of sight has triggered a memory, a regression in time. And so, the scholar-viewer possesses one more element of the interpretive keys for reading the film. It is a Proustian triggering mechanism for involuntary memory. As he reads this film, the viewer is programmed to anticipate a filmic narrative in which sensory experiences will trigger temporal dislocation.

And, as the man focuses and refocuses his gaze on the view of the city on the horizon, he leaves the present behind. As he turns his attention behind him, he and the narrative step 30+ years into the past, where only his own physical person does not regress. This unique flashback mechanism creates the potential for the "past" never quite left behind once the narrative flashes forward returning to the narrative present, in order to reflect or be reflected in some other aspect of the filmic narrative into which Luis has stepped. With the flashback/flash forward-confusion motif clearly established as a central expressive, and therefore interpretive, key, the first few minutes of Carlos Saura's *La prima Angélica* (1973) orient the viewer to read the film in terms of the persistence of memory. The traumatic events of a divided and conflictive nation, of a divided family, and of his 1930's childhood are vivid involuntary memories affecting the 1970's adult Luis.

With the early insistence on sound overlapping, where the boys singing associated with a past, traumatic event bridges into the present-tense narrative, there is a further evidence of the past never quite being left behind. As voices link visual sequences, cause-effect relationships are compressed, signaling for the viewer that past experience having a continued effect in the present is an interpretive key for concretizing filmic meanings.

Another exemplary, illustrative "case" in which a motif from a film's first few minutes serves to guide the viewer in his reading of the film comes from Alejandro González Iñárritu's highly successful 2006 film *Babel*. The very title primes the reader for a discourse that is scattered confusión

> "Come, let us go down, and there confuse their language, that they may not understand one another's speech." So the Lord scattered them abroad from there over the face of all the earth, and they left off building the city. Therefore its name was called Babel, because there the Lord confused the language of all the earth; and from there the Lord scattered them abroad over the face of all the earth [*Revised Standard Version Bible*, Genesis 11. 7–9].

But, the film's first few minutes offer the reader a "crutch" to help him straighten out the Babelian twists and turns well before the ultimate unfolding of events clarifies the ties between stories, voices, and continents.

As production credits appear on an otherwise black screen, the sounds of footsteps are heard, and then the film's title appears. The first visual, a close (but not tight)-up, is of a bearded man with a head scarf. His walking in a hilly, stony desert, and he carries something wrapped in cloth over his right shoulder. He knocks at the door of a low standing, stone home, and a man answers. They speak Arabic, there is a family inside, and the first man unwraps what he has been carrying. It is a rifle, which the other man takes as the camera takes a close-up of it and a box of 200 cartridges. Two young boys (12- to 14-ish) look on as the men haggle. The price of the sale is agreed upon, and all go outside to try out the rifle. The girls laugh at the first boy's attempt ("If he doesn't hit the jackals, at least he'll scare the shit out of them."). The two men depart, leaving the two boys with the gun.

Less than five minutes into the narrative, the film has established the rifle as the go-to interpretative motif. So, when, at 9 minutes, the narrative jumps to a house in the U.S. with two blond kids running around and a Mexican woman who answers the phone, the viewer knows it should be somehow connected to the rifle. Or when the narrative, at 14:50 minutes, jumps to an American couple ordering Cokes in the desert, or when the narrative jumps, at 19:46 minutes to a volleyball game in Japan, the viewer is primed to suspect that these people and places are somehow connected to the rifle established as an interpretive motif in the film's first few minutes.

But, the establishing moments can determine more than point-of-view or interpretive keys, as seen above. Often what is established in the first few minutes at the same time as point-of-view is also the perspective from which the film is to be read. The opening minutes can orient the scholar-viewer as to the thoughts, feelings, and attitudes that will inform the reading of the filmic discourse. This will be evidenced later in this volume in the "case study" of Ana in *El espíritu de la colmena* where in her personal subconscious, thoughts and feelings of search guide an orientation towards the reading of the film.

In attitudinal terms of perspective, a film's first few minutes can serve also to orient the viewer as to its stance *vis-à-vis* the reality is portrays. Does the film question that reality? Does it take that reality seriously? Does it wish to poke fun at that reality? Another of the ways in which the establishing moments of a film can orient the viewer is with respect to the film's overall tone. They can orient the viewer as to the tone with which his reading of the filmic narrative ought to be guided. In this regard, two of the most transparent "case studies" in Spanish-language film are instructive examples, as well as being historically important.

Two hands take a phonograph record and place it on the revolving turntable of a phonograph. The one hand places the stylus onto the record and a lively tune begins to play. Cut to a loudspeaker from which the music is broadcast and a panoramic long shot of the frontlines, complete with trenches populated with soldiers going about their daily routines. The camera follows one soldier as he travels the trenches picking up letters for the mail and things for the exchange/interchange. As he does, the viewer is privy to the gossip exchanged among the soldiers and to the frivolous conversations among them.

A pan from behind the trenches discovers a barren open space, and the camera draws back to follow the progress of the soldier clad in boxer shorts. A conversation about uniforms and the last can of sardines is interrupted by a loudspeaker announcement from across no-man's-land: "Aquí la voz del frente de la España Nacional.... Eh, vosotros.... La España de Franco quiere invitaros a una fiesta" (The voice from the front of Nationalist Spain here.... Hey, you guys.... Franco's Spain wants to invite you to a party). Less than four and a half minutes into the filmic narrative and before all of the film credits have been presented, the viewer has been clearly oriented as to the tone with which this film is to be read.

Or consider a slow traveling shot as it moves down a symmetrically tree-lined dirt road or lane to discover a suitcase in the middle of the road. After intertitles offer an explanation of a failed 1930 uprising in Jaca, following which a young man took off and began to wander the countryside, another intertitle identifies the scene as somewhere in Spain. At the end of the traveling shot, two Civil Guards kick the suitcase and it falls open. As they wonder about the owner of the suitcase, they turn to discover a young man in the weeds beside the road. When they command that he raise his hands above his head, his pants fall to his knees, as he tries to explain that he was.... When the guards ask him where he is headed, he stutters that he does not know, with a Chaplinesque look on his face that invites laughter. Suspecting he is a deserter from Jaca, the older of the guards comments on the incongruences of the young man, a Republican with a Bible, as he handcuffs him.

As the young man continues with his Chaplin face, the older and the younger guard discuss the merits of letting their prisoner go, Civil Guard involvement in politics, and the relativity of remaining apolitical. After a time, the older guard, the younger's father-in-law, decides to let the prisoner go. The two guards disagree about this action. As a result the younger guard shoots his father-in-law, then, before the still astonished now former prisoner, he removes his shoe so that he can pull the trigger of his rifle in order to kill himself, crying "Fuck all the laws ... fuck the guy who invented the public order...." And so the first few minutes of the film come to an end.

In both cases of the first few minutes of the two films just alluded to, lighthearted music, incongruent conversations, and a man in boxer shorts orient the viewer as to the tone of the two films. The two films share the same tone, as the second film continues the legacy left by the first.

The importance of the tone in these two films is historical as well as integral to the reading of each individual film. Specific references in the first filmic text, Luis García Berlanga's 1985 *La vaquilla*, place the filmic narrative squarely in the middle of the Spanish Civil War (1936–1939). Intertitular explanation and the Civil Guards' debates in the first few minutes of the second film, Fernando Trueba's Oscar-winning *Belle epoque* (1993), locate the filmic narrative in a period of Spanish national history that became increasingly conflictive leading up to that same civil conflict.

The first of the two films comes after two decades in which Spanish national cinema dedicated considerable filmic time and space to the confrontation of *cainista*[11] trauma from its civil conflict. Though this confrontation early on was aesthetically somewhat obtuse, Spanish national cinema from 1965 to 1985 seemed to take seriously the need to confront its traumatic past. The first few minutes of *La vaquilla*, however, augur a change. The establishing moments orient the viewer towards reading the film with a ludic tone, thus announcing new possibilities for approaching Spain's ideological dialectic.

Presaging theme or message is another of the ways in which the establishing moments of a film can guide the scholar-viewer as to how the film is to be read. A film's first few minutes frequently provide the viewer with an overall meaning that can resolve any internal conflicts between filmic elements and organize them into a meaningful whole. Perhaps nowhere in Hispanic film is the first few minutes' presaging of theme more apparent/

transparent than in the later "case study" of the overt presentation of filmic theme in the chapter dealing with *La historia oficial* (Luis Puenzo, 1985). But, for the purposes of this introduction's taxonomical exemplification, other equally explicit cases can be adduced.

A shadowy close-up of a goshawk among the leaves of a tree cuts to an older man wearing a beret who screams "Eh!" to the bird. As he runs through the underbrush, he laughs and continues to scream; and he looks around to see if he has elicited some response. The bird seems to respond with calls in the distance as the man continues to run. The rhythmic sounds of his paces through the underbrush give way to a non-diegetic music of the soundtrack. It is an insistent percussive, almost tribal, beat, the product of a drum and a tambourine. Intermittent close to medium shots of the man show him to be lacking teeth and to be humbly dressed.

At around forty seconds of the film's running time, there is a fade to white followed by a slow fade-in to a photograph of a humble family. The fade-in approximates a developing photograph in which the figures progressively acquire sharpness and clarity of detail. In the center are seated a father and mother, she holding a girl child wrapped in a blanket. To the right of the photograph stand two older children, who look like they could be mid- to late-teenagers. To the left stands the man seen earlier running and screaming to the birds. A bird perches on his shoulder. All look directly into the camera, but only the older man left is smiling.

The photograph acquires sharpness but as that rhythmic, almost tribal beat continues on the sound track, the photographic image continues to develop, even proceeding beyond what would be the desired clarity of detail for a usable photographic print. By one minute and twenty seconds of the film's running time the photograph is fully overexposed to the point at which the screen is nearly black.

At this point, film credits begin to appear superimposed over the remaining overexposed photograph. With the film credits, there is a shift to a different music on the sound track. Now the music is that of two plaintiff violins that offer a sharp, nearly discordant dialogue. After an identification of the producing collaboration, the first credit communicates the film's title in all lower case letters, *los santos inocentes* (The Holy Innocents).

In these establishing minutes, theme and interpretive motif combine in the opening sequence. With the opening close-up, the running free, and the perched bird of the photograph, it is clear that bird symbolism and the freedom emblematically associated with birds is to be a motif central to the filmic discourse.

The scholar-viewer has viewed the first one minute and thirty-three seconds of *Los santos inocentes*, and these establishing moments have provided a matrix for reading the film's theme. With the photograph developing and becoming overexposed, with the lowercase capital letters of the title indexing the humbleness of the family, and with the serious, driving, tribal beat that transitions to a discordant screeching, the opening minutes presage a reading of the film in terms of abrasive erasure or disappearance of this family.

Indeed, the misfortunes of the photographed family (Paco el Bajo, Régula, Azarías, Quirce, Nieves, and "la niña chica") are chronicled in a poignant struggle for survival, as victims of a *cainista* feudal system persisting in late Francoist Spain. The intense, penetrating tone set by the dialoguing violins reflects the seriousness of the treatment of the socioeconomic polarization between this family and the family of the Marquesa. This "haves and have-nots" / "vencidos y vencedores" / winners and losers theme and the film's tone are reflective as well of the thematics and tone of a decade's worth of Spanish films. This film comes during a period in Spanish national film history immediately prior to the one alluded to above in reference to Berlanga's *La vaquilla*. It comes during a decade in which the filmic confrontation of national trauma was aesthetically and ideologically direct, not shying away from a frontal engagement with a thematics too sensitive to be presented so directly during the era of official Francoist censorship.

Surely the censors did not take long in realizing the volatile theme of another canonical work of Spanish cinema. The first few minutes create a matrix for a reading that would be deemed unacceptable for the time at which the film was made.

The viewer is greeted with a non-diegetic Handel's "Aleluya Chorus" played and sung loudly behind a black and white architectural still shot featuring classic, renaissance columns. Film credits, including the film title, *Viridiana*, appear superimposed on the still background. Following the last credit identifying director Luis Buñuel, the camera opens onto the interior patio of a cloister where young male students wearing uniforms led by a nun file two-by-two across the patio. Two more *cainista* nuns stand in the distance. The Handel composition is replaced by ambient sound, the first of which being the ringing of bells. More nuns and a priest become visible. From behind, the camera discovers a group of three nuns in habit and a fourth who approaches. The latter speaks, calling for Sister Viridiana. From the group of three, one nun turns and walks toward the beckoning nun, her back still to the camera. The first nun walks eyes down and her hands drawn to her. Even as she reaches the nun who called to her, this nun does not yet raise her eyes to engage her interlocutor. The latter turns out to be the Mother Superior, and the conversation between the two nuns closes the film's establishing moments, as it establishes a conflict central to the film's readerly matrix:

> MADRE SUPERIORA: Acabo de recibir carta de su tío. No puede venir a la profesión. (I received a letter from your uncle. He cannot come to see you take your vows.)

VIRIDIANA: Está bien, Madre. (Very Well, Mother.)
MADRE SUPERIORA: No parece sentirlo mucho su caridad. (You seem unconcerned by his charity.)
VIRIDIANA: Casi no le conozco. Sólo le vi una vez hace años. Ya ni me acuerdo. (I hardly know him. I only met him once years ago. I hardly remember him.)
MADRE SUPERIORA: Pues, ahora le invita a su casa. (Well, now he is inviting you to visit him.)
VIRIDIANA: Preferiría no salir del convento, Madre. (I would rather not to leave the convent, Mother.)
MADRE SUPERIORA: Temo que no se encuentre bien. Es su único pariente y debe de despedirse de él antes de profesar. Seguramente no le verá más. (I fear that he is not well. He is your only relative. You ought to see him before you take your vows. Surely you will not see him again.)
VIRIDIANA: ¿Por qué quiere que vaya? Nunca se ha preocupado por mí. (Why do you want me to go? He never bothered about me before.)
MADRE SUPERIORA: Ha pagado sus estudios. La ha sostenido y acaba de enviar su dote. ¿Qué más quiere? (He has paid for your studies. He supported you and he just sent your dowry. What more do you want?)
VIRIDIANA: Mi deseo sería no volver a ver el mundo. Pero si Su Reverencia me lo ordena…. (My wish would be to never see the world again. But if Your Reverence orders me….)
MADRE SUPERIORA: Quedan pocos días antes de que empiece el retiro. Así que puede irse mañana. En su celda encontrará las cosas necesarias para el viaje. Procure ser afectuosa con él. (There are a few days before the retreat. So you may leave tomorrow. You will find all you need to travel in your cell. Try to be affectionate with him.)

In just over the first three minutes (3:20) of the filmic discourse, an orientation as to reading the film's theme has been established, and the censors are programmed to reject this discourse for consumption in Francoist Spain. Placed in opposition are inside and outside world, spiritual and material. On the one side, the scholar-viewer finds the combination of the "Aleluya Chorus" and the sustained still shot of a solid architecture (in which contrasts between light and shadow are highlighted), the enclosed architecture of the cloister and the regimentation of the children walking two-by-two, and all responding automatically to the call of the bells, the invocation of charity, and the humility and obedience of Sister Viridiana. And, on the other side especially, there is the theme and tenor of the dialogue between Viridiana and the Mother Superior, in which the latter ultimately sustains her argument on basis of materialism. The film's first few minutes create a matrix according to which the film is to be read as a conflict or confrontation between a strict religious orthodoxy and the outside, material world.

As mentioned earlier, recent critical practice has pushed beyond the boundaries of the text, preferring to consider artistic texts in terms of their connections with values, institutions and practices elsewhere in the culture.

Primary areas of interest in film studies have been the politics of film (cinema and the state, cinema and revolution, cinema and industry, etc.) and politics in film (be it gender politics, postcolonial politics, subaltern politics, identity politics, etc.), as was discussed, for example, by distinguished experts on Spanish-language film on a panel adjunct to a recent Latin American Studies Association (LASA) conference. It is undeniable that film is an important agent in the transmission and reflection of elements of the larger cultural context in which it is produced, and many filmmakers are conscious of these functions. But, the description of such cultural agency cannot be a substitute for the close reading of artistic texts. Conscientious close readings are the necessary prerequisite to decisions about films' connections to and reflections of their surroundings.

The approach to reading a film with a recognition of the establishing importance of its first few minutes is offered as an approach to the close reading of the film. It is not offered as a rejection of critical readings that position the filmic text in its relationship to its cultural context. It is not offered as a rigid, principled insistence upon what is within a filmic text and what lies outside of it. Allowing a film's first few minutes to provide an orientation as to the interpretation of the film can lead to rich and nuanced readings that can then serve the interests in social, historical and political dimensions of filmic practice.

Confronting concepts proposed for literary and cultural reflection, yet in a very different context from the one at hand, Mabel Moraña, Enrique Dussel and Carlos Jaúregüi condemned some propositions as "fashionable notions, [that…] when taken as totalizing critical paradigms, provide limited and limiting knowledge of Latin American cultural and political problems" (16). And, their point is well-taken. If any concept (here "the first few minutes") is taken as a "totalizing critical paradigm," it is almost guaranteed to fail the test for paradigm. To argue for any concept as having totalizing paradigmatic status is largely a rhetorical gesture and as such is essentially empty. What is proposed is less of a metatheoretical or theoretical concept and more of a tool to view and describe films in new and richer ways. The attention paid to establishing filmic moments is as an orienting tool to be used in search of networks and connections within the filmic structure so as to arrive at rich and meaningful interpretive understandings. To begin with, then, the concept of "the first few minutes" is offered here as a guide for close reading of films, not as a privileged means to knowledge about cultural and political problems.

♦ 1 ♦

Through a Child's Eyes
Víctor Erice's 1973
El espíritu de la colmena
(The Spirit of the Beehive)

> *L'Esprit de la ruche* montre comment un enfant regarde l'"Histoire…. La seule chose qui demeure pour un enfant, c'est qu'il ne faut pas parler de certaines choses. C'était cette approche-là qui m'intérssait, cette façon de voir la réalité comme un primitif. Ce sentiment a été très bien compris, je crois, mais de façon intuitive, presque inconsciente, par le public.[1]
> —Víctor Erice quoted by Alain Phillippon
> in an interview for *Cahiers du Cinéma* (March 1988)

"Érase una vez…." "Un lugar de la meseta castellana hacia 1.940…." (Once upon a time…. A place on the Castilian plain around 1940). It is with these intertitles that most analyses of *El espíritu de la colmena* seem to read how this beautiful politically metaphorical film begins. Víctor Erice's, 1973 film, though, begins with soft music playing over a series of childlike drawings of children, a cat, a mushroom, a watch, and a girl jumping over a fire, for example; along side these drawings are offered the film credits. Then, the filmic narrative opens with a paved road and the arrival of a truck into what appears to be a small town called Hoyuelos. The town seems poor and rural, and the camera focuses briefly on an escutcheon emblem of a yoke and a set of arrows, a symbol of Francoist Spain. The truck sounds its horn announcing its arrival, and a number of children appear running behind it, attempting to open the rear of the truck. The driver gets out, and as he opens the rear of the truck another man greets him. The men begin to unload, and the children ask the rather rotund man about the movie. He answers them, and the narrative jumps to a woman with a piece of paper in hand, blowing a whistle, and shouting an announcement of the movie to be shown, complete with prices for old and young.

Then, a viewing area is improvised in the town hall, as chairs are set out and people begin to be seated. As people arrive, the rotund man takes tickets, and people talk among themselves. The lights go out and the movie begins. The movie begins with a man dressed in suit and tie explaining that the film will be about the life of Dr. Frankenstein. As the camera pans the audience seated in shadows, it focuses closely on two little girls, whom the viewer will come to know as Ana and Isabel.

El espíritu de la colmena (2006). Reproduced with permission obtained through EGEDA (Entidad de Gestión de los Productores Audiovisuales) [Spain].

1. Through a Child's Eyes

The film's narrative, thus, is set in postwar 1940 in a small town on the Castilian meseta. It is Sunday when the truck arrives with the movie. In the rundown multipurpose building, a showing of the film *Frankenstein* (James Whale, 1931) is organized. For ninety minutes, the old words of the romantic myth echo through the empty streets of the small town. In the improvised movie theater, among the public, are the two little girls: the blonde, Isabel, and Ana, the "morena" (brunette with dark eyes). They are sisters, and they are completely absorbed as they follow along with the movie. The smaller of the two, Ana, asks her older sister why the monster kills and why, in the end, he dies. These are but the first questions Isabel answers with her imagination: the monster is a spirit, she has seen him, and he can appear, if a friendly voice calls him forth.

> Si eres una amiga, puedes hablar con él cuando quieras. Cierras los ojos y le llamas ... "Soy Ana, soy Ana." (If you are a friend, you can speak with him whenever you want. You close your eyes and you call him ... "It's Ana, it's Ana.")

What is for Isabel is a game involving the imagination turns into a vital reality for her younger sister Ana, who wants to see the monster. She summons the spirit. And, in her search she finds and helps a fugitive, who is killed in the darkness of the night.

The old house where the two girls live with their parents is characterized by the presence (some analyses prefer to focus on absence[2]) of something impalpable that it would appear only Ana is determined to identify. Fernando and Teresa, the parents, live out their own nostalgia and their own frustration. Never do they imagine what is going on in the little girl's mind.

One day Ana disappears and there is an anguished search for her. She is found, but nobody, except Ana, knows how the story will end.

As mentioned, most readings of *El espíritu de la colmena* seem to see the film beginning with the "Érase una vez.... Un lugar de la meseta calellana hacia 1940..."

A drawing from *El espíritu de la colmena* (2006). Reproduced with permission obtained through EGEDA (Entidad de Gestión de los Productores Audiovisuales) [Spain].

ignoring somehow the earlier drawings and soundtrack with the credits presented along with them.³ However, these two elements form part of the filmic text, and they are crucial to establishing the matrix with which the film is to be read.

As mentioned also, the series of opening drawings appear to be from a child's hand, and the viewer, in fact, learns in the closing credits that they were drawn by Ana Torrent and Isabel Tellería, the two child actresses in the film. There are twelve drawings, and, in order, they depict:

1. A beehive with a swarm of bees tracing a path between the hive and the house; to the side stands a man in a beekeeper's suit (accompanying the drawing is the film's title);
2. A beekeeper with a beehive panel in hand (accompanying the drawing is the name of Fernando Fernán Gómez);
3. A blonde woman seated at a table writing (accompanying the drawing is the name of Teresa Gimpera);
4. Two girls (accompanying the drawing are the names of Ana Torrent and Isabel Tellería);
5. A train (accompanying the drawing are the names of other collaborating actors);
6. A cat (accompanying the drawing are the names of screenplay authors Ángel Fernández-Santos and Víctor Erice);
7. A girl jumping over a fire with three female figures watching from afar (accompanying the drawing is the name of the production head);
8. A building with two doors and a red roof, and a well along side of the building (accompanying the drawing is the name of the editor);
9. A male figure wearing a hat and a cape (accompanying the drawing is the name of the person in charge of music);
10. A mushroom (accompanying the drawing is the name of Luis Cuadrado, in charge of photography);
11. A gold pocket watch (accompanying the drawing is the name of the director); and
12. The depiction of a movie viewing scene with 18 people watching a movie screen on which is represented a scene with a girl beside water and a figure of someone hiding among the foliage (ending with a zoom to the depicted movie screen as the intertitle "Érase una vez..." is superimposed).

At this point the drawings end, and the viewer enters the diegetic world as the truck bringing the film comes down the road. At this moment, superimposed is a second intertitle that reads "Un lugar de la meseta castellana hacia 1.940...." As the truck enters Hoyuelos, the camera focuses on a wall that displays the emblem of a yoke and five arrows. The background music stops, and the first diegetic sound is the truck's horn followed by the shouting of children who announce that a film is coming. Children are, in fact, the first to seat themselves to watch the film, which begins with an announcer telling of the film's craziness and finally warning not to take it too seriously. And so end the first few minutes of *El espíritu de la colmena*, some 6 minutes and 20 seconds to be precise.

The soft, almost haunting music playing behind the drawings and credits is an instrumentalization played by a lone piano and a lone flute. The form of the instrumentalization indexes the bulk of the rest of the soundtrack which is comprised of children's songs, done with the same two lone instruments. The children's songs used as soundtrack emphasize, as they remind the viewer, the centrality of the child's perspective to the reading of this film. Children's songs are musicalized and form the soundtrack for key moments throughout the film.[4]

The orientation for the viewer is clear.

Because of the drawings, the early centrality of children, and the music, the scholar-viewer knows that the film is to be read from a child's perspective, and it is not long before he knows that the child's perspective is centered on Ana.

Because of the intertitles ("Érase una vez..." and "Un lugar de la meseta castellana..." the latter indexing Cervantes's introduction to *Don Quijote*),[5] the metatextual gambit of film (story) within a film (story), and *Frankenstein*'s announcer's warning not to take the story too seriously, the viewer knows that the film is not to be read literally as a realist narrative, but rather as a fable, whose ultimate meanings respond to an allegorical-symbolical level.

Because of the intertitular reference to 1940, the focus on the escutcheon of the yoke and arrows as an emblematic, iconic reference to the Falange and the Franco regime, and the phonic echo of the name Franco in Frankenstein, the viewer knows that the film is to be read at its allegorical-symbolical level in terms of its reference to postwar Francoist Spain.

The quality of Spanish films made since 1973, the undeniable talent of their directors and the critical and financial success achieved by them nationally and internationally notwithstanding, popular and critical opinion would still place among the best films of all time a film made in Spain in 1973, two years before Franco's death and two years before the official death of censorship. Directed in 1973 by Víctor Erice, who also wrote its script, *El espíritu de la colmena* is a canonical film, and it is considered by many as the best Spanish film ever.[6]

It would be difficult to imagine a retrospective festival of Spanish film that would not include this precious film, which is available to viewers everywhere.[7]

In spite of the community of opinion regarding the film's singular quality, *El espíritu de la colmena*, as a filmic text, is commonly misunderstood or not understood at all. This undoubtedly comes as a surprise to the director, who once gave the opinion that "En *El espíritu* había algo de misterio pero nunca había factores desconocidos" (In *Spirit of the Beehive* there was something of mystery, but there were no unknown factors.).[8] Those who view the film, however, frequently end up with the same sensation that Ana's family feels at the end of the film. Though the viewer may be impressed with the techniques used in the film and the efficacy of its expression, typically he experiences doubts about the story that is narrated and its meaning. This film, *El espíritu de la colmena* by Erice, generally is characterized as "enigmatic,"[9] and the purpose of this chapter is to offer an explanation for the enigma and to clarify elements of that confusion. Key to this purpose is the matrix which the film's first few minutes offer the viewer.

As was stated in the introductory chapter, several currents of contemporary critical theory commonly have insisted upon the primacy of the immanence of the artistic text. The text's immanence, notwithstanding, elements of it can "disappear" in the absence of a knowledge or recognition of particular referential information and/or without a familiarity with certain modeling codes on the basis of which and with whose knowledge the text is evaluated and its comprehension is enriched. Textual immanence implies the reader's ability to competently decode the complex network of textual relationships. It is one thing to hear the words and see the images, to understand the dialogue and to follow the story, that is, to have a readerly competence. It is something different, though, to possess an information network that allows the reader/scholar-viewer to understand the implications of what is being read, of what is being seen, and of what is being heard, and to relate it to an implied context.

The sense of enigma or confusion felt by the viewer with *El espíritu de la colmena* in terms of the cohesion or the meaning of the film can mainly be attributed to the degree of initiation in the artistic and cultural contexts and codes that the viewer may or may not possess and which would allow him to arrive at clearer meanings produced by the filmic text. Although the viewer may appreciate individual qualities of the film, he may unable to understand its ultimate implications and its overall meaning in terms of their relationship to an implied or connoted context or message.

The sense of enigma produced by Erice's film could be seen, then, in part as the result of some lacking in "cultural competence" or in recognizing matrices offered by the filmic text itself. Such a lack manifests itself in those cultural blind spots that might inhibit this highly acclaimed Spanish film from producing clear meanings at the level of connotative abstraction. These are blind spots which range from the general, like, for example, ability and experience with artistic decodification (as, for example, recognition of the importance of the "first few minutes," central to the thesis of this volume), to the more specific. The requisite specific areas of cultural competence include what is most closely associated with a culture, like, for example, a knowledge of Spain's socio-historical context, a familiarity with Spanish 'infraculture,' and an awareness of things purely cinematographic.

It is possible that a viewer not focused on artistic decodification might enjoy watching *El espíritu de la colmena*, but undoubtedly he will end up with a fragmented, not very cohesive understanding of the film. This will be the case until the viewer seeks to find in the film's structure the elements of an organization that will allow the work to be conceived of as a signifying whole. The key concept here is "whole," and important to the whole are the first few minutes as they establish an orientation to the understanding of the whole. What is required is an ability to perceive intentionality, understood as the semantic energy which resolves tensions and contradictions between and among individual textual elements and components and gives them a specific relationship to other elements and gives a unified meaning to all of them together. Until a viewer brings to his analysis such an understanding of intentionality in art as an important modeling system, there may always be certain elements in the film that escape him or that seem to him to be loose ends.

Another kind of competence or experience that is important to allowing *El espíritu de la colmena* to produce clear meanings in its viewers is related to their overall level of contextual/referential knowledge. In order for this film to be read in terms of its unified semantic potential, it is important for the viewer to possess and bring to bear a certain network of information, a certain "data base" that prepares him to capture the implications of what he is seeing and hearing, and that allows him to relate it to an implied, only connoted, context. That is, the viewer must possess an understanding of the potential referentiality of the film. Without this understanding, there are elements and components of the film that may seem to the viewer to be empty, gratuitous, or confusing.

All educational systems have a moral goal that they hope to achieve and that informs their curricula. They seek to produce a certain kind of human being, a certain kind of citizen. In this regard, the political regime is important, as it needs citizens who agree with its fundamental principles. Nowhere is this more apparent than in the Spain of Francisco Franco. For nearly forty years, an authoritarian and paternalistic political regime controlled the cultural competence of its citizens through the implementation of a national educational curriculum and through a complex and effective censorship apparatus, both designed in order to homogenize Spanish society in tune with an archconservative, traditional vision. Any deviation from what was prescribed was severely proscribed. In terms of a film like *El espíritu de la colmena* being able to produce clearly apprehensible messages, then, it seems plausible to speak of readerly incompetencies "inflicted" on the Spanish public at the time of the production and the release of this film. "Inflicted readerly incompetencies" among a viewing public comprised of several generations, inhibits Erice's film in terms of its potential referentiality. If not altogether lost, several filmic indices to Spain's socio-historical context could become hollow or lose their potential meaning for the "afflicted" viewer.

On the other hand, non–Spanish viewers also will suffer from their own readerly blind spots. These blind spots are not, however, inflicted but rather inherent. Some elements of the film, for example, are very intimately linked to Spanish culture; they are endemic to Spanish cultural codes, and as such they are significant primarily for Spaniards. It is possible that the non–Spanish viewer, uninitiated in detailed information pertinent to the culture, may not be capable of "reading" certain elements in *El espíritu de la colmena*.

And, finally, in order to achieve the full production of meaning through the "reading" of *El espíritu de la colmena*, readerly competence implies a knowledge of and an initiation in certain film techniques, and a disposition towards resolving the tensions within the text. In many ways, *El espíritu de la colmena* is a daring film. It is not ashamed to be a film, to show itself as a film. So many films do show a particular reticence in the face of the expressive and technical possibilities that their medium offers, and they seem to prefer to take the viewer by the hand through the use of narrative techniques common to other arts, with which the viewer may be more comfortable, more familiar, or more accustomed. Director Erice, however, makes use of techniques that make film unique among the arts, and here they are consistent with the child's perspective established as matrix in the first few minutes of the film. The viewer who is not accustomed to such techniques may perhaps see certain elements of the film, if not as somewhat confusing, as examples of a poor or unsophisticated structure.

Erice, for example, makes repeated use of *dissolves*. A daylight shot of the exterior of the family house suddenly "dissolves," changing day into night. With the same dissolve technique, school morning and afternoon are compressed into seconds, as both cases produce a relativization of time that is wholly consistent with the structuring child's perspective.

The film contains an important, almost imperceptible *match cut/jump cut* combination. After school, Ana goes alone in search of the monster into the countryside to the abandoned building. The fact that this is a repeated (obsessive) act is only communicated and noted through the change in color of the little girl's stockings in the different shots that are conjoined and superimposed in the match cut/jump cut.

Far from being symptoms of inferior cinematographic structuring, as some viewers might tend to think, these technical figures, besides clearly identifying the artistic medium as cinematographic, serve the purpose of foregrounding the relativization of time. Time, which is typically compressed in film anyway, is openly compressed further in order to call attention to the continued and concentrated narrative focus from the child's perspective, and specifically to underscore the obsessive character of Ana's search.[10]

The contextualization of other referential and intentional elements referred to earlier in the search for semantic unity in the film leads to greater clarity and specificity.

One such element is the music from *El espíritu de la colmena*'s soundtrack. Quite possibly, the uninitiated viewer will ignore the importance of the soundtrack in any film, and the significance of the music in this film will escape the viewer who has no experience with details of Spanish culture. *El espíritu de la colmena*'s soundtrack, as mentioned earlier, is comprised of instrumental adaptations of children's songs "El patio de mi casa," "Tengo una muñeca," "Vamos a contar mentiras," and others. All of these songs are those which little Spanish girls have always sung when they play. And knowing this, recognizing this fact, the viewer is capable of conceiving the implications of this element so integral to the filmic discourse and so integral to the matrix established in the film's first few minutes. The character of these musical elements of this modeling system indicates to the viewer once again that the filmic discourse is structured from child's perspective, and that the narrative implications of the film are best understood from that point of view.

Just as the musical soundtrack is intimately linked to culture, so too are other elements of the film, and for this reason, they also may offer some interpretative difficulties. One of those elements is the scene in which Fernando, the father, and the two little girls are in the mountains. They are looking for mushrooms, and in doing so, Fernando carefully teaches the girls about the poisonous varieties and the ones that can be eaten. To the uninitiated viewer this episode might seem somewhat strange and disconnected with the rest of the film. It is important to know, though, that this act of passing on popular wisdom about wild mushrooms from one generation to another is a common rite of initiation in some sectors of Spanish society. Knowing this allows for an interpretation as to the meaning of the scene, and once again the emphasis is on the child's perspective since what is selected to be included within the filmic discourse is a key moment in the sociocultural initiation of the Spanish child. The internal artistic function of the scene, on the other hand, ought to be obvious to any viewer, since it is a poisonous mushroom that Ana offers to the "monster" in the hallucinatory sequence during her escape towards the end of the film. Equally important for the internal structure of the film is the possibility of Fernando's indexing the mother as he stomps on the poisonous mushroom, "the worst of them all."[11]

For some viewers, *El espíritu de la colmena* has always had two central enigmatic elements: Teresa's letters and the identity of the man who is killed in the night. These elements perhaps are enigmatic because of what was earlier referred to as an "inflicted readerly incompetence." If the viewer of this film has not been informed as to the violent and divisive nature of civil war in general, if he is not aware of the character and the extremes of the ideological excision in 20th century Spain as well as the particular consequences that violence and division had for the country in the post-war period, that viewer is not prepared to understand the significance of these two elements. The man, a wounded soldier with his head bandaged, who jumps from the train and takes refuge in the abandoned building where Ana and Isabel have been looking for the "espíritu" is undoubtedly a ***maquis***. After the end of the Spanish Civil War, there were more than fifty thousand *maquis*. These *maquis* were soldiers from the Republican army who, because they refused to accept defeat at the hands of the Nationalists, kept on fighting, because of which they were considered criminal renegades and they were hunted down. This referential information not only explains the uniform the man wears and his furtive behavior, but it also explains why he is killed by machine gun fire in the darkness of the night.

Near the beginning of the film, Teresa, the mother, without any one in the family realizing it, writes a letter to an unknown person. Only the viewer has access to and knowledge of the contents of the letter through a *voiceover*:

> Aunque me doy cuenta de que ya nada puede hacer volver aquellas horas felices que pasamos juntos, pido a Dios que me conceda la alegría de volver a encontrarte. Se lo he pedido siempre desde que nos separamos, incluso en medio de la guerra. Y se lo sigo pidiendo ahora....
>
> (Although I realize that now nothing can bring back those happy times we spent together, I pray to God that he grant me the joy of seeing you again. I have continued praying this since we were separated, even in the midst of war. And I am praying for it even now....)

The unknown, unnamed person is missed; it seems to have been a long time since Teresa has had any news from this person. Different critical speculations have wanted to identify the addressee of this letter as an adopted son lost in France or as a lover. Given the coldness of the marriage relationship between Fernando and Teresa that is seen on screen, it seems clear the letter is written to a lover. It seems equally clear that the lover to whom the letter is written is the murdered *maquis*. His having jumped from the train at this spot on the Castilian meseta cannot be mere chance. Further, and more importantly, the second secret letter, the one Teresa writes to the Red Cross, is thrown into the fire once news of the *maquis*' death is learned. In a cause-effect metonymy, the *maquis*' death causes Teresa to destroy the letter in the fire.[12] With the *maquis* dead, there is no reason to send a letter, if he is the addressee.

All of this is important as it has to do with what has been presented earlier as the central narrative perspective, the child's point of view. The conclusion to which this inexorably leads is that the *maquis* is not only Teresa's former lover, but that he is also Ana's father.[13] If the scholar-viewer is unsatisfied with leaving apparent loose ends hanging, a search, guided by the readerly orientation established in the first few minutes of the film, for the semantic energy that resolves conflicts and tensions among elements of the narrative will lead him inexorably to this conclusion. This conclusion is supported by other elements of the filmic discourse that may have gone by unnoticed, elements which from Ana's perspective, established as central to the matrix for reading the film in its first few minutes, are crucial to finding semantic unity in this work of art.

Teresa and Fernando, the parents in *El espíritu de la colmena*, are both blondes. (In truth, Fernando, played by Fernando Fernán Gómez, leans more towards being a redhead). Isabel, the older of the two daughters, is also blonde. However, in spite of these genetic precedents, Ana has hypnotic dark eyes and dark hair; she is "morena" (brunette). This difference creates a tension in the text, supported by other tensions within the family to which other critics have alluded frequently. Her different physical appearance along with her fascination/identification with the spirit/monster, raises a doubt as to Ana's birth, and from this circumstance, it is possible to speculate that Fernando is not Ana's biological father.

This speculation finds some corroboration in a match cut that connects two like-featured characters. Returning from a sojourn into the moonlit darkness of the night, and ignoring her sister's questions as to where she has been, Ana falls asleep with the left side of her face on the pillow. The close-up of the dark-haired child falling asleep dissolves into a close-up of the fugitive *maquis* in the same position as he sleeps in the abandoned building after having jumped from the train. The close-up of the fugitive foregrounds his dark features. This match cut (1:10:25 to 1:10:37) establishes a strong continuity between Ana and the fugitive as the two shots link them metaphorically (one continued in the other).

One day (the next day?) Ana returns alone to the solitary abandoned farmhouse, and she discovers the dark-haired soldier, wounded and sitting on the ground. His head is bandaged and his leg is wounded. Hearing Ana approach, he takes out his pistol, but, when he sees that it is a child, he hides the gun and accepts an apple she offers him. Later, during another visit, Ana takes him some other things he might need –bread, shoes, and Fernando's coat. All of this occurs without there being any verbal communication (with the one-word exception of Ana offering him the apple, "Ten"). However, the viewer can see that there is an apparent tacit bond in the empathy and tenderness between the two. It can be speculated to be a "spiritual" bond supported by genetics.

In the darkness of the night, machine gun fire is heard and the flashes of the fired rounds are seen and heard. The following morning, the dead body of the man lies on a slab in the place that earlier had served as the improvised movie theater. The civil guards have called Fernando, since his watch was found in the pocket of the dead man's coat. Fernando returns home to have breakfast with his family. He takes out the watch and looks at Ana, who in turn stares at the watch. She gets up from the table and runs to the solitary abandoned farmhouse, only to find the bloody traces of the man to whom she had offered friendship and tenderness. Ana then runs off, and a search for her ensues. Night falls without a trace of her having been found. The camera then presents a hallucinatory sequence that runs parallel to a similar sequence from *Frankenstein* in which Ana is kneeling beside a river looking at the reflection of the moon in the water. Suddenly, also reflected in the water, a somber figure appears behind her. It is the Frankenstein monster, but a close-up reveals that he has the face of Fernando.[14] Ana offers him a mushroom she has picked.

The "espíritu" for which Ana[15] is searching is her father. Although, because of her tender age, she is unable to articulate it, hers is an Oedipal search, motivated by an unspoken desire to answer questions and to solve the mysteries of life and of her own identity.

Clearing up artistic, referential and filmic blind spots, and tying up loose ends allows greater precision in determining the meaning of this film on the literal level and, at the same time, it creates an appreciation for what the film achieves in cinematographic/narrative terms. But, one more step remains: specifying the implications of the film on a level of allegorical-symbolical abstraction and its relationship to an implicit context. The need for this step was offered in the first few minutes of the film as part of the orientation as to how the film is to be read. Later on and shortly after those establishing moments, Isabel reinforces the invocation to read this film on another level when she tells Ana that "…en el cine todo es mentira. Es un truco." (…in cinema, everything is a lie. It is a trick.) (22:30). The film having established itself as a fable with the orientation provided by the first few minutes, it is incumbent that the scholar-viewer discover the "truco"/trick and arrive at a meaning on an allegorical-symbolical level.

This step will bring with it an appreciation for the film in terms of its worth as a historical document. In order for *El espíritu de la colmena* to produce this connotative meaning, what is first required is an intertextual reference.

Víctor Erice turned to the genre of horror film in order to create a caricature of Spain through intertextuality with the film *Frankenstein*. Dr. Frankenstein is a sinister creator whose very name instrumentalizes and creates a phonic echo of "Franco."[16] Frankenstein constructs a ghostly, spectral collage; he creates a monstrous figure who possesses no identity of his own and who possess no moral sense. This monster can, one moment, show a friendly tenderness, and the next moment he can kill, because he has lost his memory. The Frankenstein monster is a perfectly suited metaphor for the Spain created by Franco. The "spirit" of the title, at the allegorical level, is the ghost of the Civil War, after which the Franco regime set about creating an artificially unitary Spain in which many saw themselves defined by that with which they did not identify. At an allegorical level, Ana's literal Oedipal search becomes a search in which Spain is searching for its complete identity, for its origins; it is the search for a pluralistic heritage from which the country had been separated as a result of civil war. It is, then, in one sense, a search the need for which was caused by the loss of historical perspective.

But, does this return the scholar-viewer to enigma? For some, it would seem so. Sarah Thomas (2007) concludes:

> The film's ending is wide open. Ana is seen once again in closeup, and, in a repeat of her calling the monster who seems to materialize as the fugitive jumping from the train, she closes her eyes. A voice-over ... whispers "Soy Ana...." The image resonates with all the themes implicit and explicit in the film. Ana is on the threshold of becoming ... a woman? The inheritor of a new (post–Franco) Spain? ... the allegorical reading is expressly invited, yet there are too many levels for the allegory to function neatly. Ambiguity is maximized here again [196].

If ambiguity is enigma, then *El espíritu de la colmena* is enigmatic. There is no closure; in fact, what is suggested is continuity or circularity, which is underscored once again by music. Once "FIN" is shown on a black screen, the same music plays as that which served as background to the opening credits and drawings. Final film credits roll on the same black background, as this music continues to play, sending the viewer back to where he started, creating a circularity. Of course, there is no ending to the allegorical reading. In 1973, Víctor Erice could not write/film/allegorize an ending to the problematic his film describes. There is, though, a prediction or a prescription of sorts. At the end of the film, the doctor tells Teresa, "...Se le pasará.... Poco a poco irá olvidando" (...It will pass.... Little by little she will forget.).

The first few minutes of *El espíritu de la colmena* orient the viewer towards the centrality of the child's perspective and towards the need to understand Ana's search, both literally and allegorically. That search of hers is also the search for an escape from another of the film's dominant metaphors: the beehive. The house where the family lives looks like the houses typically seen in horror films. It is large; it is empty, dark, and somber. The little girls run through hallways that seem to swallow up their little forms. The windows of the house are made of a yellowish glass cut and placed in hexagonal shapes. This image equates the monotonous life of the house's inhabitants with that of the bees in the beehives Fernando tends. The loud buzzing of bees on the soundtrack supports the visual suggestivity of the windows. The color also contributes to the beehive metaphor with interior scenes having been shot through a yellow filter, thus creating a yellowing, antiquated effect. All of this must be viewed as well as figuratively and connotatively interpreted, as in the case of the Frankenstein myth, as metaphors for Spain.[17]

The need to search for precise, clear meanings at a allegorical-symbolical level for a filmic discourse created in 1973-Spain clearly responds to the existence of an official censorship apparatus, which, for nearly four decades, conditioned all semiotic output in Spain. The film's critical allegorical implication obviously "attacks the Regime and its institutions ... [and those attacks] characterize the whole of the work,"[18] and if the film had been more literal and more direct in its critique, it, in all likelihood, would not have escaped censorship. Due to that circumstance, in 1973 it was still impossible to directly and literally confront problems of national importance. Ironically, though, the existence of censorial oversight seems to have encouraged creative expression at the same time as it makes comprehension of the expression of deeper meanings problematic/enigmatic.

The relaxing, and ultimate cessation, of censorship practices and the subsequent process of facing the nation's traumatic past, have made it easier for postwar generations to have access to the richness of meanings in this marvelous film. And, this is perhaps the reason why, since its first showing in October of 1973, *El espíritu de la colmena*, instead of falling into oblivion as an enigmatic cinematographic curiosity piece, has grown in stature and has risen to assume a lofty place within the whole of Spanish film production. If director Víctor Erice's *El espíritu de la colmena* is to continue to enjoy the high esteem in which it is held, it is important that younger generations and Hispanophiles everywhere be open to the lessons to be learned in the film's first few minutes, where children's drawings accompanying opening credits with musical support have the establishing potential for the orientation towards the filmic narrative's child's eye point-of-view. Similar to Erice's *El espíritu de la colmena*, as was shown in the introductory chapter of this volume, Pedro Almodóvar uses fashion magazine cutouts accompanying opening credits to *Mujeres al borde de un ataque de nervios* to prime the viewer for a women's eye point-of-view filmic narrative.

In both films, the opening minutes offer the scholar-viewer a matrix for interpreting the point-of-view that structures the filmic discourse and the point of view from which it should be read. And, in both films, point-of-view and perspective are quickly united with establishing close-ups. In *Mujeres al borde* ... it is in a sleeping/dreaming Pepa, whose search will be for answers as to why her relationship was "unsavable." In *El espíritu* ... point-of-view and perspective come together in the focal child Ana, whose literal, personal search seems tied to Oedipal questions and identities central to the allegorical meanings.

1. Through a Child's Eyes

The elements of the opening of Víctor Erice's *El espíritu de la colmena* make clear another of a film's first few minutes' possible orientations, as detailed in the introduction. *El espíritu*'s opening minutes establish interpretive keys for reading the film. With the cues of "Érase una vez…" (Once upon a time…) and the metatextual device of film (story) within a film (story), the scholar-viewer is programmed not only to clarify the enigmas of the film's literal narrative, but also, and more importantly perhaps, to read it as a fable, whose deeper meanings play out on an allegorical-symbolical level.

Alerted to point-of-view and perspective, and programmed to read not only literally but allegorically, the first few minutes prepare the scholar-viewer to access the aesthetic and semantic potential of this rich and complex filmic text, where John Hopewell, as indeed does all of the bibliography dedicated to *El espíritu de la colmena*, points out that "Ana's story is open to psychological, cinematic, and historical readings, all of which naturally overlap" (205).

◆ 2 ◆

REFLECTIONS OF ART AND LIFE
Carlos Saura's Flamenco Trilogy:
Bodas de sangre (1981), *Carmen* (1983),
El amor brujo (1986)
*(Blood Wedding; Carmen;
Love, the Magician)*

> Commentators sometimes refer to Carmen as myth, implying ... the timelessness of her story, an idea that implies that somehow Carmen has always been with us in Western culture. And Carmen's story taps into age-old concerns about sexual and ethnic otherness. The specific origins of Carmen have been much more recent ... a short story by the French writer Proper Mérimée. This novella offers us Carmen's story at third hand: it is told by an imprisoned don José to an unidentified traveller, who in turn recounts it to us the readers.... The refusal of patriarchy to allow Carmen to speak for herself is of a piece with the misogynistic tone struck from the very beginning of the story's preceding epigraph, which informs us that women are bitter as gall and only offer any pleasure when they are either in bed or in the grave.... Mérimée first offered us Carmen, subsequent attempts to tell Carmen's tale trace the struggle between her efforts to tell her own story and those of others to tell it for her.
> —Ann Davies, Introduction to *Carmen.*
> *From Silent Film to MTV*

First the viewer hears the rhythmic sounds of stomping feet and clicking fingers, and then a group of women appears, as the viewer watches from behind; a man leads them. They are dancing flamenco in a studio in front of a mirrored wall. Suddenly, the viewer realizes that the man among them is directing the dancers. He stations himself in front of and facing the dancers as he observes them. The reflection in the mirror allows the viewer to see the women dance while the camera focuses on the man, who continues observing the women closely. The camera, from the directing man's perspective, focuses on several women individually. He, then, claps and he asks the women to organize themselves again. They begin dancing again, first with his help, then, alone. The man stops them, and he calls forward one woman and he asks her to dance. First one, then another and then another. He, then, calls Cristina, a woman seated somewhat away from the scene, and he asks her to take over rehearsal with the women.

The man steps down from the mirrored rehearsal area to speak with a seated Paco, guitar in hand; he asks him when he plans to go to Seville. He tells Paco that, during the trip, he should visit the dance academies and look for a woman for the role of Carmen, because none of the girls in the studio at that moment convinces him. Something is not right with each one of them; they are not bad, but he does not see any of them as Carmen. While he smokes a cigarette, the smoke floats among them.

Suddenly, the viewer hears the sound of an opera; the screen shows sketches of opera costumes and scenes depicting 19th century garb and style. The sketched engravings are by Gustave Doré, further anchoring them in the 19th century, and over the sketches, the film credits begin to be superimposed. The music becomes louder. The sketches present women dancing, images of women with tambourines, and even an engraving with a bat and macabre-faced characters reminiscent of Goya's *Caprichos*. One sketch shows a woman with a cape and sword dancing around a reclining bullfighter. Given the reference already to the role of Carmen, and as one of the superimposed credit titles gives the title of the film, *Carmen*, it is possible for the viewer to conclude that the drawings and sketches are from, or that they index a subtextual *Carmen*.

Because the characters (dancers, choreographer, guitarist…) that appear here are associated with their real-life field of endeavor, the initiated viewer will easily identify them. The director is quickly identifiable as Antonio Gades (1936–2004), nationally and internationally known for his dancing and for popularizing the art form. His assistant is Cristina Hoyos (1946–), well-known female flamenco dancer and the one who actually danced the part of Carmen when this dance troupe did, in fact, tour Europe with the show they are rehearsing in the film. The guitarist is Paco de Lucía (1947–2014), famous Spanish flamenco guitarist also popular as a crossover artist in classical and jazz forms. The woman singing flamenco is Pepa Flores (1948–), also known since the early 1960's as Marisol, famous child star and popular culture icon. The easy recognizability of these stars and the fact that they are doing what they do, that is performers preparing a performance, identify these people in "real" life.

Because Antonio steps down from the rehearsal stage to converse with a friend and colleague, two different levels are suggested, art and life. Because of the presence of the mirrors, two different levels are further suggested, the image and its reflection. Because of the presence and ultimate blending of multiple textures (flamenco, operatic, visual, guitar, orchestral), intertextual or intermedial mixture, or cacophony is suggested. With theses cues, the first few minutes of the film have oriented and prepared the viewer to read Carlos Saura's *Carmen* as confronting art and life in a confusion of textual levels.

With dozens of characteristic feature-length productions to his credit since 1959, director and screen play writer, Carlos Saura is among the pioneer filmmakers of contemporary Spain. In addition, with great filmic successes that range from *Los golfos* (1959), *La caza* (1965), *El jardín de las delicias* (1970), *La prima Angélica* (1973), *Cría cuervos* (1974), *Elisa, vida mía* (1977), the 1980's flamenco trilogy, *Bodas de sangre* (1981), *Carmen* (1983) y *El amor brujo* (1985), through the 1990's ¡*Ay, Carmela!* (1990), *Flamenco* (1995), *Tango* (1998), and *Goya en Burdeos* (1999), to the recent millennium-beginning *Buñuel y la mesa del rey Salomón* (2001), *El séptimo día* (2004), *Iberia* (2005), *Fados* (2007), and *Flamenco, flamenco* (2010), Saura is one of the most important and prolific directors in contemporary film.

Beginning as a young disciple of the classic Spanish film director, Luis Buñuel, Saura was ideologically committed to opposition to the Franco regime, and in this vein he produced a series of early works that explore the meaning of life in a repressive society and the enduring effects of civil war in Spain. In a 1976 interview after Franco's death, Saura said, "Franco was like a wall, a barrier, beyond which it was impossible to advance...."[1] But Carlos Saura managed to advance, and in order to do so, he had to evade censorship; to escape it, he created productions that were personal allegories and that clearly criticized the realities of Franco's Spain and the Cainist divisions that had given rise to civil war.

With films like *La caza*, *El jardín de las delicias*, *Ana y los lobos* and *La prima Angelica*, which, although not without some difficulty, were able to pass censorship, Carlos Saura was so successful that he came to be associated very closely with a difficult cinematic syntax. The use of symbols, metaphors and allegories, veiled allusion, childhood memories, the use of flashback and more, all are stylistic techniques that characterize Saura's *auteurist* expression as well as characterizing an aesthetic that came to be known as the *estética franquista*.[2] The narrative ambiguity and confusion required the viewer to participate very actively in the semiotic process of the production of hidden meanings. At the same time, the existence of censorial restrictions during the Franco dictatorship, obligated directors to express their sociopolitical critiques in an indirect way.[3]

In 1975 Franco dies and two years later official censorship disappears. With this, also disappearing is the need to create a demystifying discourse to subvert Francoist myth. Gone, too, is the urgency for historical recovery, and cinematographic directors, free of the censorial bonds, can take on themes of current import. In the face of new possibilities and new creative exigencies, Carlos Saura responds, again revealing the influence of Luis Buñuel.

If previously Saura had shown himself to be an inheritor of Buñuel's surrealist tradition, now the Aragonese filmmaker's influence is visible in the importance that is given to what is Spanish, what is Hispanic. Through his films, Buñuel had taught younger directors that *lo español*, what is Spanish, the country's literature and culture, history, legends, myths and traditions, is a rich source of themes for cinema. Picking up on the rich cultural heritage with its deep roots in Spanish tradition, Saura discovers flamenco music and dance, and in the early 1980's, he makes a series of films inspired in turn by things Spanish. They are films inspired respectively by a dramatic work by Spanish poet and playwright Federico García Lorca (*Bodas de sangre*, 1981), by a legendary cultural arquetype (*Carmen*, 1983), and by a ballet by Spanish composer Manuel de Falla (*El amor brujo*, 1985).

The trilogy of flamenco music and dance films from the 1980's represented a change in Saura's focus towards a more private and intimate world. In these works, the filmic discourse is richer, more complex, and more allusive. The films can be interpreted as ingenious, artful metaphors for the relationship between art and life, between creation/creativity and death.

As seen from the summary of the first few minutes, *Carmen*, by Carlos Saura, presents a real-life contemporary Spanish modern dance troupe, the well-known company of the renowned Antonio Gades. The narrative line of the film follows the company as it prepares and rehearses its own eclectically interpretive version from the novel *Carmen*, a 19th century novella by French writer Prosper Mérimée, and from the opera *Carmen* by Georges Bizet, itself inspired by the Mérimée novel.

The Mérimée novella is comprised of four parts, and it is written as a kind of travelogue in which the author relates the story through his experiences on a trip to Spain in 1830 during which he is searching for a battle site in Andalusia. Central in the novella, is Don José, a robber whom Mérimée meets during his search. In Part 1, Mérimée befriends the robber known as Don José Navarro and helps him escape.

Later, in Part 2, Mérimée meets Carmen, a beautiful gypsy woman; he goes to her home to have a fortunetelling, which is interrupted by Don José. Months later, when Mérimée learns José Navarro is to be executed, he visits him and listens to his life story, the subject of the novella's third part.

The robber is really a Basque hidalgo, who had killed a man in a fight and fled to Seville, where he joined a police unit. Don José reveals himself to be a man of ardent, if naïve passions. In Seville, the dragoon meets Carmen, a worker in a tabacalera (cigar factory), who sings and dances with Andalusian charm. Unlike others in his unit, he ignored Carmen, which caused her to tease with him. After a row in the factory in which she cuts a co-worker, bound by duty, José has to arrest her and take her to jail. However, José helps her to escape because she convinces him she is half Basque. For this, Don José, eventually, is imprisoned for a month and demoted.

After his release, Don José, who has fallen in love with Carmen, meets her and she repays his kindness with a day of bliss. Allowing some smugglers to pass his post, he is rewarded with another day with Carmen. Later, when José looks for her, he finds her with his lieutenant. In a fight, José kills the lieutenant, and he flees to Carmen's outlaw band, where he moves from smuggling to robbery and he lives a harsh life, contrary to his character. He does so, just to be close to the woman he loves.

Sometimes he was with Carmen, but he suffered from jealousy as she used her charms to further business; and he learned that she was married.

Carmen, who at first may have been in love with Don José, is in fact married under gypsy ritual, and her husband has just been released from jail. The ex-commandant, Don José learns of this; he seeks out the husband, and, provoking a knife fight, he ends up killing him. Carmen becomes José's wife. He then asks Carmen to go away with him to America to start a new and honest life. Carmen refuses and falls in love with a bullfighter, Lucas. At a bullfight, José realizes that he has been deceived. Mad with jealousy, he threatens Carmen, trying to get her to go with him, and, when she continues to rebel, not so much for any love she may feel for Lucas, but to preserve her freedom, José kills her. Carmen had said she had known from omens that he was fated to kill her. José blames the gypsies for the way they raised her.[4]

The four-act Georges Bizet opera *Carmen*, which is one of the most well known operas in the world, is based mostly on part three of the Mérimée novel, and it follows essentially the same story, with a few notable differences appropriate and important to a consideration of Saura's filmic text. The opera, for example, does not include Carmen's gypsy husband. The singing roles for females had no counterparts in characters of the novel. Additionally, major musical compositions highlight and heat up Carmen's fatalistic seductive attraction. The musical score highlights as well the role of the bullfighter, in the opera called Escamillo, not Lucas as in the novella. Carmen knows her fate, but not from reading cards but from other omens.

In Carlos Saura's *Carmen* the audience is witness not only to the Gades troupe's rehearsals as they prepare their unique interpretive performance of the classical work, but they are witness also to the lives of the very actors, dancers, and musicians who are members of the dance company. Narrative structure for the rehearsals comes from the story line of the Mérimée novel and major musical moments of Bizet's operatic *Carmen*, while the dance company members' lives are seemingly narrated by the omniscient, omnificent, all-seeing eye of Saura's camera.

Yet, is this really the case? As the film progresses, the viewer realizes that the Spanish dancers,' singers,' and director's lives and emotions become amazingly more and more like those of their fictional counterparts. Antonio

Carmen (1983).

Gades, company director and the dancer who is to interpret the part of Don José, in an effort to convincingly fill the role of Carmen, goes to Seville to visit dance studios in search of talent. There he discovers Carmen, a young, buxom, haughty, typically Andalusian beauty who dances in a gypsy flamenco *tablao*. In rehearsals, Carmen shows herself to be independent, strong-willed, and seductive. Outside rehearsals, Carmen and Antonio fall in love. In their relationship, it is the younger Carmen who is stronger than Gades. His love for her becomes a consuming obsession. After a time, Gades learns that his Carmen is married and that her husband, whom she claims to no longer love, is in jail on drug charges and will soon be released. Gades gives money to Carmen to be passed on to the husband so that he will disappear. After one particularly intense rehearsal, following which it seems that the studio is empty and all the dancers have left, director Gades discovers Carmen "fooling around" with another man in the properties/wardrobe room. Carmen's response to the obsessive, possessive Gades is, "Suéltame.... Quiero ser libre y hacer lo que me dé la gana." (Let go of me. I want to be free and to do what I feel like.).

From the summary of story lines it is easy to see how the literature-opera-film intertextual/intermedial foundation allows Saura's layered narrative discourse to brilliantly intertwine the levels of fiction inherent in a dual-role structure as an artful metaphoric exploration of the relationship between life and art. So skillful is Saura's narrative that at times the viewer can be confused and not know for sure if he is viewing a rehearsal of fictional events, or, on the other hand, if he is witness to the real-life interplay among the Gades company principals.

In the first few minutes, where a film normally declares its position *vis-à-vis* reality by setting up a matrix to orient the reading of the film itself, an orientation for its own interpretation, the viewer is notified as to the complex relationship between this film's history and its discourse. The fusion-confusion of narrative levels, of subtext(s) and text, is quickly enunciated; it is immediately made apparent. Foregrounded in the first five minutes is textual-subtextual juxtaposition. As we have seen, it is in this timeframe in which the film opens in the Gades' dance studio. Women are rehearsing flamenco dance steps under Antonio and Cristina's direction. Suddenly there is a jump to the film's credits, which are rolled against a background of drawings that look like they could be libretto scene sketch studies. Music from the Bizet opera accompanies the rolling of the credits.

The viewer knows, then, that what follows the film's first few minutes are juxtapositions of levels between the real preparations of the dance troupe and the artistic subtexts. The viewer further knows to expect an intertextual confluence, since classical music and flamenco music, the movement of the dancers and the stasis of the drawings, the 20th century and the 19th century are opposed, superimposed, and juxtaposed. From the first few minutes, then, the scholar-viewer knows that intertextual interplay is a key to the interpretation of the filmic text.

The fusion-confusion of narrative levels, of subtext(s) and text, is further underscored, and almost immediately following the establishing sequences, through the use of sound simultaneity. Again, in the Gades' studio, guitarist Paco de Lucía, singer Pepa Flores and others work on a flamenco song, a *bulería*, for the dance company's production. Someone arrives and gives a tape to Antonio. He puts the tape on the tape player and plays it to listen to it. It is music from the Bizet opera. Both musics, the flamenco of the group and the classical from the recording, blend in foregrounding cacophony.

A short time later, during a rehearsal, this simultaneous layering of subtext/text becomes further complicated with the visual effect of a mirror image and a voiceover quotation from the Mérimée novel. This occurs while Cristina, Gades' assistant, is rehearsing only the women. The camera intermittently shows them, their reflection in a wall of mirrors, or both them and their mirrored reflection. Gades silently observes as the audience hears a voiceover interior monologue quotation from the Mérimée subtext:

> Carmen era de una belleza extraña y salvaje.... Sus labios, algo carnosos pero bien perfilados, dejaban ver unos dientes más blancos que las almendras desprovistas de la piel. Sus cabellos eran negros, largos, brillantes, y, como el ala de un cuervo, tenían reflejos azulados. Sus ojos tenían una expresión voluptuosa y hosca al mismo tiempo que no he vuelto a encontrar en una mirada humana. Ojos de gitano, ojos de lobo ... dice un refrán español.
>
> (Carmen had a wild and strange beauty.... Her lips, full and well-shaped, opened onto small teeth, whiter than almonds with their skins removed. Her long, black shiny hair shimmered with blue like a raven's feathers. Her eyes had a voluptuous but surly expression that I've never been able to find again in a human gaze. Gypsy eyes, wolf eyes ... as the Spanish saying goes.)[5]

The voiceover quotation technique is also used by itself in order to intertwine subtext and text when Gades is sitting in a dance studio in Seville looking over a group of girls rehearsing flamenco dance. He discovers the girl who is to play the lead in his production; he discovers his Carmen. While he watches the dancers, the voiceover quotes from the Mérimée novel narrating the first encounter with Carmen,

> Levanté los ojos y la vi. Era un viernes y no lo olvidaré jamás. Al principio, no me gustó y volví a mi trabajo. Pero ella, siguiendo la costumbre de los gatos, que no vienen cuando se les llama y vienen cuando no se les llama, se detuvo ante de mí y me dirigió la palabra.
>
> (I looked up and I saw her. It was Friday.... I'll never forget it. At first she did not please me. I went back to my work. But, as is customary with women and cats who don't come if you call but come if you don't call, she stopped in front of me and spoke to me.)[6]

Characters in "life," dance company members become identified with the roles they are to play in the flamenco dance version of *Carmen*. This is achieved in plot duplication in two-part scenes. The reflection or mirroring of life and art in the case of the sexual attraction between the principles becomes literal at the end of a rehearsal when Carmen and Antonio face a mirror as they portray Carmen and José.

From these few examples it is clear that this film situates the viewing audience within a world of fusion-confusion of narrative lines, a world of intertextual madness. It is a filmic *demimonde* into which various elements from Mérimée's literary subtext or Bizet's operatic subtext are absorbed and transformed.

Kiril Taranovsky, picking up the heritage that began in Jurij Tynianov and continued in Mikhaïl Bakhtin and Jan Mukařovsky, offers some useful categories for considering *subtext/text* relationships. In his *Essays on Mandel'stam*, Taranovsky classifies subtexts into four categories:

> 1. that which serves as a simple impulse for the creation of an image; 2. the borrowing of a rhythmic figure and the sounds contained therein; 3. the text which supports or reveals the message of the later text; 4. the text which is treated polemically by the poet.[7]

From the previous summary of the narrative lines for Mérimée's novel, Bizet's opera, and Saura's *Carmen*, and from the few examples of the film's complex history/discourse relationship, it is evident that the literary and operatic subtexts fit Taranovsky's first category. The literary and operatic subtexts clearly serve as impulse for the creation of the filmic text. Additionally, the voiceover quotations from Mérimée's novel and the use of Bizet's musical compositions clearly constitute the "borrowing of a rhythmic figure and the sounds contained therein" as described in the second category of Taranovsky's taxonomy. But, as Taranovsky himself observes, the mere pointing out of the borrowing of a determined rhythm or image "does not necessarily contribute to our understanding…."[8]

In the case of Saura's *Carmen*, the identification of subtexts or elements thereof that constitute the similarity relationship between subtextual sources and the film itself does not really help to better understand the semiotic process of the phenomenical (surface) structure of the filmic text. The interest lies not in stating that certain determined literary or operatic elements serve as an "impulse" for the creation of Saura's filmic text, but rather it lies, on the one hand, in analyzing the dialogical relationship between the film and its literary-operatic backdrop, which, on the other hand, indicates the allegorical-symbolic message contained in the filmic text. Both of the questions are related respectively to subtextual relationship types 3 and 4 of Taranovsky's typology.

2. Reflections of Art and Life

As Saura selects passages, episodes, events, and musical compositions from the literary or operatic subtextual material for the narration of certain episodes of his film *Carmen*, he very often respects their linguistic or musical configuration, to the point, as we have seen, of quoting directly several times. However, such fidelity to subtextual material at a linguistic or musical level does not guarantee the respecting of other important aspects of those subtexts. A purely linguistic juxtaposition or regrouping of a text fragment detaches it from any previous or pre-existing dialogical relationships.

The consideration of the selection of literary or operatic documents that are found in Carlos Saura's *Carmen* cannot be done without analyzing how this material is inserted in the film as part of the structural and signic filmic whole. As part of the narrative structure of the film, the literary and operatic material loses much of the signifying value it had as an independent sign in order to gain new significance in relationship to the new structure of which it forms part. There are two aspects of the novel (literature) and the opera that are obliterated in the transposition to the filmic code: the chronological character that the material possessed as a syntagmatic-syntactical element of and within the subtext, and the referential character that the material had within the subtexts' particular semiotic structures.

The linguistic or motif fragments taken from Mérimée or Bizet, as they are combined with the rest of the elements that configure *Carmen*'s [Saura] structure, become pieces in the *collage* composition of the film. The breaking or negation of chronological linearity is a characteristic of Carlos Saura's *Carmen*'s structure. The break in the order of the *chronos* affects the perception of the literary/operatic fragments inserted in the filmic discourse. On the one hand, the fact that they are often direct quotes would lead the viewer to read them as such; but, on the other, the fact that they appear integrated into a structure that often negates temporal succession—through the fragmentary presentation of narrative nuclei or through the simultaneous presentation of elements whose relationship is not established within a spatial/temporal logic—makes the viewer's reading them as literature or opera impossible. Scholar-viewers are carried along the narrative thread towards a reading of the literary/operatic as the simple raw material for the composition of the film's narration. The destruction of temporal succession is one of the ways in which Saura's film works to erase the distinction between art and life.

There is a tension between the particular literary and operatic elements used as material for the filmic text and their abstraction and synthesis at the narrative level that strips them of their subtextual referentiality and presents them as simple concrete examples that are repeated. This tension permits the interpretation of the subtextual elements on two planes. As literary and operatic facts, they show the particularity of the subtexts that concretize them. But, within the film, because they are subject to a process of synthesis and abstraction that the work imposes on them, they become symbols that lose referentiality to concrete subtexts as they enter into semiotic relationships with other textual elements.

Narrative activity demands an intellectual process that subjects subtextual elements to a process of abstraction that turns them into symbols in relation to reality. In this process of generalization, systematic relationships between elements tend to be established. If the superpositioning/superimposing of different elements (literary-operatic-filmic / art-life) can be considered as a way of removing concrete referentiality from the subtextual elements, in Saura's *Carmen* the generalization process is favored further by the very choice of archetypal content.

In this way, then, the viewer realizes that in *Carmen*, **Art**, in general, and the literary/ operatic material, specifically, utilized in the film are treated polemically. The polemical relationship is reflected in two aspects. First, the break with the chronological character that supports the subtextual story line upon being inserted into a narrative structure that breaks temporal linearity and leads to a conception of Art as one more entity within the film text's changing and static "life." And further, the polemical relationship is reflected in the abstraction and synthesis of the literary/operatic elements realized in the narrative process that emphasizes the symbolic. As a consequence, it strips them of their concrete artistic ties and makes them applicable to any case.[9]

The relaxation of the rigid temporal succession of chronological linearity leaves the viewer with the sensation of a chaotic reality. At a literal level, this chaos reflects the chaotic state of the obsessively enamored Gades' emotions. At an allegorical-symbolic level, it is a reflection of a historical period of chaos and confusion that characterizes 1980's man-woman relationships in Spain in particular and in the Western world in general. Thematically, Saura leaves behind his obsession with the civil war and its related themes, in order to focus of themes of sexual and social politics.

At a pole opposite from the chaos and confusion is the static sensation of the filmic text. In spite of the constant shifts from subtext to text, from literature/opera to film, from art to life, stasis is reflected in the fact that none of these shifts supposes any real change.

Nowhere are the results of the polemical relationship between Art, the literary/operatic subtextual material, and Life, the subject of the filmic text's discourse more apparent than in *Carmen*'s final scene. In the film's ending, the entire dance company, featuring a bullfighter, Carmen and Don José, is rehearsing a flamenco style dance to a song about jealousy. Suddenly, Carmen [Carmen-life?] and Don José [Antonio Gades?] break away from the rehearsal group [Art?]. Arguing, they leave the studio stage [entering Life?]. After Carmen tells Antonio that it's over, she tries to enter the dressing room. Gades grabs her, and, in the doorway half-hidden from the viewer's gaze, he stabs her to death. The confused viewer might ask if Antonio really kills Carmen; the answer must be yes. While these moments of the film's final scene are played out, the "Toreador Song" ("Votre toast, je peux...") from Bizet's opera is heard progressively more loudly as if to underscore the lack of change between textual and subtextual narrative lines.

Since the same schemas are repeated in each mode, the man-woman relationship is presented to the film's audience as profoundly static.[10]

Seeing the final scene, viewers may be momentarily confused. Are they seeing Saura's *Carmen* featuring the Gades dance company's personal relationships [Life], the Gades dance company's rehearsals for its *Carmen* [Life or Art?], Mérimée's *Carmen* or Bizet's *Carmen* [Art]? The answer to the questions raised by the intertextual fusion/confusion, in fact, is not so important because the story is the same: it is again the story of Carmen, of the gypsy girl and the soldier, of a mystical and abstract Spain,[11] of the archetypal *femme fatale* and of *amour fou*. Since the subtextual story does not change, it is clear that life has imitated art. It is Carlos Saura's *Carmen*, and through his narrative technique that confuses and erases distinctions between Art and Life, the story becomes more violent and real, more modern, even more Spanish[12] and, at the same time, more universal.

Francoism had taken over the cultural heritage of the country and it had manipulated it in order to move its own agenda forward. In order to recover a more pluralistic cultural heritage, it was necessary to recuperate the historical, artistic, and literary past and to reinterpret it. Free from the obsessions born of the censorial repression of the Francoist period, and with the rise of feminism in the Europe of the 1970's and 1980's, Spanish storytellers, in literature as well as in film, occupy themselves with sexual politics. The theme of women-object is repeated in multiple forms. Notwithstanding a postmodern aesthetic in which the allegorical techniques of an *estética franquista* are replaced by less politically charged metaphors, Carlos Saura's 1983 *Carmen*, through its intertextual madness, reveals that, although they have survived the Franco years, Spaniards have a long way to go in order to overcome the social and moral habits of a traditional ideology.

The first in Carlos Saura'a 1980's flamenco trilogy had been *Bodas de sangre/Blood Wedding* from 1981. Short by feature film standards at 71 minutes, *Bodas de sangre* structurally is composed to two large narrative blocks. The first shows a dance troupe in their dressing room readying for a performance rehearsal. The second block consists of that very rehearsal in which the troupe dances and sings its interpretation of Federico García Lorca's 1932 play of the same name.

As with any film, the first few minutes provide the viewer with an orientation as to how the film is to be read. And *Bodas de sangre*, in its first few minutes, creates a matrix within which the concepts of art and life are again central, as was to be the case with *Carmen* and later *El amor brujo/Love, the Magician*.

While credits appear superimposed upon a background that is a posed photograph of what the viewer later learns to be a dance troupe performing a flamenco-style version of *Bodas de sangre*, a lone guitar slowly plays a theme that will be repeated later and during final credits.

Then, with only ambient sound and the non-diegetic lone guitar, a properties master turns on the lights of multiple makeup stations in a dressing room, and he readies costumes such as the bridal veil and bouquet. Dressed in street clothes, performers, led by Antonio Gades, begin to arrive and prepare their makeup stations. They find their places and open their makeup cases amid vaguely distinguishable conversations where sporadically something is understood, like "Do you have an aspirin?"

Antonio Gades, before readying his makeup station, asks the properties master for "the" photo. Taking the photo, Gades places it on his mirror, and the camera pauses to zoom in on the black and white photo of a group of people sitting on and surrounding a truck.

The others prepare their makeup spaces as well. They put photographs on the mirrors, like a photo of a child or an image of Jesus; they take out personal items such as a troll doll; they begin to put on makeup, with one man, for example, applying makeup to another. With a guitar warming up in the background, they speak among themselves; there are comments about how they will interpret the music. As Gades applies his makeup and smokes, the viewer listens to an extended voiceover in which Gades details his beginnings in dance, and the steps he has taken to get to where he is.

The photograph featured in these first few minutes of Carlos Saura's *Bodas de sangre* is of *La Barraca*, the traveling theater company started by the Ministry of Culture and Public Information in the early years of Spain's Second Republic (1931–1939) and directed by Federico García Lorca and Eduardo Ugarte. The dance company and performers featured in these first few minutes of Carlos Saura's *Bodas de sangre* are Antonio Gades' dance company and performers well-known in contemporary Spain.

Unlike what the viewer was to see two years later in *Carmen*, there is no look into any part of the performers' lives that is not a preparation for their art, in this case, the rehearsal. There is no look into anything other than art, not even a view of the "real," outside world through the windows as is the case in establishing shots in *Carmen*. The tight shot of the photo of *La Barraca* emphasizes a lifestyle in which artists lived art by taking classic national theater to places where there was little cultural activity. Parallel to that dedication, Gades' voiceover centers solely on his life in art, or, better still, on his life becoming art, as he details being discovered by Harry Flem-

Bodas de sangre (1981).

ming, dancing first in a cabaret, his discovery by and admiration for Vicente Escudero, and his studying dance in Paris, etc.

Like what the viewer was to see two years later in *Carmen*, there is an early central presence assigned to mirrors. There is a central presence assigned to dancers, musicians, and singers, who, while they are reflected in mirrors putting on makeup, are seen "in real life." Though there are indices of life outside (personal photos, amulets, etc.), they are presented only in terms of their life as artists.

So, the orientation as to how to read *Bodas de sangre* is clear. With the central presence of mirrors, the viewer knows that he is oriented towards reading the film in terms of reflection. With the entrance of real life performers, with their preparations for rehearsal, with their headaches and so on, and with Gades' review of aspects of his life, the matrix for interpretation indexes real life. With Gades' singular focus on his coming to art, with the troupe's preparations singularly focusing on a rehearsal, the matrix for the film's interpretation privileges art. Again, and unlike what will be seen in *Carmen* two years later, *Bodas de sangre* offers no look into these artists' real-life lives and emotions. It offers no opportunity to compare and contrast the two, to distinguish one from the other. In a situation that puts into play the two great suggestive concepts of Life and Art, the viewer knows that for this film the two concepts are synonymous; life is art or art is life. And, privileged between them, is art. The orientation for the viewer is to focus on the art, not on any life aspect extraneous to art (love affairs, midnight trysts, husbands, etc., as seen in *Carmen*). True to this orientation, *Bodas de sangre* offers a rehearsal performance that in several ways obligates the viewer to focus on "art."

The Gades' company's interpretation of García Lorca's *Bodas de sangre* is done without dialogue. In what is clearly a polemical relationship with the subtextual material, this stylized flamenco version makes most of García Lorca's verbal text disappear.

While the story does not disappear, it is told without the words of the literary/dramatic subtext, which give way to mostly silence filled with stylized flamenco choreography. The communication of emotions and the narration of events are left to costume, gesture, posture, facial expression, music, and, above all, dance. If the viewer is unfamiliar with the subtext, he finds it difficult to follow the narrative, perhaps. But, with the white dress, the dark suits, and so on, and with the floral bouquet, there is enough costuming and there are enough props to suggest a wedding. But, what the filmic discourse conveys of the rehearsal with its corporal expression, facial gesture, allows the viewer to easily capture emotions, and the viewer is asked to focus on the art of the performers in the rehearsal.

In its intertextual/intermedial tug of war with the subtext, the showpiece of Gades' company's interpretation of García Lorca's *Bodas de sangre* is the five-and a-half-minute long slow-motion dance scene that plays out a knife fight between Leonardo and the Groom, in which the both combatants die.

This is polemical, of course, because in the García Lorca subtext, the deaths occur offstage, and the reader/spectator begins to learn of them when, before the curtain at the end of the first scene of the third act, the moon appears, violins play, two screams are heard from offstage, and the beggar woman appears bringing absolute silence. The two deaths become very certain in second scene with the symbolic colors, the depth of the groom's mother's poetically expressed sadness (for example, her son is now "dried flowers"), and the explanations of the beggar woman.

The fact that the subtextual deaths do not occur on stage and yet are so privileged in the stylized flamenco version calls additional, special attention to the inclusion in the Gades' company's/Saura's movie version of the tragic story. It is the *pièce de résistance* of the dance portrayal because of the astounding artistry displayed by the two dancers. The performance was earlier described as slow-motion, and it is. But, it is choreographed and danced in slow-motion. It is not a slow-motion playback of a dance routine. It is a knife fight scene that is danced in controlled slow-motion/slow movement, and the viewer can but marvel at the physical control, the stamina, and the geometry of the art he witnesses.

The two great ideas of Life and Art are put into play again in the third of Saura's stylized flamenco choreofilms, 1986's *El amor brujo* (*Love, the Magician*). True to a concept of trilogy, there are familiar threads; there are several elements that link this film with the first two. Once again, the bulk of the filmic narrative is carried out by the Gades dance company, and centrally featured are Antonio Gades, Cristina Hoyos and Laura del Sol. Once again, the filmic subject matter comes from something Spanish. The first of the trilogy, took its subject matter from the work of a Spanish playwright and poet. The second drew from the mystical Spanish stereotype of the *femme fatale*. And this third film takes its subject matter from the Spanish composer Manuel de Falla and his 1915 (then 1925)[13] *El amor brujo*. Once again, in Saura's third film, the focused art form is flamenco.

Although the director will later return to flamenco as inspiration and as a topic for cinematic creation,[14] this is the last of the 1980's flamenco trilogy, and its first few minutes create a matrix for its reading, a reading different from those of the previous two films in the series.

Beginning with a black screen upon which are superimposed initial intertitles reporting the film's rating and its sponsorship by the Ministry of Culture, the audience hears soundover that mixes sounds of an orchestra's violins warming up and street noise. After 15 seconds, the visual image shows a large soundstage garage door open onto an alley as the non-diegetic orchestra begins to play the overture from *El amor brujo*. The large garage door descends slowly for about 30 seconds, and the overture music is interrupted, as the door slams closed.

With the sounds of violins signaling tension and the continued orchestra music, the camera pans right into the interior. What is revealed is a movie soundstage with its flats and braces, catwalks, scaffolds, lighting and so on, as the camera moves to the set. Arriving at the set, the soundtrack becomes a mix of the orchestra music and ambient diegetic sound. First the camera pans the set, which is comprised of a group of shanties around three sides of an open dusty area. The back is a blank, lighted horizon punctuated by utility poles. In the dusty central area, children are playing, clapping as they jump rope, shouting as they play bullfight. Around the edges of this area, adults gather or are seated at tables. As the camera continues to pan, it begins a slow zoom-in, and the sound mix soon becomes only diegetic sound. The zoom-in finally focuses on two pensive men who are drinking, one of them singing.

The first man comments how the other's daughter, Candela, has grown. The second man places his hand on the shoulder of the first and he tells him that Candela will be his son José's. Each man then calls his child over, and they explain the pact to them. As they do, the camera cuts to a third child, a boy, who, rising, watches seriously. The fathers shake hands and seal the pact by pouring wine over their clasped hands, toasting ("Por los niños" [To the kids]) and embracing. Almost expressionless, the third child watches the sealing of the pact from afar. The camera zooms in on the boy's face. The film's credits begin to appear superimposed to the right of his face, which, for the minute and a half that the credits last, morphs slowly into the face of an adult male.

This adult male is the familiar Antonio Gades. This last sequence of the slow morph of the boy child's face into the adult male face is accompanied not only by the credits but also by the soundtrack that is a woman singing in flamenco style. It is Rocío Jurado singing "El fuego fatuo" (The Fatuous Fire), a song from the de Falla ballet.

After the first few minutes, about eight and a half minutes, the orientation as to how to interpret the film is clear. The viewer is aware that, in spite of the similarities with the first two films in the trilogy, the matrix for reading *El amor brujo* is quite different.

With the dark eyes of the morphing face reflected in the "ojos negros" of the foolish fire song, the viewer knows that, in the narrative, his interpretation must make room for superstition and room for love's suffering.

With the slamming of the door to the sound studio and the leaving of ambient sound outside, the viewer knows that (real) life is being left behind. Unlike the previous two films in the trilogy, there is no presence of the "real life" of the artists. As it is left behind, there is little possibility for a dialectical tension between "real life" and art, as was the case in the two earlier films of the trilogy.

With the following traveling and pan of the sound studio, the move is away from life outside and into art, and the viewer knows the focus is on art.

The entrance into art stops at the shantytown set. The somewhat allegorical backdrop of reflected light with no other silhouettes than the utility poles, in combination with ambient noise that includes indications of traffic, speaks to a marginal settlement on the outskirts of a city. The camera arrives at a set where nothing seems to speak of costuming, makeup, or even acting. In fact, it might even be said that the two fathers "underact" the promising sequence. With this evidence, the viewer knows, though, that he has arrived at a set that he is being asked to read as real, if not infrareal, life. With the two great concepts again indexed, the first few minutes of *El amor brujo* orient the viewer to reading the film in terms of art reflecting life.

With the marginality of the community, with the physical appearance of the children and the adults, with the speech pattern and pronunciation, with the music (both the de Falla score and Rocío Jurado singing) the reader further knows that the interpretive matrix includes gypsies.

The remainder of the filmic narrative tells the *El amor brujo* story, with a few variations from the subtext. As promised, José and Candela marry, although her affections belong to Carmelo (the subject of the morph), and José's to Lucía. During community celebrations for Christmas, José steals away with Lucía. In a group knife fight precipitated by a man who wants to take Lucía away, José, trying to defend her, is killed. When the police arrive, Candela and Carmelo are with the dead body, and the police arrest Carmelo.

The ghost of José continues to haunt Candela, who goes every night to evoke his presence and to dance with him (Danza del terror/Dance of fear).

Four years later, Carmelo returns, determined to win Candela for himself. Candela, now a widow, is desirous of having a relationship with Carmelo, but she is not free because she continues to be haunted by José.

Carmelo gets advice from the wise gypsy aunt who tells him that a ritual dance is necessary to cast the ghost off (Danza ritual del fuego/Ritual dance of fire), but it does not work.

Carmelo convinces Lucía[15] to go with him at night accompanying Candela as she goes to meet José. Since he died for her and she still loves him, she can be with him, freeing Candela from his obsession. As Candela's dance with José begins, Carmelo and Lucía join in. During the dance, José and Lucía begin to dance together, and the two finally go away together, leaving Candela and Carmelo.

Dawn breaks, Candela and Carmelo embrace, finally free to enjoy their love.

While the filmic narrative is again punctuated by flamenco performances, this art form is not the sole vehicle responsible for carrying the narrative line. In fact, the flamenco numbers seem as responsible for conveying emotion as for moving the plot along. In the 100 minutes that the film lasts, there are a dozen flamenco numbers.[16] And, these dance and song numbers integrate nearly seamlessly into the structure of the narrative flow, built as well on movements from one part of the shantytown to another, dialogue, and performance of daily activities (ironing, making beds, hanging clothes out to dry, socializing, etc.). In effect, the filmic discourse includes enough daily activity for the viewer to accept the narrative as the life of the marginalized gypsy subcultural community. This is a subculture characterized not only by its marginality, but also by its artistic passions and its adherence to pre-modern superstition and ritual.

When Carmelo visits the old gypsy woman for the second time in search of her wisdom, she tells him that "La felicidad de unos siempre es a costa de la felicidad de otros" (The happiness of some always comes at the expense of the happiness of others). Carmelo realizes that this means death for Lucía. And, the follow up commentary of the wise aunt serves as much as consolation to Carmelo as it does to underscore for the scholar-viewer what the film's first minutes establish as the way in which the film is to be read. She says, "Así es la vida" (This is how life is). In a reading in which art reflects life, how life is reflected in *El amor brujo* is in its range of human emotions, in feelings of: happiness, sadness, jealousy, violence, and injustice.

With the presence of the Gades' dance troupe and subtextual material taken from the Spanish artistic archive, the first few minutes of each of the three films in Carlos Saura's 1980's flamenco trilogy place the great concepts of Life and Art face to face and they are indexed as central to interpreting the films. Yet, each film's narrative is different, creating a different relationship between the two concepts. And, the possible combinatory equations for the Life/Art confrontation are played out. In *Bodas de sangre*, life is art; in *Carmen*, life imitates or reflects art; and in *El amor brujo*, art reflects life.

And, with this genetic perspective, we can return to *Carmen*, the canonical[17] and "indisputably the best of the three films" (Edwards [1995] 113) and the focus of this chapter's attention. The critical bibliography dealing with *Carmen* seems to coalesce around themes of identity politics (including gender politics), stereotypes and clichés, and artistic technique.

Of the latter group, the most suggestive study may be that of Linda Willem (1997). Her focus on *Carmen's mise en abyme* not only supports a reading of the film from the perspective of life imitating art, but also it is suggestive in terms of the trilogy's artistic status, as it situates the films along side touchstones in the history of Art.

Focusing on dance and Gades' choreography, for example, Rosella

El amor brujo (1986).

Simonari (2008), emphasizing choreography's vital role in revisiting the Carmen tradition, concludes that

> Devoid of all the ornamental elements characterising a flamenco performance, his [Gades] approach helps to delineate Carmen as a figure who is at times both fragile, assured, and charismatic. By showing the development of character through the very process of choreographic invention, Gades and Saura undermine the stereotype of the femme fatale, interrogating traditional representations of Carmen, and breaking the illusion of the Carmen myth [200].

This conclusion obviously leads to an overlapping with that group of studies that focus attention on stereotype, myth and cliché.

An early approach to *Carmen* from the point of view stereotype is found in the pages John Hopewell dedicates to the film in his 1986 *Out of the Past: Spanish Film after Franco*. Using *machismo*, along with marked forms of flamenco, as a concept to unlock meaning, the analysis ends by indexing political-historical implications: "In a post–Franco Spain the characters still bear the marks of centuries of authoritarian government: 'freedom' for them seems less a right than a vicarious form of escape" (157).

Very often, studies emphasizing the Carmen myth or stereotype index identity concerns. This is the case for studies like those of Ann Davies (2004) and José F. Colmeiro (2005). In the latter's case, the point is that Carmen is rehispanized because she is returned to the gypsy roots of the flamenco culture from which she had been appropriated. At the same time that there is a consciousness of the constructedness of it all, this is a search for cultural authenticity. Even when such studies posit identity search, they recognize the *españolada* dimension and quality of the myth in question.

Continuing to be one of the most cogent and cited of the identity studies is that of Marvin D'Lugo (1987). Interestingly, D'Lugo seems to share assigning establishing importance to a film's first few minutes. His study separates, for example, "the first full narrative sequence of the film"[18] (56) from what for him are non-narrative, establishing, orientational "pre-credit" (55) sequences, where the spectator discerns the problematic relationship of the Spaniard to texts that have created for him ideas of his personal and collective identity. For D'Lugo, Saura questions the imposture of misrecognized, deformed Spanishness bound up in colonizing aesthetics of foreign perceptions of Spain. With that as the focus, he can conclude, speaking of the film and its director,

> But his own lucidity about the volume of deforming cultural ideology which has shaped the Spaniard's image of himself in the world will not allow him to posit so simplistic a narrative Utopia as the end of performance. Instead, he makes the final shots of the rehearsal hall the moment for the real spectator to confront the ambiguity of a cultural narrative without performance or closure, to witness for himself the margins of a history yet to be lived by Spaniards, yet to be written by Spaniards [61].

Most all of these studies add depth to the critical reception and understanding of Carlos Saura's *Carmen* and its companion films in his flamenco trilogy. While some of the studies find establishing value in the first few minutes in which Gades works with the female dancers as he looks for his Carmen and still others call attention to the indexical value of the Gustavo Doré engravings, none of the studies uses the film's (films') first few establishing minutes to orient the reading of the film. The matrix for reading therein established prepares the scholar-viewer for the confusion, and mixing of fictional levels he will encounter, as it prompts for a reading in which life will imitate art. This reading does not exhaust the semantic potential of the film, but since it is a reading established by the film itself, it does point to dimensions that other studies ought to keep in mind as they look for implications for artistic techniques, gender politics, myth manipulation, and identity search as well as the relationship of these films to the whole of the director's filmography.

♦ 3 ♦

Through a Woman's Eyes
Maria Luisa Bemberg's 1984
Camila

> Este largo cansancio se hará mayor un día,
> y el alma dirá al cuerpo que no quiere seguir
> arrastrando su masa por la rosada vía,
> por donde van los hombres, contentos de vivir.
>
> Sentirás que a tu lado cavan briosamente,
> que otra dormida llega a la quieta ciudad.
> Esperaré que me hayan cubierto totalmente …
> ¡y después hablaremos por una eternidad!
>
> Sólo entonces sabrás el porqué, no madura
> para las hondas huesas tu carne todavía,
> tuviste que bajar, sin fatiga, a dormir.
>
> Se hará luz en la zona de los sinos, oscura;
> sabrás que en nuestra alianza signo de astros había
> y, roto el pacto enorme, tenías que morir.
>
> —Gabriela Mistral, "Sonetos para la
> muerte" in *Desolación* (1922)

On a sunny day with birds singing, along a road covered by overhanging trees a caravan approaches, soldiers riding on horseback escorting a carriage. The road leads to what is apparently an estancia, a hacienda, or a ranch. Suddenly, some well-dressed children appear, shouting to Camila that grandmother is coming. A woman appears from inside the house walking towards where the children are, and where there is also a child in a goat-drawn wagon. The woman shouts to Adolfo to come because of the arrival. The little girl in the wagon has a woman of color at her side as if giving her special attention.

Camila tells the other children that they are going to greet the grandmother and that they must behave. As the grandmother in the carriage pulls up with the group of soldiers, one of the children asks why soldiers are escorting her, if it is so she will not escape. Another child asks why the Perichona [Little Pigeon] would want to escape. Camila tells her not to refer to the grandmother like that; even if others do it behind her back, she should not. The other child also asks the mother why they are detaining her; and if it is because she is a spy. Quickly thereupon another even smaller child, judging by her voice, questions what is a spy.

The carriage and the soldiers now are very close to the house, a salmon colored mansion with a second floor in the shape of a tower. Finally, when the carriage stops in front of the house, the grandmother is about to get out. It is a moment of total silence in which all that is heard is the singing of the birds and sound of the carriage's wooden door opening so that she can step down. The perplexed look on all the faces of those who have come out of the house is intense. In spite of the fact that the grandmother is being escorted by soldiers for reasons still not clarified, she is treated like a lady, a status that her form of dress avows. The camera focuses on the face of each of the house's residents, and they reflect a surprise and clear respect at the arrival of the disgraced grandmother. All are bowed as the carriage door opens, and a man elegantly dressed in white, as are all the other white residents of the house (there are servants of color), approaches the carriage and extends his hand to receive the grandmother. She, too, extends her hand, with a grace that only education and time can teach. When she steps down, the viewer sees her dress, which is the same color as the mansion, and she wears a veil that falls from the rim of her large hat and beneath which her face is visible.

The man tells the grandmother that it is pleasure to receive her at the house and that he hopes her stay there is as pleasant as possible. The "Little Pigeon" answers aggressively and dryly, with rigidness of posture, saying that her stay has nothing of pleasantness about it. The man insists that she be thankful for the generosity of the authorities in allowing her to spend her jail time in the house instead of a cell. She responds to this with the same tone, reminding Adolfo that he not forget that she is his mother. She moves away from him, and she approaches the house. She proceeds to greet a woman who appears to be the woman of the house with a baby. Then, she approaches a little girl seated in the wagon, and she says that she does not know her, since the girl was born while she was in Rio de Janeiro. She asks her name, and the little girl responds, "Camila, grandmother." The grandmother tells the child that it is a beautiful name. Leaning closer to the little girl, the grandmother asks her if she likes love stories. Little Camila responds, "No sé" (I don't know).

At 3 minutes and 20 seconds into the filmic narrative, the arrival scene ends, and the screen goes to black. A new scene opens with a superimposed intertitle that reads, Buenos Aires 1847. This flashforward shows the exterior of an urban house with a colored servant sweeping the sidewalk. A man on a mule hands him a package, which he in turn takes into the house, passing through an interior garden, where a colored female servant tells him to hurry because the master is waiting. The house is large and there are many servants at work. The voices of children playing are heard, and film credits continue to appear intermittently superimposed.

Questions are heard enquiring as to Camila's whereabouts as the servant takes the newspaper and breakfast to the master. As he is bathed by the manservant, Adolfo reads the newspaper and comments on the political and economic news, mocking the servant's ignorance of the issues. Camila's brother finds her in the attic, where the joy in her face reflects her discovery of some newly born kittens. From a scowling Adolfo ominously witnessing this scene from the shadows, there is a cut to a servant with a gunnysack on a beach. The servant fills the sack with rocks, and he tosses it into the sea. At just over 7 minutes and 20 seconds, the film credit identifying the movie's director as María Luisa Bemberg appears superimposed, and the screen goes to black. An intertitle appears on the black screen that dedicates the film to the memory of Camila O'Gorman and Ladislao Gutiérrez. Quickly, another intertitle characterizes the narrative as "Versión libre 1984" (Free Version 1984). This dedication ends the film's first few minutes at 7:28, as it offers to the viewer the last of the establishing cues in the orientation as to how the film is to be read.

At the end of these first few minutes, the orientation for the viewer as how the film is to be read is clear. With the grandmother's arrival under house arrest for espionage, and with reading of the newspaper's political and economic news, the reading of the film must have political connotations. Also, with the grandmother's question to Camila, the viewer knows that what will follow will be a love story. Further, with that question ("¿Te gustan las historias de amor?" [Do you like love stories?]), a matrix is invoked in which history and storytelling are privileged. Thus, a reading of the film should privilege historical implications and elements of storytelling.

With the exchange between Adolfo and his mother, these opening scenes establish a matrix for reading that also must take into account conflict with authority.

Equally important to the orientation as to the reading of the film is what is not established in the first few minutes of *Camila*. While the viewer may begin to pick up on sympathies, especially in the exchange between Adolfo and his mother in which he comes across as cold and harsh or in Adolfo's cold stare at Roberto, Camila and the kittens, there is little attempt (perhaps with the exception of a closeup of the very young Camila) to identify the narrative perspective with any of the characters there present.

3. Through a Woman's Eyes 67

The first-few-minutes-ending dedication, however, does identify a structuring principle of the narrative. The viewer is clearly oriented towards a reading sympathetic to the two characters he will come to know as Camila O'Gorman and Ladislao Gutiérrez.

Further, the very last of the establishing cues in a matrix for the film's reading offers multiply nuanced indicators. In "Versión libre 1984," the viewer encounters a reference to a third date. Just prior, the viewer reads of the year 1847 in which he meets a young adult (20-ish) Camila, realizing that the earlier opening scene (where Camila is apparently a 5-year-old-ish child) is a flashback to another year (ca. 1832). The attention paid to dates, two specific years identified by intertitles and a third implied in flashback, cues a reading of the filmic narrative as it relates to history.

"Versión libre" is a polysemic establishing cue. In one sense, "free" can refer to the freedom of the presentation and reportage of historical events. Thus, while notions of history are clearly actualized, the filmic narrative does not ask necessarily to be judged or interpreted on its merits as an accurate historical document.

Other studies have proposed *Camila*'s potential as historical allegory (For example, Foster [1992], Bach [1994], Hart [2002]). Because his focus is on the encryption/inscription of the film's discourse within the melodramatic genre, Stephen Hart is lead to Doris Sommer's *Foundational Fictions*. Hart believes that Bemberg's "pot-boiler" filmic tale can fit into the model of historical allegory in which love story and nation story have interesting implications in their complimentarity. Surely, Sommer's ideas can inform the analysis of historical allegory in Camila, but it is not necessary to recur to her ideas in order to justify such analyses. Given the orientation of the film's first few minutes, which is continually supported, reinforced, and developed by multiple elements of the filmic discourse, such an allegorical reading is not only justified but called for by the film's own establishing orientation as to how it should be read.

"Free" in "Versión libre," especially since it appears accompanied by the year 1984, also evokes the conditions under which *Camila*'s filmic discourse is produced. In this case, "free" has clear historical connotations, given that the immediately previous period of Argentine history was not "free." The viewer, then, is oriented towards reading the film as a free adaptation and as an expression of freedom.

The present chapter is not the first study to emphasize the importance of this film's first few minutes, as other also studies have placed analytical importance on the opening sequences of *Camila*. None, though, have viewed them as establishing a matrix for the reading of the film. Jorge Ruffinelli (1996), for example, sees the film opening, or "prólogo," composed of "microrrelatos" (microstories) with a will toward structuring the narrative. But rather

Camila (1984). Reproduced with permission obtained through EGEDA (Entidad de Gestión de los Productores Audiovisuales) [Spain].

than seeing their structuring potential and the revelation of theme, he asserts that "Después de estos microrrelatos que componen el preámbulo, el tema no demora mucho en conformarse" (After these microstories which make up the preamble, the theme does take long in revealing itself) (19). For this reader, the opening sequences merely open accounts that need to be settled.

Claire Taylor (2005) focuses on performativity and citation in two of Bemberg's films, *Camila* and *Yo la peor de todas*; and because she does so, the opening carriage sequence in the first film holds importance for her. There she sees a wink or citation of Buñuel's *Belle de jour*, which also opens with a carriage sequence. This coincidence suggests "a certain link to *Belle de jour*." The desire to find citation ignores the vast differences between the two films' scenes: open vs. closed carriage; distant trees vs. close, overhanging trees; lone carriage vs. solider-accompanied carriage. And, though Taylor recognizes the narrative disparity between the two filmic visions, a performativity search for parallels between content and meaning leads to the conclusion that through this coincidence "Buñuel's film locates itself not in the realm of the protagonist's waking life and reality, but in her daydreams [fantasy]" (114).

The identification of another text or the opening sequence thereof that might seem to offer similarity with a text that herein is the object of study does not necessarily help to better understand the semiotic process of the borrowing text. Perhaps Bemberg's film brings to mind material from another narration or other narrations, even seeming to respect their visual, musical or linguistic configuration. However, such fidelity to the subtextual does not guarantee the respecting of other important aspects of those subtexts. Even disregarding the differences alluded to above, any purely visual juxtaposition or regrouping of a text fragment detaches it from any previous or pre-existing dialogical relationships. The consideration of the selection from a Buñuel piece cannot be done without analyzing how this material is inserted in *Camila* as part of its structural and signic whole. Being detached from *Belle de jour* and being inserted as part of the narrative structure of the new film, the opening sequence material loses much of the signifying value it had, in order to gain new significance in relationship to the new structure of which it forms part. That significance is better determined by *Camila*'s first few minutes than by any coincidental features it may share with earlier performances.

Argentine film has always been among the best of filmic traditions in Latin America, and, for that reason, it has received ample critical and scholarly attention. In particular, Argentine cinematographic production of the post-military-dictatorship period of the 1980's has been the object of well-deserved critical and commercial interest. Representative of the notable production of the time, two films from the period have entered the canon, with the first being the award winning *La historia oficial* (Luis Puenzo, 1985). A year earlier, another excellent Argentine film, *Camila*, was released, and it has since entered the canon.[1] The film was good enough to attract sufficient attention to be nominated for an "Oscar" as best foreign film for that year, an award which, of course, fell to *La historia oficial* the following year. *Camila* is the work of a female director. María-Luisa Bemberg is the film's director as well as a co-author of its screenplay.

Camila is a historical film. It uses capital-H History—a historical event from Argentina of 1847—as a pre-text for its cinematographic representation. A historical film (and/or its discourse) is always a *sign*, which is sometimes more direct but more often figurative with respect to the History to which it refers. Even when the historical events it describes are presented just as they occurred,[2] they can acquire a meaning within the filmic discourse that can completely differ from the meaning they had in History.

The filmic discourse is the very expression of that history. It is the whole of visual, linguistic, and formal elements that constitute the filmic text. Regardless of the definition or conception one chooses for the director of a film, it is that person most responsible for the organization and structure of the filmic discourse. The director, especially as the case with *Camila* in which Bemberg shares responsibility for the screenplay, is the individual through whom referential raw material must pass as it is transformed into a film. The relationship or correspondence between life and art, or in this case between history and film, is mediated by the director. Historical events and experiences are not represented directly in the film, nor are they transferred directly into film. Rather, they pass through the director. As this transference occurs, it is involuntarily subject to the director's immediate and long-term acquired experiences, on the one hand; and, on the other, it is the direct result of an intentional search aimed at the creation of a film. As relates to creation of the work, the director is a personality, which becomes the common denominator for the work. But, the relationship between the director and the creative work does not refer to personality as an indistinguishable whole, but rather to all of the individual aspects of personality and the relationships among them. All sorts of a director's acquired and inherent attitudes and inclinations (character, talent, ability, psychology, etc.) as well as her very own typology can become manifest in the film as a work.

It is through these different components of the directorial personality that referential raw material much pass as it is transferred to film. Several aspects of a director's personality can influence the organization and the structuring of the filmic discourse. Directorial attitudes and inclinations influence selections, focus, and detail of referential raw material in its filmic form. In terms of the present consideration of *Camila* by María-Luisa Bemberg, this chapter seeks to examine how the director's feminine/feminist, political/ideological and aesthetic attitudes and inclination might be seen to focus and structure the filmic discourse in terms of the orientation for the viewer that is offered by the film's first few minutes. It will be important to examine the form and the degree to which these dispositions are present in the filmic text and their implications for the viewer's reading of it.

Among the problems attendant to the director and his/her work is that of the subject of the work; that is, the artistic "I" from which the work emanates as communication and the one who is perceived of as the intrinsic contributor of thought and emotion. The subject is the perspective from which the structure of the film can be viewed in all its uniqueness and complexity.

These considerations are important because, as we have seen, *Camila*'s first few minutes orient the scholar-viewer to read the film with political connotations.

The fact that María Luisa Bemberg's film carries the name of one of its protagonists as its title does not necessarily mean that the film is made through an identification with this character. On the contrary, one of the characteristics of the structure and organization of *Camila*'s filmic discourse is its scarce identification with the characters. The filmic discourse, for example, does little to prepare the way for the two main characters' falling in love, and it goes even less into their feelings. It might be said, in fact, that if the filmic discourse identifies in any way with some character, however momentarily it might be, it is with the young priest and the crisis of conscience he suffers in Goya, Corrientes, after having abandoned his ministry. In spite of the attention paid to this crisis of conscience, this brief preoccupation with Ladislao's psychological state is far from defining it (or Ladislao for that matter) as the subject of the filmic discourse.

The subject in *Camila*, however, is not hidden or obscure. In fact, it is strongly suggested in the first few minutes, and it attains a high degree of fulfillment. The perspective from which the film *Camila* is best read in all of its uniqueness and complexity is a feminine/feminist perspective.[3] Substantiating this inflection suggested in the opening scenes of the grandmother's arrival to the familial estancia, there are several components of the filmic discourse that reveal the role of the feminine and/or feminism as a structuring or modeling system. Among them, there are at least four that for the purposes of this chapter ought to be mentioned:

1. The importance ascribed to the *word*;
2. The view of eroticism;
3. The role of the maternal;
4. The anti-machista tone.

From the opening scenes, this film makes it clear that the *word* is important to the structuring of the discourse. In the opening flashback that presents the return of Grandmother O'Gorman under permanent house arrest, the old woman meets little Camila for the first time. After asking her name, the grandmother asks her, "¿Te gustan las historias de amor?" (Do you like love stories?). Later, young adult Camila and her prisoner grandmother will spend many leisure hours together re-reading and dramatizing old love letters. The relationship between the two of them, no matter how precarious due to the old lady's imprisonment and Camila's father's prohibitions, is, in this way, a relationship built and solidified by the *word*.

The first meeting between Camila and the young priest takes place primarily as a function of the word. Camila goes to confessional and she tells her "sins," thinking that her usual, older father confessor is listening to her. When the priest finally speaks to her from the other side of the confessional lattice, Camila realizes that it is not Father Félix but someone else, and she leaves. Somewhat later, at the family home, Camila's birthday is being celebrated. The guests are playing blind-man's-bluff; when suddenly the presence of someone new is noticed. With her eyes blindfolded, Camila approaches this person, feeling his arms, his shoulders and his face, but she does not recognize him. But, when Ladislao speaks (directing words to her) wishing her a happy birthday, Camila says "Ya sé quién es. Es el nuevo cura de provincias" (Now I know who it is. It's the new priest from the provinces).

She recognizes Ladislao by his voice, by his words. And, for Camila the *word* will always be the tie that binds them. That is why, much later and again in the confessional, where the only possible relationship between them is through the word, Camila tells him,

> Me gusta hablar con Ud. ... Ud. me ordena los pensamientos.... Para poder hablar con Ud. voy a tener que inventar muchos pecados ... (I like to talk with you.... You order my thoughts.... In order to be able to speak with you, I am going to have to come up with a lot of sins.)

Just like in her relationship with her grandmother, it is the *word* that cements the human relationship with Ladislao.

Corresponding to priorities and values that are more generally feminine, this importance assigned to the *word* is also manifest in the way in which Camila defines her possible future husband. After having listened to the moving and daring sermon given by the young Ladislao, Camila, when her sister announces that she is going to get married, says that she herself does not necessarily want a man who is handsome and socially well-placed, rather she wants a man of whom she can be proud –so proud as to shout (employ the *word*) in the streets "Este es mi marido" (This is my husband).[4]

What the *word* means for the two sexes is revealed in a scene that has to do with the exiled Romantic writer Esteban Echeverría. Camila, after having furtively obtained a copy of a book by the proscribed author, reads a passage to Ignacio, Camila's suitor and, according to others, "el mejor partido de Buenos Aires" (the best catch in Buenos Aires). Camila is all moved and enthusiastic with the ideas that Echeverría expresses about exile and what the homeland means to a person. Poor Ignacio, with his look of an idiot, does not even realize that Camila is reading him these emotional words. The only thing he is worried about is looking at Camila's face and asking her when she is going to stop tormenting him and allow a date for their wedding to be set.

There will be an allusion to a final and powerful example of the feminine importance granted to the *word* near the end of this chapter, and many others could be adduced. For now, however, attention is turned to the view of eroticism in the film.

In general, *Camila* is not an openly erotic film, but there are two or three scenes of an erotic nature, and in them, the erotic perspective is feminine. One of these erotically oriented scenes in particular manifests the feminine structuring perspective of the filmic discourse through the curiosity that is shown for male sexuality.[5]

Through their meetings in confessional, the young priest becomes aware of the nascent feelings of love that Camila feels for him; and, at the same time as he realizes the desires that Camila awakens in him. As a result, then, Ladislao confesses with the father superior. He flagellates himself and falls rather ill. In his cell, delirious with fever and writhing in an obviously erotic dream, Ladislao receives a visit from Camila. They kiss, and he grabs Camila's hand to press it against his naked torso. As he draws her hand towards his groin, she withdraws frightened. The structuring feminine curiosity is revealed here as the camera focuses on the now solitary male form, facedown, groaning as if ejaculating.

The perspective of the other few erotic scenes also reflects a curiosity for male sexuality. In these cases, the feminine perspective makes manifest the self-centered, self-focused value that the sex act can have for the "other." The filmic discourse includes two occasions when the two protagonists make love. In both cases, the act seems be realized in response to a "male" need. In both instances, Ladislao is anguished, confused; he is afraid of the consequences of what he has decided to do. And, he is shown to seem to seek refuge from his own anguish and his own insecurity in the sex act.

Other evidence of the structuring feminine perspective of the filmic discourse is found not so much in the curiosity about the "other" as in the knowledge of what is peculiar, unique and important to one's own self. The role of the maternal and the importance granted to it with *Camila*'s discourse reveal "(s)elections" that would seem only to respond to a focus from a feminine viewpoint.

Throughout the film, one of the only ways in which a woman is realized as a person is through her sensibility to the maternal instinct. Fulfilling the role of mother protects women from the affective coldness and hostility of the environment that surrounds them. This is true for mothers with their children as much it is for Camila in her relationship with her brother. The maternal instinct elevates woman above (if not physically, then, morally) the male world. From very early in the film's flow of events, it is clear that the maternal instinct is a value for the organizing viewpoint of the discourse, and, that it is, besides, a quality that lifts women above the cold dominant world around them.

Following the initial flashback, the filmic narration presents the viewer with the Buenos Aires mansion of the O'Gorman family. Everyone is very busy and they ask as to Camila's whereabouts. Her brother finds her, alone and hiding in the attic. Bathed in a white light entering from above, she is there with some kittens that have just been born. Camila asks her brother to be quiet and not to say anything about the kittens to their father, because they both know what he will do with the little creatures. At that moment, the father climbs quietly and unnoticed to the attic, and the scene ends as the camera focuses on his insensitive and cold face that contrasts with the vision of a smiling Camila dressed in white and bathed in a soft, pure light. Immediately following, the viewer sees a servant of the O'Gormans beside the sea. He is carrying a cloth sack; he fills it with rocks and throws it into the water. At the same time as the kittens drown, the opposing maternal instinct becomes identified as a superior value for the structuring perspective of the filmic discourse.[6]

The structuring directorial vision later takes this value to an even more transcendent plane. If the maternal protects a woman from the danger of loosing her identity in the face of a more powerful worldly system of values, the maternal can "save" her at a different level. After having been in Goya, Corrientes for a while, the couple witnesses a procession of penitents carrying a crucifix. This sight brings about a crisis within Ladislao's (now Máximo) conscience. He spends a sleepless night, obviously repentant for having betrayed his love of God. Camila intuits these thoughts, and, at daybreak, she asks Ladislao, "Si yo llegara a tener un hijo tuyo, sería una señal de que Dios no está enojado, ¿no es cierto?" (If I were to have a child of yours, it would be a sign that God is not angry, isn't that right?). In this way, the viewer comes to understand that for the organizing principle of the filmic discourse, motherhood and the maternal instinct are not only valued as superior to other reigning circumstantial values, but that they are seen as transcendently and universally superior. Such a valuation would seem also to respond to a feminine set of values.

The last of the earlier-listed structuring perspectives of the filmic discourse is not, however, only feminine; it is also feminist. This focus as well structures and organizes the filmic discourse in such a way as to critique and to show the errors, even the comic absurdity, of a set of values and a social order that excludes an active and positive feminine participation. Beyond the obvious feminism inherent in a story about a young woman whose actions and ideological curiosity challenge social, moral, and political codes of conduct in an environment dominated by men; beyond the obvious symbolism inherent in a grandmother confined as a prisoner by those same codes dictated by men, there are other elements specific to *Camila*'s discourse which are anti-machista or militantly feminist.

Ladislao's father confessor, following the daring sermon that the young priest delivers, scolds him for the "desagradable sorpresa" (unpleasant surprise) which his sermon brought. From within the authoritarian doctrine of the Church, as an institution dominated exclusively by men, the father superior admonishes him even more. As if intuiting the future relationship between the young priest and Camila, the father superior warns Ladislao that "la mujer puede ser instrumento del demonio" (Women can be the instrument of the devil).

The atmosphere dominated by men in all institutions—the Church, the family, the government, and society in general—is presented as affectively cold and without sensitivity; it is an atmosphere that suffocates and stupefies the feminine person. There are numerous examples of this throughout the film, but a few of those episodes are really worthy of mention. Most often the presentation of this atmosphere dominated by men as oppressive is done subtly or indirectly without really insisting too much. There are occasions, though, in which the influence on the filmic discourse exercised by a feminist focus of an anti-machista bent is very clear.

During the O'Gorman family meal after the young Jesuit's audacious sermon, there is a discussion (among the men, of course) about how inappropriate the priest's commentaries were and how appropriate the violent political reprisal that gave rise to them was. Camila intervenes briefly. Such is the shock produced by the fact that she, a woman, would dare to opine about matters of such transcendence that everyone stops eating. Camila's authoritarian father asks her to repeat her comment, but Camila at first answers alleging not to have said anything. When her father insists, Camila repeats her comment. But, not only does she repeat it, she expands upon it with a brief but at the same time strong defense of the provincial priest and with a critique of violence as a viable political solution. To this, her father responds by sending her away from the table (censoring her speech, taking the *word* away from her).

Man, however, does not only oppress woman by excluding her participation by means of his authoritarian posture; he dominates her as well with his paternalistic attitude. The paternalism that governs all man-woman relationships within the world as it is presented in *Camila* is unmasked in the episode that revolves around the bookstore and Mariano the bookseller. When Camila goes to the bookstore, Mariano gives her a book that he wraps up in a newspaper so that no one can see it. At that moment, Ignacio arrives. He comes to the bookstore no so much to accompany Camila as to protect her because, as he explains to her with a paternalistic tone and somewhat enigmatically, "hay libros y hay libros" (there are books, and there are books). That same night, Rosas troops come and kill Mariano the book vender.

The feminist viewpoint that organizes the filmic discourse not only lays bare the fact that machista paternalism restricts the movements and thoughts of women with its desire to "protect" them, it also is what blocks communication between men and women. As he arrives at the bookstore, Ignacio, because he is "bien situado" (well connected), obviously is already aware of the reprisal planned against Mariano. His machista paternalism, however, does not allow for that information to be shared with Camila. Any possible communication between the two of them ends in the enigmatic "hay libros y hay libros" and, ultimately, in the perhaps preventable death of a friend.

Another scene that should be mentioned here as evidence of the anti-machista tone of the filmic discourse does not focus so much on the oppressive quality of the machista environment as it does on the comic (at least for a late-20th century scholar-viewer) absurdity inherent in some of its systems and ways of thinking. One evening, while Camila, her mother and father are spending a quiet time at home, her father decides that it is an opportune moment to discuss his daughter's future. As the two women listen more or less attentively, the father explains that Camila has reached an age when she must decide what she plans to do with her life because "la mujer soltera es un caos" (the single woman is chaos). What's more, according to her father, being a woman, she has only two options: either the convent or marriage. And, since Camila never has shown much of an inclination to dedicate herself to the Church, Don Adolfo concludes that she must marry. Exactly … she has to get married because it is good for the country since it lends it stability, order, and so on. But, when his daughter protests saying she does not love Ignacio, the father replies saying that "la realidad, Camila, no es una novela francesa ni el amor una miradita entre jazmines…." (Reality, Camila, is not a French novel nor is love a passing glance among the jasmines). It is at this point at which a brief visit from Ladislao interrupts the father's speech. The young priest is there for only a few minutes, and when he leaves, Camila's father asks, "¿En qué estábamos?" (What was I saying?). The response that comes from his normally submissive wife makes very plain the comic absurdity of the interrupted machista rhetoric. The choice of the response again makes manifest that a structuring principle of the filmic discourse is feminist. With absolute calm, the wife replies, "En que el matrimonio es como el país y que la mejor cárcel es la que no se ve" (You were saying that marriage is like the country and the best jail is the one you cannot see). Adolfo sternly reacts, "No dije eso. Dije que la mujer tiene que casarse, eso es todo" (I did not say that. I said that a woman has to get married, that's all). "Es lo mismo" (It's the same thing.) his wife retorts, putting a final touch on this very revealing scene in which a feminist spin mocks the machista mindset.

Man does not only oppress woman by means of authoritarianism or through paternalistic attitudes, he dominates and determines discourse. So it is with the key concept of "madness."[7] Both Camila and her grandmother are labeled as mad by Adolfo. This self-identified arbiter of acceptable discourse is quick to condemn Camila and ascribe her actions to madness as he compares her to her grandmother, "Primero mi madre, ahora ella" (First my mother, now her), and later, "Lo lleva en la sangre, es como mi madre" (It's in her blood, she is like my mother). Even Ladislao allows himself to tell Camila, "Tú estás loca, Camila" (You're mad, Camila). They judge and ascribe "madness" from the perspective of their male dominant discourse.

But, "madness" can be defined as and by the "other," and that is what happens in an end-of-film sequence at the O'Gorman home in which a feminist mockery of the machista mindset and the importance of the *word* converge with the historical dimensions of the film in order to subvert the machista woman/madness binary. As a retort to Adolfo's ascription of madness, his wife proclaims

> En vez de pensar en tu hija, lo único que te preocupa es tu apellido. Tú estás enfermo de orgullo. Todos están enfermos ... de violencia, de sangre. ¿Alguien levanta la voz para salvar a mi hija? Nadie. Nadie piensa en ella. La Iglesia piensa en su buen nombre, vos pensás en tu honor, Rosas en su poder, los Unitarios en cómo derribar usando este escándalo....
> (Instead of thinking about your daughter, the only thing that worries you is your name. You are mad with your pride. All of you are sick ... from violence, from blood. Does anyone raise their voice to save my daughter? Nobody. Nobody thinks about her. The Church thinks about its good name, you think about your honor, Rosas about power, the Unitarians about how to win by using this whole scandal....)

As she indexes historical forces of Church, State, oligarchy, and politics, she condemns their desire for power as the real causal "madness."

At the same time as this feminine/feminist code determines the structure and organization of the film, it links it with other female voices. One such voice from 20th century Latin American letters is that of 1945's Nobel laureate for literature Gabriela Mistral. In the last scene of the film, a firing squad executes Camila and Ladislao, who for some time prior have been isolated separate from each other. Both bodies are thrown into the same coffin; thus, the two will rest for all of eternity in that pine box. In voices-over, the dead Camila asks, "Ladislao, ¿estás allí?" (Are you there?), and he replies, "A tu lado, Camila" (By your side, Camila).[8]

This scene not only demonstrates one final time the feminine focus through the importance granted to the *word* as an eternal bond, but it also represents filmically the same feminine spirit that infuses the Gabriela Mistral sonnet used as the opening epigraph for this chapter. In their community of spirit, the importance of the *word* is highlighted ("hablaremos por una eternidad"/we will talk for all eternity) as well as the way in which death is viewed. In both the poetic and the filmic texts, death is seen not from its tragic side, but rather as a final means of union with the loved one.

It would be an error, however, to see Bemberg's work as only a feminine or feminist film. The first few minutes of the film have prepared the viewer for other aspects and nuances of the film's reading. The material selected and included by the director responds to other criteria as well. One criterion, which must be mentioned because of its importance to the structuring of the filmic discourse, is the prevailing aesthetic principle.

It has already been said that *Camila* is a historical film. The events that it narrates are real events from mid-nineteenth century Argentina. The use of History as subtext or pre-text for artistic and filmic representation is nothing new. In fact, the establishment of this practice as an aesthetic norm dates from the very early beginnings of film; for example, the work of D. W. Griffith, and followers attracted by spectacular epics based on the great events of History have continued the genre as a staple of cinematographic practice. In the timeframe surrounding María Luisa Bemberg's *Camila*, some narrators and other cotemporaneous directors, however, had begun to signal the path towards a new type of historical film and historical narration. Some films from the same timeframe as *Camila*, like *Apocalypse Now* (Francis Ford Coppola, 1979), *Le retour de Martin Guerre* (David Vigne, 1982), *La nuit de Varennes* (Ettore Scola, 1982), and *Le bal* (Ettore Scola, 1983) among others, augur a new path for historical film. Like *Camila*, these are historical films, but, instead of telling the great events of the sweep of History, they prefer to base their narrations on "little histories" or "stories."[9] By pulling on the threads of the historical tapestry woven by these "stories," one comes to an understanding of the History to which the filmic discourse refers. Instead of an iconical organization and structuring of the filmic narrative, this new kind of historical film narrates a "story" that points toward or indexes History.

Camila, a film from 1984 and a product of the directorial vision of Argentine María Luisa Bemberg, adds itself to this trend in the creation of historical film. The aesthetic matrix that focuses on historical material in *Camila* is **indexical**.[10] The enchanting and powerful "love story" (little history) about a young Catholic women from Buenos Aires high society who falls in love and takes off with a Jesuit priest in 1847 Argentina points out or indexes a whole of sociopolitical complexities from the period of the tyrant Juan Manuel Rosas in the history of Argentina.

If this type of aesthetic approach places de *Camila*'s filmic discourse within the cinematographic "vanguard" of filmic storytelling of the time, there are other elements at the textual level that correspond to a more or less traditional aesthetic. So traditional are they, in fact, that their prevalence as artistic norm even precedes film. There are, for example, within the filmic discourse aesthetic elements that are proper to literature. That is to say, that one can even say that *Camila*'s filmic discourse has a literary quality to it.

As the filmic discourse is structured and organized, it takes advantage of, for example, some commonplace symbols from Western culture that have been consecrated or fossilized by literature. This is especially true with the symbols of **light** and **water**. While the execution is visual, which is immanently cinematographic, what is employed is a symbolical value that is established in a long literary/cultural tradition. These two symbolic elements are employed at a textual level in the film as purifying forces. In terms of light, we have already mentioned that the first time the viewer sees Camila as a young adult on screen is when she is in the attic with the kittens. Dressed in white, she is bathed as well in a soft white light whose symbolic force helps to establish the central polarization of the filmic discourse.

Water is also employed as a purifying force. After having been discovered, Ladislao and Camila spend some months in jail awaiting a decision on what is to become of them. Finally, when their fate has been decided, a priest visits Camila to listen to her confession. He gives her a cup of water to drink, telling her that this will purify the soul of the unborn child that Camila carries in her womb.

Not all symbolic borrowings, however, have such transcendent implications, though they do serve to polarize the different elements of the discourse. On one occasion, for example, a commonplace symbol is employed as a kind of "wink" to the viewer. After having focused on the aroused and moaning priest visited by Camila, there is a jump to the following morning. Father Félix is seated, eating his breakfast. When Father Ladislao enters to join him, he grabs an apple, he takes a big bite of it, and he sits down to have breakfast with the father superior. Given its biblical symbolism, the scholar-viewer can but think "What symbolism! What foregrounding!" as he realizes that Ladislao is about to succumb to earthly desire.

Yes, another device with strong precedents in literature that is employed by the aesthetics structuring *Camila*'s filmic discourse is foreshadowing. After presenting the clandestine escape by Camila and Ladislao, the discourse presents a scene that at the time and in its placement within the narrative flow seems somewhat enigmatic. Don Adolfo has gone to the countryside. He is at his estancia, and the camera focuses on him smoking a pipe and drinking mate. In front of him, the camera focuses on two gaucho types and a felled cow. The two decapitate the cow, they slice open its womb, and they remove a calf. Edited contiguous to the beginning of the adventurous escape of the two lovers, though at first it might seem gratuitous, this scene foreshadows the end of that adventure as well as Camila's and her unborn child's ultimate fate.

Although later it will be necessary to return to a consideration of aesthetic selections or choices and, in particular, to the analysis of the preference for index, in order to complete the view of aesthetic choice, it is important to consider other choices as they influence the filmic discourse's focus. Also governing choices reflected in the organization and structure of the filmic discourse is ideological/political principle.[11] At one level of interpretation, it has already been seen that various components of the filmic discourse place in conflict two sets of values defined by gender: the institutionalized dominant machista complex and the subjugated feminine world. The orientation established in the film's first few minutes compels the reader not to be satisfied with an interpretation that does not go beyond this level. Those opening sequences create a matrix for a reading of the film with political connotations. And, *Camila*'s narrative discourse is, in part, organized and structured by the codes of an ideology that is politically liberal, democratic and anti-authoritarian.

Earlier in a reference to the episode with the kittens, it was mentioned that the episode serves to identify the maternal instinct as a superior value. In that episode as well, two distinct ideologies are placed in contrast: one authoritarian and oppressive, and another that, as Camila herself might define it, "está al lado de la vida" (is on life's side).

The subject of the filmic discourse is identified, clearly, with the second of these ideologies, and it is the same ideological-political structuring principles that are responsible for laying bare the fear, suffering, and horror caused by that dominant ideology. That is how it is in the case of the reprisal against the bookseller Mariano. It is nighttime, and the tranquility of the O'Gorman household is broken by a spine tingling scream that is heard coming from outside. Camila and her brother look out of the window, from which they see the quick and raucous withdrawal of some soldiers mounted on horseback. "Otra vez como cuando éramos chicos" (Again, like when we were kids) is the commentary. In the face of the fear and terror aroused by this event, all they can manage to do is to question, "Dios mío, ¿hasta cuándo?" (My God, how long will this go on?).

The next day, the severed, bloody head of Mariano the book vender is publicly displayed on a stake. The justification of such an act and its display—"Dice Rosas que veinte gotas de sangre derramadas a tiempo evitan derramar veinte mil" (Rosas says that twenty drops of blood spilled in good time can keep from spilling twenty thousand.)—rings hollow in contrast with the concomitant mournful scream of Mariano's widow—"¡Asesinos! ¡Asesinos!" (Murderers! Murderers!).

Index and ideology converge. While it is true that the "story" (historia) in *Camila* indexes the Rosas period of Argentina's history,[12] narrative activity demands an intellectual process that, as such, subjects particular events to a process of abstraction that converts them into symbols in terms of their potential reference to reality. And, in this process, there is an association established between and among particular events. Even the most summary of considerations of Argentine history in particular, and of Latin American history in general, evidences the repetition of concrete situations from many different periods that are similar to those narrated in *Camila*.

The narrative discourse of *Camila* not only indexes the Rosas period in the history of Argentina; at an allegorical-symbolical level, it indexes similar complexities from the Argentina of the time of the film's making, and it indexes similar conflicts common to the history of Latin American in general. It is impossible to view this 1984 film without thinking about the immediately previous military regime under which thousands of Argentines unjustly "disappeared," as well as other authoritarian dictatorships that constitute the whole of Latin American history.

This whole consideration of the perspective from which the filmic material is focused and structured is in one sense nothing more that an artifice in order to be able to approach the film's intertextuality. Through the different codes analyzed and present in *Camila* (and others), as it was created by María-Luisa Bemberg, the filmic discourse is related and connected to social, political, historical, and artistic texts and contexts. The filmic text is the intersection of these multiple codes, and the filmic discourse is defined by political and artistic codes that govern its structure and organization.

That said, *Camila* is perhaps best defined by the feminine/feminist code that determines its structure. It is the feminist code that places in opposition the contrary worlds in *Camila*: the dominant world based on an order whose hierarchies are upheld by force and authoritarianism, and the other "possible" world. This latter world, however, cannot flourish because of the first world, and the filmic discourse makes this very clear. While they are in Goya, Camila and Ladislao experience that "possible" world; they live in peace; they live peacefully and productively. They live a life based on a rather feminist set of values: equality between the two sexes in every sense. But, on Easter Sunday, the happiness of that world comes apart, and the filmic discourse shows it in terms of the established dichotomy. The lieutenant "steals" Ladislao for a few minutes as he asks Camila's indulgence, telling her that "es cosa de hombres" (it's men's business). It is the return to the first of the two worlds, and this sentence signals the beginning of the end of the feminist "experiment" that the two were carrying out.

The bibliography on *Camila* reveals that canonical readings of the film take two directions: the first, a popular view, and the second, a more academic, theory-driven view. The first reading often does not go beyond a reading activated by *La Perichona*'s question from the opening arrival sequence, "¿Te gustan las historias de amor?" As the cover of Cinemateca's 2002 DVD release of the film puts it, *Camila* offers "Love Against All Odds."[13] Others, picking up on the love story angle, study the inscription of this narrative within generic antecedents, especially melodrama.

The second of the directions of canonical reading sticks very closely to the reading from the feminine/feminist perspective, and that, too, is a matrix point established in the first few minutes through the introduction of a female whose freedom is being restricted.

While each of these two sets of common readings of *Camila* finds its initial justification in the film's first few minutes, neither pays full attention to all of the cues offered in those, the film's establishing moments. Neither of these common readings of the film goes far enough in their analysis. Both ignore the film's implications at an allegorical-symbolical level indexed as political by the establishing first scenes. But the fact that *La Perichona* is a political prisoner orients the viewer toward a reading of the film on a political level also. This orientation is substantiated in the indexing of the Federalist promotion of the link between the government and the Catholic Church, and in the repressive censorship that inhibits intellectual and artistic expression ending in the exile of intellectuals.

Camila is an intertextual blend of film and historical and literary subtextual material. Intertextuality should be understood as a transposition from one sign system to another in which the transposition implies a change or transformation. In *Camila*, as the film is structured and organized through the mediation of the director's artistic vision, personality, gender, ideology, etc., the transposition/transformation from pre-text/subtext to filmic text creates a strong and singular cinematographic statement at the same time as its filmic perspective offers the viewer a unique and emotional experience. And, it is through an application of the orienting matrix offered by the film's first few minutes that the scholar-viewer is able to discover *Camila*'s rich meanings at many levels.

Understood as a people's accumulated past, History is central to this film, as *Camila*'s story is based on actual events from the mid–1800's. One of its allegorical implications is that the tyranny and repression suffered by Camila and Ladislao and the structures of repression of the period foreshadow similar tyranny and repression contemporary to the film's making. In this regard, the film participates in Argentina's post-1983 redemocratization process, along with the next film to be analyzed, *La historia oficial*, whose establishing minutes clearly index that contemporary history as they, too, create a matrix for reading the film.

◆ 4 ◆

FROM BYSTANDING TO STANDING FOR

Luis Puenzo's 1985
La historia oficial (The Official Story)

> Our Commission was set up not to sit in judgment ... but to investigate the fate of the people who disappeared during those ill-omened years of our nation's life. However, after collecting several thousand statements and testimonies, verifying or establishing the existence of hundreds of secret detention centres, and compiling over 50,000 pages of documentation, we are convinced that the recent military dictatorship brought about the greatest and most savage tragedy in the history of Argentina ... we cannot remain silent in the face of all that we have heard, read and recorded. This went far beyond what might be considered criminal offences, and takes us into the shadowy realm of crimes against humanity. Through the technique of disappearance and its consequences, all the ethical principles which the great religions and the noblest philosophies have evolved through centuries of suffering and calamity have been trampled underfoot, barbarously ignored.
>
> —Ernesto Sábato, Prologue to *Nunca más*, Report of CONADEP (National Commission on the Disappearance of Persons)–1984

With intertitles that appear on a black background, the viewer learns that Historias Cinematográficas present Héctor Alterio and Norma Aleandro in a Luis Puenzo film entitled *La historia oficial*. The film begins with this title in light blue letters that look a little like a neon sign, as the sound track includes muted crowd noise. This title appears diagonally on the screen, with the left side lower than the right. Suddenly the image is broken in two as if the screen were a sheet of paper being torn, with the tear splitting the screen in the middle horizontally as each half moves away, one going up, and the other going down. This visual is accompanied by the very same sound of tearing paper.

The first filmed diegetic image to appear is a close-up shot of three loudspeakers attached to a pole near which various small, light blue Argentine national flags are hanging from other poles. An orchestral song begins to play through the speakers; it is the national anthem of Argentina. The camera moves to the right to a high angle shot, and as the camera moves, the view is from behind the supporting structure of the roof. The camera moves to the high angle where it discovers a school assembly at an all-boys school. Students, dressed uniformly in sport coats and ties, are assembled in a courtyard or patio. As the camera continues to move right, it discovers among the boys some older people, presumably teachers. Over the wall of the courtyard, a street and tress are visible. There is the sound of airplanes mixed with the music that continues. A train or trolley passes by on the street outside the wall. Those present begin to sing the Argentine national anthem beneath a misty rain, for which some of the adults are carrying umbrellas. Though it is somewhat difficult to hear the singing because of the sound of the passing train, what is very clearly distinguishable is the refrain "Libertad, libertad, libertad" (Freedom, freedom, freedom). The assembly solemnly sings[1]:

¡Oíd, mortales!, el grito sagrado:	Hear, mortals, the sacred cry:
"¡Libertad! ¡Libertad! ¡Libertad!"	"Freedom! Freedom! Freedom!"
¡Oíd el ruido de rotas cadenas	Hear the noise of broken chains,
ved en trono a la noble igualdad.	see the noble Equality enthroned.
Ya su trono dignísimo abrieron	For their most honorable throne has opened
Las Provincias Unidas del Sud	The United Provinces of the South.
y los libres del mundo responden:	And the free of the world reply:
"¡Al gran pueblo argentino, salud!"	"To the great Argentine people, hail!"
"¡Al gran pueblo argentino, salud!"	"To the great Argentine people, hail!"
Y los libres del mundo responden:	And the free of the world reply:
"¡Al gran pueblo argentino, salud!"	"To the great Argentine people, hail!"
Y los libres del mundo responden:	And the free of the world reply:
"¡Al gran pueblo argentino, salud!"	"To the great Argentine people, hail!"

The camera moves through the assembly, focusing close-ups on individual faces of some those assembled, the young men and a well-dressed woman with her hair pulled tight upon her head. She seems to scan the assembly with her eyes, as the man beside and behind her briefly looks to the sky.

With the sound of a school bell, there is a cut to an interior; it is the hallway of the school where students move quickly to their destinations. Following the ceremony, everyone enters the school, and the woman earlier highlighted shows up walking down the hall. Briefly the man and woman featured in the previous close-up greet and go on their way.

There is a cut to a close-up of a page from a school log, and a hand writing the date, 14 marzo 1983 (March 14, 1983). It is the hand of the woman teacher that the viewer has come to know, and a medium shot discovers her seated very erect, signaling discipline, at her teacher's desk, glasses half way down her nose and a map of Argentina on the wall to her right. The students talk among themselves, and the woman closes the folder and puts down her pen, takes off her glasses, stands, and clears her throat.

> Silencio, señores, por favor. Silencio, por favor. Mi nombre es Alicia Marnet de Ibañez.... Algunos ya me conocen.... La materia que vamos a ver juntos es historia argentina.... Según consta en el programa, vamos a tratar sobre las instituciones políticas y sociales desde 1810.
> (Quiet, gentlemen, please. Quiet, please. My name is Alicia Marnet de Ibañez. Some of you already know me.... The subject matter we are going to see together is Argentine history.... As stated on the syllabus, we are going to deal with political and social institutions since 1810.)

She asks for their silence and introduces herself. She tells the students that the course will be three hours a week, and it will be about Argentine political and social institutions since the year 1810. Further, she warns the students that she does not like to waste time, that she believes in discipline, and that she does not give grades away. Shot reverse shot technique reveals the reactions of the students as well as the teacher giving her remarks.

In addition, the teacher goes on to explain that:

> Comprender la historia es prepararse para comprender el mundo.... Ningún pueblo podría sobrevivir sin memoria. Y la historia es la memoria de los pueblos.... Éste es el sentido que vamos a darle a la materia.
> (To understand history is to prepare oneself to understand the world.... No people could survive without memory. And history is the memory of the people.... This is the meaning we are going to give to the subject matter.)

She tells her students that to understand history is to prepare oneself to understand the world, and that no people can survive without memory. She tells them that history is the memory of the people. The teacher sits down again at her desk. She begins to take attendance, and the students respond indicating their presence ("Presente") without much enthusiasm. When one student responds uniquely, "Acá, señora" (Here, Ma'am), the others laugh at him.

At this point, the first five minutes and twenty seconds of the filmic narrative have elapsed, and periodically throughout, different credits have appeared superimposed on the images. Here, the last of the film credits appears, identifying the film's director, Luis Puenzo, which often can be taken as the end of a film's first few establishing minutes.

If, as we saw in *Camila*, the grandmother's question to the child Camila (Do you like love stories?) primes the scholar-viewer for a film to be read as a love story with political overtones, in *La historia oficial* Alicia's extremely direct introduction to her course, and at the same time, to the film, clearly tells the viewer that this film is to be read as a study of history. What viewers are going to see together are lessons in Argentine history, lessons in which "official" understandings will be torn asunder in order to fill gaps in memory and to prepare the viewer to understand the world. However melodramatic the following filmic narrative might become, the scholar-viewer has been

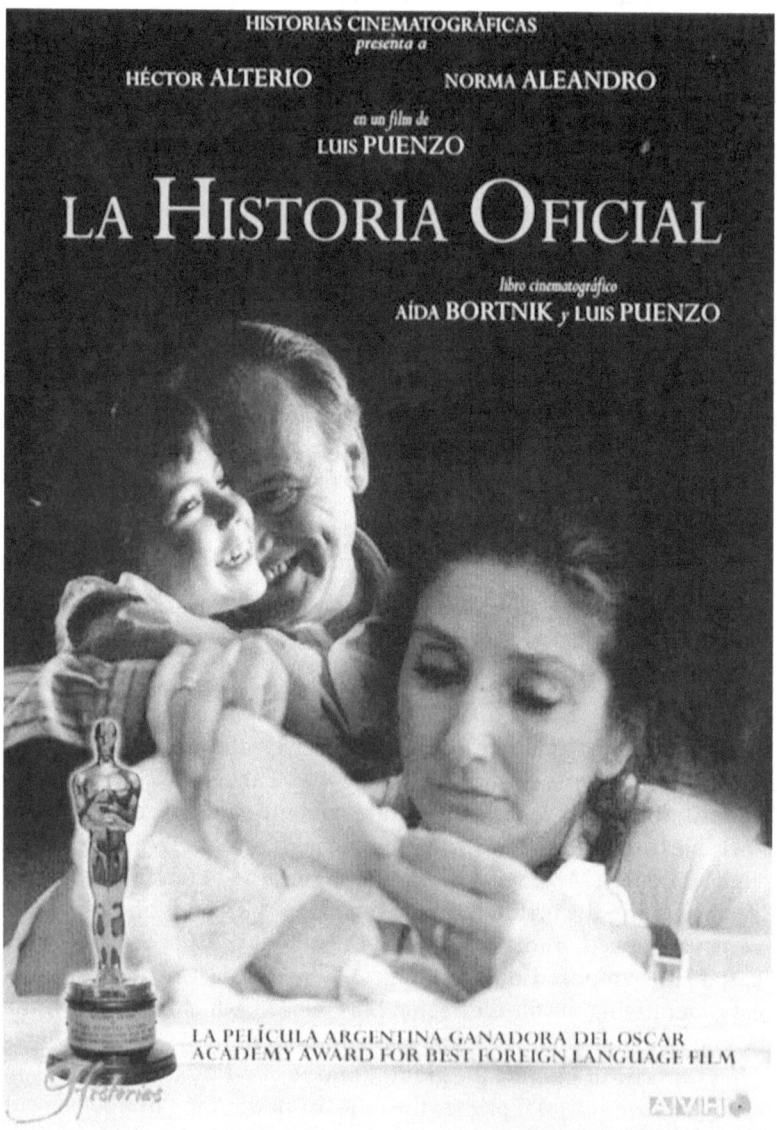

La historia oficial (1985).

primed to read the film's meaning in terms of its lessons about Argentine history.

If the viewer is to read the film as history lesson, Alicia's dating of her school log gives him a precise orientation as to the historical period about which lessons will be taught. When she writes March 14, 1983, she locates the filmic narrative in the waning months of a historical period referred to variably as the "Guerra Sucia" (Dirty War), military dictatorship, and "Proceso de Reorganización Nacional" (Process of National Reorganization).

With the camera movement at times forcing the spectator to view from behind, he knows that there is to be an element of spying, of looking behind in his reading of the filmic narrative. On this point, there is agreement from another study of the film. And, the agreement is not just on the importance of the filming technique but also on the establishing of an early frame of reference.

Stephen M. Hart (2004), as he posits the importance and the significance of the blocking shot in *La historia oficial*, seems also to recognize the importance of the film's first few minutes when he writes:

> The establishing shot of the film, for example, gives a hint of what is to come ... the camera focuses on the school playground, but our view is consistently blocked by the concrete structure of the roof behind which the camera is placed. This blocking shot, i.e. there is something interrupting the vision of the spectator from the main action, is an early indication that we will be seeing a behind-the-scenes version of Argentine reality. This establishing shot, indeed, draws attention to one of the key techniques used in the film, namely, snares which offer a tantalising view of an event but without telling us the whole truth [121].

What Hart refers to as "seeing a behind-the-scenes version of Argentine reality" is a reference to part of the orientation to the reading of the film as history. Alicia tells the viewer that the subject matter of the film is Argentine history. Since this orientation comes from a teacher of history at a school, the reference is assumed to be to history with a capital H, History. But this orientation to "behind-the-scenes," while it indexes a clandestineity of the events of the dirty war to be uncovered, also indexes history with a small letter h, the history, or better the story, that reveals reality behind capital letter History.

With the filming technique of the first few minutes shooting close-ups of individuals as the anthem's lyrics refer to "el pueblo argentino" (the Argentine people), there is a suggestion of the relationship between individual and the whole. From this establishing cue, the viewer is prepared to read the film as a metonymy.[2]

The centrality of the metonymical device, in which the relationship of individual to the whole allows the individual to index the whole, is almost immediately underscored. The ritual affirmation of nationality introduced by the singing of the national anthem in the film's first few minutes is followed by the meeting of the first class of the academic year. Alicia introduces herself ("Mi nombre es Alicia Marnet de Ibañez"), and she calls roll announcing the individual names of the students (Alara, Sebastián.... Álvarez, Rodrigo.... Artemi, Rubén.... Beláustegui, Manuel.... Burman, Alejandro.... Costa, Horacio.... Cullen, Martín...). The contiguity editing places the very personal in immediate association to the generic in the prior evocation of national identity. At the same time, this contiguity keys a metonymy in which individual indexes whole as a key component of the matrix for reading *La historia oficial*.

If one were to explain that a film spends precious narrative space to showing a history teacher taking attendance on the first day of class, it perhaps would be hard to believe that the same film is also an award-winning work. But, it is easy to justify the use of so much narrative space for the calling of roll in the scene's importance for creating a matrix for reading the film. To begin with, and as suggested above, this sequence serves to corroborate the metonymical nature of the reading of the film in terms of the relationship of individual representing the whole.

Further, the sequence, with its shot reverse shot technique in which the students are alternately focused upon, serves to characterize one generation, Argentina's youth, as disengaged with an older generation. This disengagement, visible in the youths' body language as well as the lack of enthusiasm in their responses, is symptomatic and it foreshadows other societal disengagement. Additionally, the surnames themselves offer the viewer a first history lesson.

If, as Alicia announces in the first view minutes, the matrix for reading the film is that film viewers, observers of the narrated world together with the participants in that world, are to see together the history of Argentina, this roll call is a first lesson in Argentine history. In the list of last names that Alicia reads off and in the visuals of the students seated in her class, different national origins are indexed. The different surnames and the origins they index offer a history lesson into the different immigrations in Argentine history that have been important in the formation of Argentina as a nation. With this list, there are at least allusions to Spanish, Basque, Italian and English ingredients in the Argentine historical mix. In that same vein, the visuals speak as much with what they portray as with what is absent in their portrayal. Even though what is presented is a Latin American context, it is clear from the physiognomies offered that the history lessons will not contain indigenous or Afro ingredients.

As the scholar-viewer reads the film prompted in search of Argentine history, he receives lessons in three different ways. The first is very direct, and most certainly less related to the *raison d'être* of the film. Offered, for example, are direct history lessons in the form of classes at school. In this regard, for example, the viewer learns of Mariano Moreno. Moreno was a late 18th and early 19th century criollo lawyer, journalist, and politician who played a decisive role in Argentina's first independent national government, created after what Argentine history refers to as the May Revolution. And, in Alicia's class, there is a discussion of Moreno's "republican spirit" and of civil rights such as freedom of the press.

When the discussion turns to how Moreno died, there is an assertion that he was poisoned, but Alicia refutes the assertion as something that was once believed, but for which there is no proof. Ironically, it is a student who gives the film's first history lesson as he responds to this notion of proof. The student Costa interrupts Alicia "No hay prueba porque la historia la escriben los asesinos" (There's no proof because history is written by the murderers/ assassins!). A different take on the often-cited claim that History is written by the victors, the reference here is, of course, to capital H history or, as the film's title might suggest,[3] to official [hi]story.

The students later offer another "in-class" history lesson for the viewer. When Alicia enters the classroom, one student is already reading aloud to the others from a text by Moreno. Two students hold watch in the hallway awaiting Alicia's arrival. When they enter to warn the others, the rest of the students listen with great interest. One student reads from Moreno's essay published on the 12th of June 1810 in *La Gaceta de Buenos Aires*. The essay speaks of a people's need for the truth. The backdrop to the interrupted reading is Alicia discovering that the students have papered the chalkboard with newspaper clippings. Among the clippings, there are obviously visible texts related to appeals for information about the "disappeared."

A final in-class history lesson comes late in the film, when Alicia is returning papers to the students. The viewer learns of Juan José Castelli, another of the leaders of the May Revolution. Jailed for his beliefs and "silenced," Castelli offers parallels to and indexes contemporary events. The student Costa has asserted that Castelli's tongue was cut out to silence him. Though Alicia warns Costa of the need to document such assertions, she assigns to him a very good grade, signaling an important step forward in the process of the awakening of her consciousness.

"La literatura siempre se encuentra con la historia" (Literature always meets up with History) is another of the direct history lessons that the viewer takes away from a classroom experience in *La historia oficial*. And, the *double entendre* of this lesson is the words pronounced by a somewhat embarrassed Benítez as Alicia interrupts his rambunctious literature class. In the class, teacher and students read and act out portions of the novel *Juan Moreira*, a classic *gauchesca* novel by the 19th century Argentine writer Eduardo Gutiérrez. An important text in Argentine literature and a good example of Latin

American Romanticism, the romantic novel itself was inspired by a real-life story of the legendary gaucho Juan Moreira who was killed by police in 1874.

In each in-class case referred to above, the history lessons contain a liberal slant, focusing on liberties and freedom, and the tenets that supported Argentina's move away from colonial domination by Spain to independence.

A second way in which the viewer learns history as he reads the film is through documentary. While *La historia oficial* is a fictional narrative whose script is the product of director Luis Puenzo and collaborator Aida Bortnik, the filmic narrative does contain documentary (or documentary-style) footage.

Reference here is made to the demonstrations in Buenos Aires' Plaza de Mayo. Important to contemporary Argentine history are the Madres de la Plaza de Mayo (The Mothers of the Plaza de Mayo). The *Asociación Madres de Plaza de Mayo* was an association of Argentine mothers whose children were "disappeared" between 1976 and 1983, during the Dirty War of the military dictatorship. Beginning with a group of fourteen mothers, they organized as they tried to find out what had happened to their sons and daughters. On April 30, 1977, they began to march at the Plaza de Mayo in Buenos Aires, which is in front of the Casa Rosada presidential palace.

Most people were afraid of attracting the government's attention because of its efforts to eradicate opposition. Taking strength together by marching in public, with some coverage by the press, and with time, hundreds of women participated, gathering in the Plaza for weekly demonstrations. They made and carried large placard signs with photos of their children and displaying their children's names.

The filmic discourse of *La historia oficial* registers this public defiance of the government's state terrorism intended to silence all opposition as it presents footage of the Mothers of the Plaza de Mayo marching as passersby stop to observe them. The Mothers' association was formed by women who had met each other while trying to find their missing sons and daughters. Many of the "desaparecidos" were believed to have been abducted by agents of the Argentine government during the years known as the Dirty War (1976–1983); the "disappeared" were often tortured and killed before their bodies were disposed of in rural areas or unmarked graves. The filmic narrative links these historical acts with the fictional events by placing Sara (metonymy) among the Mothers marching.

In that period, the government tried to marginalize and trivialize the Mothers' work by calling them "*las locas*" (crazies, madwomen). And, the filmic narrative creates another close tie between fictional and historical events as Roberto uses this very term in his initial reaction to the presence of Sara in his home. After Alicia introduces Sara as possibly Gaby's grandmother, an enraged Roberto shouts "Vos estás completamente loca" (You are completely crazy/mad), and he refers to Sara as "la primera loca que encuentras por la calle" (the first crazy/madwomen you find in the street). As Roberto turns to these epithets, as spokesman for the oppressors, he links the two narrative levels.

Faced with increasing public opposition and severe economic problems, the military tried to regain popularity by occupying the disputed Malvinas/Falkland Islands. It lost any remaining favor in its lopsided defeat by Britain in the resulting Malvinas/Falklands War, and, in disgrace, it stepped aside for the restoration of democracy. The timeframe represented in *La historia oficial* is the chaotic period prior to fall elections that would mark the beginning of that restoration.

Of course, in addition to the history lessons this documentary or documentary-style footage provides, it serves a vital structural function. The demonstrations are captured in documentary style reminiscent of that of Patricio Guzmán, for example, in his *La batalla de Chile*, and some version of the events undoubtedly exists in the public imaginary. If the filmic narrative includes footage of "real" demonstrations in the streets and plazas of Buenos Aires, the suggestion for the viewer is that the narrated events of the lives of Alicia, Gaby, Roberto, Sara and Ana are real as well.[4]

Imbedded in the filmic narrative there are other "documents" that have the meaningful and framing function. In an early scene at home, just before Roberto returns home, a television news program is on in the background, and the viewer hears an editorial lament about how some news media abuse their rights because they preach destabilization and encourage subversive ideas. As the newscast indicates that the army is preparing to confront the infiltrators, it clearly indexes a real-life political situation in which the military dictatorship was losing its grip. And as it does, it indexes the repressive nature of the military, the cause of the film's historical subject matter.

Alicia gives Benítez a ride as she is going downtown. When they arrive and are surrounded by a great deal of traffic, hustle and bustle, the viewer sees, along with Alicia, in the background a large street demonstration. The street is littered with flyers, and visible are large signs and banners being carried that identify demonstrators as "Familias de desaparecidos y detenidos por razones políticas," "Madres y abuelas de la Plaza de Mayo" and "Trabajadores" (Families of the politically disappeared and detained/Mothers and Grandmothers of the Plaza de Mayo/Workers), and they demand the return of the disappeared to their families as well as mental health legislation. Audible are chants that demand an end to killing and to know where the disappeared are, and that protest against the Malvinas war, foreign debt, and corruption.

The demonstration consists of hundreds of marchers whose movements appear to be captured by a nervous handheld camera where the image is intermittently interrupted by passersby or vehicles. And, the audio is an unscrubbed mix of chants, people, and traffic noise. Seemingly, Alicia has come upon a newsworthy, historical event, and her gaze on the demonstration links the two narrative levels, historical reality and fiction, as she goes on to Roberto's office.

Later, much further along in the filmic narrative's process of raising Alicia's consciousness, the viewer, along with Alicia, watches another demonstration in the Plaza de Mayo. The sequence offers every indication of being documentary, as Sara marches with a multitude of other demonstrators. In footage worthy of the evening news, the filmic narrative registers demonstrators' diegetic chants: "Queremos nuestros hijos," and so on (We want our children. No pardon. No amnesty. We want them alive.), and viewers see banners that read, "Familias de desaparecidos y detenidos" (Families of the Missing and Imprisoned). Again, as a link between narrative levels, Sara and Alicia catch each other's gaze.

The third, and most prominent, way the viewer receives history lessons is through the already alluded to metonymical gambit in which story ("historia") indexes History. The story or stories of Alicia, Gabi, Roberto, Ana, Benítez, and Sara will stand for the History of Argentina. The blending of their stories will offer the viewer a lesson, not in the 'official story,' but in the 'real History.'

As already described, Alicia, the protagonist, is a teacher at a private all-boys school, and her husband Roberto is a prominent businessman. Together they have an 'adopted' daughter, Gaby. They are the image of a normal upper middle class Buenos Aires family on the eve of celebrating the child's fifth birthday.

Ana is Alicia's friend, and they are reunited at a high school reunion. Later Ana and Alicia are at Alicia's home, and Ana confesses revealing information to Alicia. Her tearful and startling confession is the motivation for Alicia's search into her daughter's past, as she herself had asked no questions. Eventually, Alicia finds out that her daughter is actually the daughter of a *desaparecida*, after Gaby's biological grandmother informs her.

Ana represents the thousands of Argentines who were detained and tortured during the Dirty War. She confesses to Alicia that she had been tortured while detained. As the viewer also learns about History, Ana also tells Alicia of the brutal treatment that the officials used on the victims, including the fact that they took babies from pregnant women, to be sold or given away to people who were willing to accept them, no questions asked.

Following a scene in which Alicia and some old friends have a kind of class reunion, where special friend Ana has returned from exile and shows her liberal side, Ana has dinner with Alicia and Roberto. He insults her by telling her that Europe seems to have polished her. Later, while Roberto cannot seem to sleep, Ana and Alicia talk into the night, with a sisterly tenderness

4. From Bystanding to Standing For 93

and an alcohol-induced lack of inhibition. Alicia asks Ana why she left, why she left in such a hurry, and why she never wrote. Beginning by telling how they ripped up the poster of Gardel she had on her door, Ana recounts having been kidnapped by the police. Ana tells about being tortured, water torture ("Después de siete años todavía me ahogo"/After seven years I'm still drowning). She was told the torture went on for thirty-six days. The only torturer whose face she saw saved her from being raped, but only because he told the others he planned to rape her himself. Ana confesses that she continues to be terrified that she will hear his voice on the street or on the subway. Throughout, Alicia seems perplexed: "Pero, ¿por qué te hicieron eso? ¿Por qué te hicieron eso?" (But, why did they do that to you? Why did they do that to you?).

Speculating that he was already dead by the time they tortured her, the torturers repeatedly asked about her lover, Pedro, whom she had not seen for two years. Alicia asks if Ana had reported it ("¿Hiciste la denuncia?"/Did you file a report?). Ana looks quizzical and asks ironically if Alicia has any idea as to whom she would have reported. Ana goes on to explain emotionally:

> Ese lugar estaba lleno.... A veces era difícil saber si era yo la que gritaba o los otros.... Había mujeres embarazadas que perdían allí sus hijos.... Y otro que se los llevaba.... Pero volvían solas porque el chico se los daba a esas familias que los compran sin preguntarle de dónde vienen.
>
> (That place was so full.... At times it was difficult to know whether I was the one screaming or the others.... There were pregnant women who lost their babies there.... And another guy who took them away from them.... But the women came back alone because the guy gave the babies to those families that buy them without asking him where they came from).

And, as Ana mentions the babies of torture victims that are given away, seemingly coming to a sudden and disturbing realization, a horrified Alicia asks: "¿Por qué me dices eso a mí?" (Why are you telling *me* that?). Evidencing the end of these moments of sisterhood and her lingering trauma, Ana answers referring to her own tortured past: "Increíble.... Me siento culpable" (It's incredible.... I still feel guilty).

As an emotional counterpoint and index to the Argentines who ignored the historical events alluded to by Ana's tale, Gaby sleeps peacefully in her bedroom while Ana talks about her being tortured.

Another important and primary story (small letter "historia") in the metonymies that index Dirty War capital-H History is that of Benítez. Leaving school he catches up with the hurrying history teacher, and he rides downtown with Alicia in order to talk with her.[5] In conversation, Alicia asks him why he was fired from his university position in Cuyo. Benítez clarifies that he wasn't fired. He tells of having his rooms ransacked and his papers destroyed. "Así que entendí el mensaje, yo solito" (So, I got the message ... all by myself).

Alicia mentions that her students hung clippings about the disappeared and missing babies in the classroom, and showing him a folder containing the clippings, she asks if such reports are true. Bothered by her naiveté, Benítez scolds Alicia with:

> ¿A usted qué le importa lo que puede ser cierto? ¿Qué problema se hace? ... Siempre es más fácil creer que no es posible, ¿no? Sobre todo para que sea posible se necesitaría mucha complicidad, mucha gente que no lo puede creer aunque lo tenga delante, ¿no?
>
> (What do you care whether it's true? Is it your problem? It is always easier to believe it is impossible, right? Above all, for it to be possible, it would require much complicity, many people who cannot believe it, even when it is right in front of them, right?).

If the combination of these stories ("historias") creates a view of a History in which the military quieted its torture, disappeared and robbed babies, other narrative elements provide depth to the History. Alicia, for example, goes to confession, where she tells the priest about being lied to when her parents were killed in an auto accident. Saying she can no longer believe what she has been told, she confronts the confession priest, who was with Roberto when he obtained Gaby and brought her home. The priest stubbornly and dismissively refuses answer Alicia's questions. He absolves her of her sins, and closes up the confessional.

Leaving the confessional, the camera follows the priest as he walks through the shadows of the dimly lit church. This image is an indexical reference to the Church's complicity with the Dirty War.

La historia oficial portrays the traumatic effects that the Dirty War had on the Argentine people. It indexes divisions in the country, and it articulates struggles of winners and losers. As a winner, Alicia struggles to come to terms with the history of Gaby. Sara, Gaby's presumed grandmother, is a loser, and she belongs to the Abuelas de la Plaza de Mayo, a subdivision of Las Madres. The viewer sees, when Sara and Alicia sit at the café for instance, the heartache and suffering that this woman had endured over the loss of her daughter and son-in-law. Alicia learns from this woman that her daughter and son-in-law were kidnapped and disappeared. Sara describes her daughter's courtship and wedding, and she also describes their kidnapping. She has only four old photos of her daughter and son-in-law, which she shows to Alicia. She teaches Alicia, and the viewer, two of the film's important lessons of history.

First, she teaches about the importance of memory, as, while showing the photographs, she tells Alicia, "No quedó nada ... nada ... estas cuatro fotos solamente de ellos ... y nuestra memoria" (Nothing remained ... nothing ... these four photos of them, that's all ... and our memory).

Recognizing the resemblance between Gaby and the young daughter, especially in one of the photos, Alicia realizes that Sara is probably Gaby's grandmother and she begins to cry. At this point, Sara teaches the second of the important lessons of history as she tells Alicia, "No llore. No llore, llorar no sirve. Yo sé porqué se lo digo, eh. Llorar no sirve." (Don't cry. Don't cry, crying doesn't help. I know what I'm talking about. Crying doesn't help).

As testimony to the activism of the Madres and Abuelas, their metonymical representative, Sara, reveals their lesson of history. While lament may be necessary for the individual dealing with trauma and loss, it does not help ("no sirve") at a societal level. In order to move past the trauma, there is a need to act, to seek answers.

Furthermore, Ana's testimonial is an accurate portrayal of the actual horrors that the victims who were part of History underwent in the detention centers. Also, the filmic narrative's portrayal is not as one-sided in its presentation of internal Argentine conflict. There is sympathy for Alicia and the pain and confusion that she endures over her ignorance regarding her daughter's origin. There is sympathy for Sara and the pain and indignation she endures at the loss of her daughter and son-in-law. There is sympathy for Ana and the pain and lingering trauma that she endures seven years after her torture and exile. There is sympathy for Benítez and the indignation that he displays and his resilient attention to the youth. There is sympathy for Gaby and the confusion that she may have to endure. But, there is no sympathy for Roberto, who is an excellent representation of the secretiveness, authoritarianism, and denial of the "dirty war" dynamic. It is his refusal to inform Alicia of anything regarding Gaby and his violent insistence on power over her that result in what would seem to bring the end of their marriage.[6]

One of the history lessons that the viewer is to learn is the importance of memory and its recovery. In her introductory remarks to her class, Alicia emphasizes that a people cannot survive without memory, and that history is their memory. She and the filmic discourse give this meaning to history, and through Alicia, this is how the film asks to be read.

That memory and its recovery are vital to the reading of this film there can be little doubt when the filmic discourse corroborates this component even at the level of its soundtrack. When the viewer first meets Gaby, she sings "En el país de No me acuerdo" ("In the country of I don't remember"), she invokes the need to recover memory. She invokes, and represents, an Argentina that has lost memory of itself and of its history. Her invocation of national historical memory loss is quickly reinforced by the soundtrack inclusion of María Elena Walsh's version of "En el país de Nomeacuerdo."

As part of the establishing matrix that the first few minutes provides through Alicia's introductory remarks to her class, and hence to the viewer of the film, history is to be viewed as memory, and especially as memory necessary to a people's survival. The opening remarks would seem to indicate a need to recover memory, and that need is immediately corroborated, as already noted by Gaby's singing and the soundtrack. The words of the song are as follow:

En el país del no me acuerdo	In the country of I don't remember
Doy tres pasitos y me pierdo.	I take three steps and I get lost.
Un pasito para allí,	One step that way,
No recuerdo si lo di.	I can't remember if I took it
Un pasito para allá	One step the other way
¡Ay, qué miedo que me da!	Oh, it makes me so afraid!
En el país del no me acuerdo	In the country of I don't remember
Doy tres pasitos y me pierdo.	I take three steps and I get lost.
Un pasito para atrás,	One step backwards,
y no doy ninguno más,	and I don't go any farther
porque yo ya me olvidé,	because I already forgot
donde puse el otro pie.	Where I put my other foot
En el país del no me acuerdo,	In the country of I don't remember
Doy tres pasitos y me pierdo …	I take three steps and I get lost.

Indexed is the Argentina of the "Proceso," a country in which Argentines have lost their way. The expression of being lost and lost memory indexes the need, articulated in the first few minutes by Alicia, of the Argentine people to recover memory in order to move ahead.

With the filming technique of the first few minutes and the establishing cues suggesting the relationship between individual and the whole that prepare the scholar-viewer to read the film as a metonymy, there is also an orientation to the need for metaphorical awareness in the interpretation of the film. The viewer will remember the presence of the walls that separate the schoolyard from the street life outside. These walls suggest a metaphor in which the "pueblo argentino," incarnate in the individuals present and singing the national anthem, is closed off from some reality. In the specific case of *La historia oficial*, it is the people closed off from truth, from the true "story" of their recent history. This metaphorically represented situation creates a need for the Argentine people to recover their memory of recent history because, as Alicia tells her class and the viewer very directly, no people can survive without memory. The breaking down of these metaphorical walls becomes Alicia's personal and vital project[7] as well as the project for the filmic narrative.

Metonymy and metaphor combine in Roberto and some, if not most, of his actions. As beneficiary of and partner and associate to those in power during the "Proceso," Roberto comes to be a metonymy representing authoritarianism in Argentina. When the viewer first meets Roberto, he comes home with a birthday present for the daughter: a new, life-size doll for Gaby. This is an obvious metaphorical reference to an event of five years earlier when Roberto returned home with Gaby, a gift for his wife. This indexes what later

Ana will reveal as a practice during the dirty war years of babies being taken away from mothers who were disappeared and selling them to "esas familias que los compran sin preguntarle de dónde vienen" (to those families that buy them without asking where they come from).

Secretive, patronizing, antagonistic to liberals, when he smashes Alicia's hand in the door jamb, Roberto ultimately shows himself to be the metonymy and metaphor for violence, like the military dictatorship responsible for torture and disappearances that he represents.

If metonymy and metaphor combine as structuring devices for *La historia oficial*'s filmic narrative, it is perhaps in a scene during Gaby's birthday party where they combine most effectively. It is a scene that involves the doll that Roberto has purchased as a gift for the couple's daughter. Not entertained by the clown hired to work the birthday party, Gaby goes off to her room alone to play with the doll.[8] As she tenderly cares for it, some boy party guests explode into the room with their toy pistols and arms. Gaby's panicked screams of terror index and reproduce for the viewer what were certainly the reactions of those individuals targeted by the dirty war as police invaded their homes to take them prisoner.

As mentioned earlier, the words of the national anthem are significant to the interpretation of the film. The modern version of the anthem is sung and it is quoted earlier.[9] Only the first two choruses of the modern version of the anthem are sung, ending with the repeated "¡Al gran pueblo argentino, salud!" The use of a shortened version allows a highlighted presence of the parts of the anthem that are sung, particularly this four-times repeated refrain and another. As the members of the school, teachers, administrators, and students alike, sing the anthem, what stays with the viewer is the clear repetition of one impactful line, the repetition of "Libertad, libertad, libertad" (freedom, freedom, freedom). In its insistence on the absence of freedoms during the "Proceso," the filmic narrative metonymically indexes lack of freedom of expression and lack of free access to information as well as more egregious violations of human rights, corruption, and fraud.[10] The lack of freedom is attributed to repression by authoritarianism.

One of the film's best metonymies for the repression of freedoms comes during Benítez' class. As Benítez conducts his literature class, the students and he read and interpret aloud. There is laughter, much movement, and a visibly free and relaxed atmosphere. At the height of the class's theatricality, Alicia enters the classroom, her hair tautly pulled into a bun, her stance erect, and her gaze disapproving. The entrance of the teacher who, to this point, has been associated with the imposition of discipline and correct behavior, puts an end to the freedoms enjoyed by Benítez and his class.

With the film's title that is presented to him at a slant, the viewer knows that the film is to be read from a "left-leaning" perspective. If there is any doubt as to the sympathies of the filmic narrative, an often alluded to sequence from the film removes it. Roberto, Alicia, and Gaby go to his parents' home for a family dinner on the patio. It is obvious from his accent that Roberto's father is Spanish, and his accent strongly contrasts with the thick Argentine accent of his son. Soon the contrast between the two becomes ideological when a discussion about predicting the weather turns aggressive. The Papá tells Roberto that he would look up at the clouds only if it were raining dollars, going further to say he raised his son for more than that, and accusing him of being too fond of money. Taking offense, Roberto retorts, "Pero sí, seguro. Vos me querrías mucho si yo fuera un fracasado" (But yes, sure…. You'd love me a lot if I were a failure). The end of the conversation summarizes the feeling of a nation at the same time as it underscores the ideological divide that is indexed originally by the tearing sound and visual of the film's title during the establishing first minutes. The conversation underscores the ideological divide that was played out by the Dirty War.

> PAPÁ: Todo el país se fue para abajo … solamente los hijos de puta, los ladrones, los cómplices y el mayor de mis hijos se fueron para arriba!
> (The whole country collapsed … only the sons of bitches, the thieves, their cohorts, and the eldest of my children struck it rich!)
> ROBERTO: … Siguen repitiendo las mismas boludeces anarquistas de toda la vida…. La guerra de España terminó y ustedes la perdieron…. ¡PERDIERON! Y me quieren hacer sentir culpable a mí porque yo no soy un perdedor. No, no, yo no soy un perdedor. Eso métanselo bien en la cabeza. ¡No soy un perdedor!
> (…You keep repeating the same stupid anarchist sayings as always…. The war in Spain is over and you lost it. You lost it! And, you want me to feel guilty because I'm not a loser. No, no, I am not a loser. Get that through your head. I am *not* a loser!)
> ENRIQUE: Y esta otra guerra –la guerra que ganaste vos con los de tu bando, ¿quién la perdió? ¿Sabes quién la perdió, hermano? Los pibes, los pibes como los míos porque ellos van a pagar los dólares que se afanaron. Y los van a tener que pagar no comiendo, no pudiendo estudiar. Porque vos no vas a pagar, claro, ¿qué vas a pagar vos?, si vos no sós un perdedor!
> (And this other war -the war you and your bunch won. Who lost it? You know who lost it, brother? The kids, kids like mine because they'll be paying for the dollars that were swiped. And they'll repay them by not eating and not studying. Because you won't repay them, of course! What should you pay? You're not a loser!)

With the strong Castilian accent of the father and the allusion to a lost war, reference is made here to the Spanish Civil War (1936–1939), in which liberal Republicans lost to archconservative Nationalists. As a result many liberals, like Roberto's father, left Spain, many, for example, for Argentina, Mexico and other Latin American destinations. Roberto, in his insistence on not being a loser, equates himself with the fascist military dictatorship those emigré losers left behind.

In the conversation, "losers" accuse "winners," left accuses right. With little or no sympathy created for a brooding Roberto who is secretive, authoritarian, and recommends not thinking, the sympathies of the filmic narrative are clear; the sympathies are with the losers and with the victims of the "winners."

That *La historia oficial* is a canonical film in the realm of Hispanic Studies, there can be no doubt. As Thomas Bloomers (2002) points out, "it has become a staple in many Latin American culture courses throughout the U.S. and Europe." The film has gained such a status, which it continues to enjoy, in part because of its relevance to historical-cultural concerns such as the "desaparecidos," "dirty wars," and memory.

Of course, the film's canonical status is not only attributable to its capacity for cultural reference. Its position within the genre is established as well by its filmic achievements and the weight of the acting performances. The year of its release, *La historia oficial* essentially swept the Silver Condor Awards (Argentine Film Critics Awards), winning, for example, best film, best actress, best cinematography, best screenplay, and best director. As is well known, internationally, the film won an Oscar, a Golden Globe, and a Los Angeles Film Critics Association Award as best foreign film; and Norma Aleandro was Cannes' pick as best actress. This level of critical recognition coupled with the film's commercial success establishes it as one that must be dealt with among the standard-bearers for Latin American film.

La historia oficial's critical success, notwithstanding, a portion of the critical bibliography dealing with the film is comprised of opinions that find the film lacking both artistically and critically. In this regard, Vicente Zito Lema, in the daily *La Voz*, wrote that *La historia oficial* "[a]penas roza el grado de conciencia pública alcanzado sobre el tema. Su utilidad es relativa, el mensaje está dirigido hacia los sectores más retrógrados, los más ciegos y sordos" (barely scratches the surface of the public's awareness of the topic. Its usefulness is relative as its message is directed toward the most retrograde sectors, towards the most blind and deaf); and in *Punto de Vista*, Raúl Filipelli similarly wrote that "*La historia oficial* ... es tan exterior a la política que, modificándole dos o tres escenas del guión, se convertiría rápidamente en un film sobre las desventuras de una madre adoptiva" (is so far from the political realm that, if two or three scenes in the script were modified, it would quickly turn into a film about the misfortunes of an adoptive mother) (both quoted in Manrupe [2001], 280).

Among those critical of *La historia oficial* were even the Madres de la Plaza de Mayo, who criticized the film because it fails to include any mention of the political antecedents and motivations, and the ideals of the victims. The Madres would have preferred a film stronger in its accusation of the oppressors. Implicit in their denunciation, and that of others, is the view that the film's creators were co-opted by international production norms, and that they lacked ethical commitment due to the Hollywood tradition that the film seeks to emulate.

Critics of the film see it as commercially produced mainly for an international film market where it would sell and gain prestige, and where international audiences could identify with its simplified, neatly packaged historical themes. Its focus on the middle class mediated an orientation towards Argentina's middle class and U.S. and European markets in a revisionist portrayal of bourgeois anguish that obscures the idea that "[t]he Junta was embraced with open arms by the national bourgeoisie ... and for years refused to acknowledge its atrocities, benefiting at the same time from the Junta's *plata dulce*" (Barnard [1986], 60).

One of the most extreme criticisms of *La historia oficial* produced by opinions rooted in this desire that Puenzo had made the film differently or a different film is that of Tamara Falicov (2007). Falicov's emphasis on film policy, Eurocentric production values, Argentine *espejismo*, and so forth, leads her seemingly to ignore aspects of the film and to conclusions difficult to sustain with filmic evidence. For example, she writes that in the film "[i]t becomes evident that it is mainly the poor who are disappearing and being killed fighting in the war..," an assertion that ignores that it is Ana, clearly not poor, who speaks for and indexes the tortured, exiled and disappeared. The disgust for the middle class and assumed middle class aesthetics leads to difficult to sustain generalizations like "[t]he real-life protagonists who truly did lay their lives on the line were not members of the universally regarded middle class" (68). And, Falicov summarizes this current of criticism of the film and its interpretation of it thus,

> *La historia oficial* is a film about bourgeois individualism. It is one woman's story, a *Bildungsroman* in which Alicia chooses to leave her morally corrupt husband, raise her own consciousness and return her daughter to her rightful grandmother. It is a story told for a middle-class audience, in which the main characters are universalized as middle-class and successful.... The historical events retold in *La historia oficial* deal with the dictatorship's slow decline and how it was able to maintain power for seven years. Alicia's obliviousness to the violence that surrounds her is symbolic of the middle class ... shielding themselves from the horrible realities of the terrorist state [70].

Ideological expectations here lead first to reading things in the film that are not there, such as the return of Gaby to her "rightful grandmother" and Alicia's "choice" to "raise her own consciousness," and to reading the filmic narrative as a retelling of historical events. But, more importantly, the critic's ideology leads her to ignore that the film, in its first few minutes, establishes metonymy, in which the individual stands for the whole, and sustains metonymy throughout in order to index a historical period about which there was much ignorance, providing the basis for a historical memory necessary for the Argentine people to go forward.

This same type of critical conclusion is repeated by Laura Podalsky (2011) when she writes:

> Puenzo's film allows the spectator a comfortable position from which to (re)view the Dirty War by privileging the perspective of Alicia, an "innocent" woman who discovers that her adopted daughter is the child of one of the disappeared. In focusing attention on the emotional discoveries of an individual "bystander," the film ignores the traumatic suffering of those who were tortured and killed and, one might add, handily avoids the difficult question of societal complicity [6].

A judgment of this nature seems itself to ignore the importance of the film's first few minutes in orienting a reading of the film. This judgment, and others similar to it, fails to recognize the important metonymical aspect of filmic discourse. To the contrary of Podalsky's assertion, *La historia oficial*, through metonymy, does not ask that the individual "bystand," but rather "stand for"; as Ana, for example, stands for "the traumatic suffering of those who were tortured..."; as Alicia stands for, not an "innocent," but rather an "ignorant" woman who actively discovers an "uncomfortable" complicity.

Perhaps, those critical of *La historia oficial* ought to consider the opinion offered by historian Mark Szuchman in his appraisal of this film (as well as María Luisa Bemberg's *Miss Mary*, from the same period), when he concludes:

> Historical cinema joined the national debates that fueled the division of a country that in the 1970s and 1980s questioned authority as well as received historical truths.... *The Official Story* give[s] us added dimensions to the observation and analysis of the Argentine past that go beyond traditionally bifurcated perspectives: liberalism-conservatism, nationalism-internationalism, federalism-centralism, and other historical antagonisms ... the nature of the medium itself—and the many commercial and financial considerations that go into the production of films—inhibit fuller explorations of historical phenomena and analyses of historical problematics ... exploring the past can be done well or poorly, regardless of the medium. These productions are richer than [history] texts but only in the context of their own confines, raising more questions than answers and serving to remind us that, as historians, we can still learn a thing or two about nuanced meanings [198].

Offering and exemplifying metonymy as a structuring device central to the filmic discourse that sets out to offer history lessons to and about "el pueblo argentino," the first few minutes of *La historia oficial* prepare the scholar-viewer to understand and appreciate nuance expressed thus. And, established at the same time is an interpretative perspective from which to read and to judge the film's achievement of the objectives, not those others would expect of it, but rather those it sets for itself in its first few minutes.

♦ 5 ♦

FOR THE LACK OF
Tomás Gutiérrez Alea's 1993 *Fresa y chocolate* (*Strawberry and Chocolate*)

> Sabemos que hay sacrificios delante nuestro y que debemos pagar un precio por el hecho heroico de constituir una vanguardia como nación. Nosotros, dirigentes, sabemos que tenemos que pagar un precio por tener derecho a decir que estamos a la cabeza del pueblo que está a la cabeza de América. Todos y cada uno de nosotros paga puntualmente su cuota de sacrificio, conscientes de recibir el premio en la satisfacción del deber cumplido, conscientes de avanzar con todos hacia el hombre nuevo que se vislumbra en el horizonte.[1]
>
> Che Guevara, "El socialismo y el hombre en Cuba" (1965)

The 1993 Cuban film *Fresa y chocolate* (*Strawberry and Chocolate*) is based on and has a strong intertextual/intermedial relationship with a novella subtext, *El lobo, el bosque y el hombre nuevo* by Senel Paz, a work that had won the Juan Rulfo Prize in 1990. Paz, then, wrote the script for the film, which is the work of Tomás Gutiérrez Alea, who, because of health issues, enlisted the collaboration of Juan Carlos Tabío to help him direct. Though it is a product of the ICAIC, *Fresa y chocolate* is a co-production with backing from Spain and Mexico. The film generated much interest and was an enormous success, both at home and internationally. In Cuba, where it won popular and critical awards, as well as a Catholic Church's award for exemplary films, it ran for months straight, with patrons frequently standing in line to get in to see it (Interestingly, though, the film had to wait 13 years before it was shown on Cuban TV). At the Berlin Film Festival, *Fresa y chocolate* won the prestigious Silver Bear Prize, and in 1994, it became the first Cuban film to be nominated for an Oscar as Best Foreign Film.

The early excitement and success experienced by *Fresa y chocolate* put it firmly on the road to canonical status. The years and a continued presence as an object of academic study and as the object of a growing critical bibliography have confirmed that status. In the first instance, in the United States, the film figures in pedagogical texts among a select, limited number of films for students to study and discuss.[2]

In the scholarly arena, the film is included among the canonical films studied by important histories of Latin American and Cuban film. Such is the case, for example, in Stephen A. Hart's Stephen *A Companion to Latin American Film* (2004), where *Fresa y chocolate* is one of twenty-five landmark films, ranging from the 1931 ¡*Qué Viva México!* (Eisenstein) to the 2002 *Cidade de Deus* (Meirelles). *Fresa y chocolate* is obviously part of the canon when it figures, as it does, among the key films in Michael Chanan's *Cuban Cinema* (2004), a crucial English-language guide to the island's cinematic history. The chapter on "The Cinema of Cuba" in the 2010 volume *Splendors of Latin Cinema* opens with a two-paragraph description of opening sequences of *Fresa y chocolate*, a clear indication of the film's achievement of canonical status. *Fresa y chocolate* is among the 29 films selected to be analyzed in the French volume *Cuba: Cinéma et Révolution* (2006), but the inclusion of the film is only part of the case for its canonical status. The cover of the volume is composed of a simple black background, the title, and drawings of two large ice cream cones, one strawberry and the other chocolate, an image whose immediate recognizability attests further to the film's iconic status.

Within the critical bibliography dealing with *Fresa y chocolate*, the preponderance

Publicity poster for *Fresa y chocolate* (1993). Reproduced with permission from the Instituto Cubano de Artes e Industrias Cinematográficas (ICAIC).

of studies read the film in terms of its extraordinary thematics, that is, its treatment of homosexuality in Cuba, and *vis-à-vis* the revolution. Studies range from how homosexuality is acted out to implications for Cuban politics and Cuban identity to audience reception. Most of these studies include obligatory references to the history of the treatment of gays in Cuba and their scant presence in Cuban cinema. Other studies look at the film stylistically, focusing on genre or comparing it to other films directed by Gutiérrez Alea.

As for the film's engaging the question of homosexuality, one summative judgment that best represents the preponderant critical view of *Fresa y chocolate* is, perhaps, that expressed by Arnaldo Cruz-Malavé (1999), when he proclaims:

> En la que es seguramente la interpretación más difundida de la obra de José Lezama Lima, *Fresa y chocolate* ... homosexualidad y cultura nacional se contemplan, cierran filas, se asimilan y se funden. Convocada inicialmente por los signos de lo artificioso—el helado de fresa, el doble sentido, el desliz sémico de la frase—o lo extranjerizante y traicionero -la pronunciación francesa, los libros prohibidos—la homosexualidad se revela aquí al final como la figura o espacio mismo de convergencia de cierta identidad nacional criolla ... se despoja paulatinamente de su carga semántica y sexual de cueva y madriguera ... hasta constituirse en el privilegiado punto de mira desde el cual el protagonista heterosexual, David, descubre no sólo su pasado cultural sino la continuidad de ese pasado con lo que es ... la sinécdoque de la nación -La Habana.... ¿Pero quién asimila a quién? [130].

> (In what is surely the most widespread interpretation of the work of José Lezama Lima, *Strawberry and Chocolate* ... homosexuality and national culture are contemplated, close ranks, assimilate one another and fuse. Convened initially through signs of artifice -strawberry ice cream, double entendre, meaning slippage of sentences—or the foreign or treacherous -French pronunciation, banned books—homosexuality is revealed here finally as the figure or the very convergent space for a certain Creole national identity ... it slowly loses its sexual semantic charge of cave or den ... ultimately becoming the vantage point from which the heterosexual protagonist, David, not only discovers his cultural past but also the continuity of that past in what is ... the synecdoche for the nation -Havana.... But, who assimilates whom?)

Here, Cruz-Malavé touches on key topics of numerous readings of the film: homosexuality, national culture, homosexual markers, national identity, and politics. Studies focusing on these topics similarly see *Fresa y chocolate* as a film about homosexual/heterosexual encounter and the implications of that encounter for Cuban national identity. But, that reading would seem to ignore the orientation provided to the scholar-viewer by the film itself in the establishing first few minutes. There, *Fresa y chocolate* offers an orientation as to how it should be read. Readings that focus on the homosexuality theme and its ramifications for Cuba, for the most part, have been excellent and thorough, and they undoubtedly have enlightened the understanding of the film.

Those readings, however, do ignore a wider understanding of the filmic discourse, of which the homosexuality motif is but a part. The relationship of this theme to a larger meaningful whole is made clear by the film's first few minutes.

For about 40 seconds, film credits appear superimposed on a blank, black screen, as an organ plays slowly and softly. At 1:20 the door to a hotel room opens; ambient sound is heard, within which car sounds are distinguishable; the room is dimly lit, but the viewer sees that paint is peeling from plaster walls. A young couple enters; she is reticent as she looks around and questions, "¿No había otro lugar?" (Was there no place else?). "El lugar no importa, Vivian" (The place is not important, Vivian), he answers, hesitating to make his move. He kisses her on the cheek, then, shyly he observes how hot it is, so he will take off his shirt. When he asks her to take of her blouse, she asks him to turn off the light.

Reaching for an exposed switch by the door, he tries to turn off the one light hanging in the middle of the room, but the switch does not work. He reaches up and unscrews the light bulb. The two laugh nervously and they kiss, as the kissing becomes more passionate. He takes off her blouse, and as they continue to kiss, he fumbles with her bra. They stop kissing momentarily so that she can unhook her bra. Once he removes her bra, she pulls him to her breasts, then, they lie back on the bed with him on top of her. At this point, she says she needs to go to the bathroom.

He stands up, checks himself out, pulls back the curtain slightly and looks out the window into the street below. There in the darkness the camera focuses on an illuminated red sign that reads "CDR no. 20 Municipio Habana Vieja." He hears a noise, a woman's moaning and heavy breathing, and he turns away from the window and puts his ear to the wall. Hearing the moaning and breathing even louder, he steps back and looks around furtively. Looking up, he sees a hole plugged with paper, which he removes as he hears "Ay, qué rico." He gets a stool, climbs up, and peeks through the hole. There he sees a couple having sex, a large-breasted woman moving erotically on top of a man. He quickly re-plugs the hole, turns away, and busies himself with picking up clothes and placing them on a chair.

Surprised by Vivian who appears in the bathroom doorway, naked with a towel in front of her, his face demonstrates delight. She moves to the bed, gets in and covers up. As he sits on the bed, she turns away. The camera discovers her naked back. He stands and begins to remove his pants, and as he does, Vivian begins to sob. With his pants around his knees, he leans in to re-assure her, telling her he loves her. Complaining a little about "this place," she buries her head in the pillow and turns face down. "Sólo te interesa el sexo, como a todos" (You're only interested in sex, like all men), she tells him. He leans in and places his hand on her shoulder. When she pulls away and continues to sob, the young man sits back, looking perplexed. Standing up with determination and pulling his pants back on, he tells her that he will not touch her until their wedding day, and then it will be in the room of a five-star hotel.

Vivian turns to look at him, no longer sobbing. "Vístete y nos vamos" (Get dressed, we're leaving), he tells her. "¿Cómo?" (What?), she responds perplexed.

At this point, at around six and a half minutes into the filmic narrative, the screen goes to black, and the title *Fresa y chocolate* (*Strawberry and Chocolate*) appears superimposed. While there is still a black screen, a soundover of a horn playing "Here comes the bride" is heard. Then, there is a cut to Vivian dressed as a bride; she is getting married in a civil ceremony. The camera discovers a groom who is not the young man from the opening hotel room scene. That young man, instead, is among the onlookers surrounding the wedding couple.

The narrative cuts to David. Though he is surrounded by a few men talking, he sits and drinks alone at a street side bar, as the soundtrack plays "Qué triste estoy / sin su amor" (How sad I am without her love). This is followed by a cut to two young men, one carrying a bouquet of flowers, walking through park, when they stop to look at David walking in the distance. With what is a rolled up newspaper in his right hand, profile shots of David as he walks offer interesting phallically suggestive images. The two others watch with interest as he crosses in front of a mural that exclaims "Somos felices aquí" (We are happy here).

The film's first few minutes end when directors Tomás Gutiérrez Alea and Juan Carlos Tabío are identified with their names superimposed on a black screen.

These first eight and a half minutes of the film provide the viewer with an orientation as to how to read the film, and the orientation starts with a general orientation as to the when and where of the narrative. When David drew back the curtain and peered into the night, he (and the viewer) saw the red sign illuminating the darkness. Reading "Municipio Habana Vieja" on that sign lets the viewer know the narrative where. "CDR" on that sign stands for Comités de Defensa de la Revolución (Committees for the Defense of the Revolution), and this adds something of the when to the where of reading the film. The film is to be read within the context of the Cuban Revolution. But, CDR not only contextualizes the film's reading in terms of where and when, it offers cues for some of that to which the scholar-viewer is to be attuned as he views the film.

The Committees for the Defense of the Revolution compose a system of neighborhood watch committees through the country. Established at the beginning of the revolution, it is a network that is to function to promote social welfare and to report counter-revolutionary activity. While the organization has monitored the activity of residents in every neighborhood or block, the CDR's history has not been without controversy. And, as David peers into the nightscape, the camera pauses on the CDR sign, emphasizing a vigilance aspect to the reading of the film. As if to further punctuate the establishment of this aspect of the matrix for reading the film, David turns from the window and "spies" on a couple in the adjoining room, as he waits for Vivian to come out of the bathroom.

When David draws back the curtain and peers into the night to then turns and spy on the couple noisily having sex, the dominant perspective for reading the film is established as well. It is David's gaze.[3] The focus from the hegemonic subject of Cuban discourse is the perspective from which the first few minutes establish that the film is to be read.

Using this as a point of departure, Enrico Santí (1998) asserts that *Fresa y chocolate* is not a homosexual film. The opening minutes establish the film's narrative focus as heteronormative, so it cannot be homosexual. And, this is consistent with the declarations made by both of the film's directors in interviews (for example, West [1995]). More importantly, this is consistent with the entirety of the filmic discourse, in which there are no relations between members of the same sex. In fact, as several analyses have pointed out (Foster [2003], for example), the closest thing to homoerotic behavior occurs between two heteronormative Communist youths, Miguel and David, dealing with the latter's hangover in the bathroom. With the two of them in underwear, Miguel's tap on David's buttocks, and his comment on them approximates the homoerotic more than anything Diego does in the entire film.

Only at the end of the establishing first few minutes, when Diego and Germán appear, the former carrying flowers and both fixating on David in the distance, is there a suggestion that homosexuality is part of the matrix for reading the film.

In the case of *Fresa y chocolate*, the first few minutes are important establishing moments as much for what they contain and for what they do not. In the film's first few minutes, there is no sex for David and Vivian, there is no marriage for David, there are no luxuries for David and Vivian, and there is no privacy. On the contrary, there is vigilance, there is postponement of gratification. Thus, the matrix for reading the film is now clear. The film is to be read as a declaration that, in the late 1970's[4] Cuba of the Revolution, **there is no ...** (No hay...). *Fresa y chocolate* is a film about **there is no ...** (No hay...); it is a film about **lack**.

The filmic discourse sets about to examine or display lack in several different spheres that range from the personal to the political to the economic.

From the moment David gazes upon the CDR sign, from the moment he spies through the peep hole on the couple having sex, the viewer knows that the film is about the fact that in Cuba there is no privacy. Like all of the film's motifs, this theme is developed further in the sequences occurring in the *guarida*, Diego's apartment. In a wink to the viewer, there is a CDR sticker on the inside of one of the apartment's doors, visually announcing again the omnipresence of "la vigilancia." And the intromission into personal space or lack of privacy is incarnate in one of the central characters of the film, Nancy. Even before any sequence in the *guarida*, as Diego and David first arrive at the apartment, they hide beneath the stairs in order to avoid being seen by Nancy ("la de la Vigilancia" / the watchdog lady) as she descends.

Once they are in his apartment, a number of acts follow up on the already activated privacy motif. On the first visit, the apartment door is left open so that David will feel more comfortable knowing that what goes on inside will be more easily accessible and less private. This is a tacit recognition of the constant vigil under which life in Cuba is lived. When the two men are in the *guarida*, Diego plays music so that neighbors cannot listen in on their conversations, indexing again the lack of privacy. There is even a tacit recognition of the private being open to the public in Diego's seduction plan. Though he does not seduce David, he carries out a part of the plan, which is to signal his conquest by hanging David's shirt from his window. Through this metonymy, Diego signals clear recognition that private behaviors are constantly subject to public scrutiny.

Though Nancy is identified as the watchdog lady ("la de la vigilancia"), not even she is free from scrutiny. Following the day they spend out and about, David appears at Nancy's door with flowers. A neighbor lady, with the door to her apartment open, is sweeping her floor within earshot of a happy Nancy and her visitor. As the two enter Nancy's apartment and close the door, the neighbor puts up her broom and scurries within. Seeing this, the viewer presumes that the neighbor will spy on Nancy, and that even the "vigilancia" is subject to "vigilancia."

Privacy indexes other areas of the personal domain where there is lack. As the scholar-viewer reads *Fresa y chocolate* as a film about lack in Cuba, the filmic discourse displays for him that there is a lack of freedom of expression. The lack of freedom of expression in the personal domain is related to the lack of freedom of expression in the public domain. As a reaction to the denial of a request to exhibit Germán's sculptures, Diego decides to write letters of protest expressing his personal disappointment with the decision, expressing at the same time his personal disappointment with the Revolution.

> DIEGO: ... si estoy que muerdo.... No sé cómo puede haber gente tan estúpida y que uno tiene que quedarse callado.... Prohibieron la exposición de Germán en las provincias.... Dijeron no y se acabó. Además, uno no puede discutir como ellos mandan.... Sólo aceptan pintores naif, oficiales o esos que se van de modernos pero en el fondo ni dicen ni

innovan nada. Son pura decoración.... Pero no pienses que me quedé callado.
(... I'm pissed off.... I don't know how there can be such stupid people and one just has to keep quiet.... They prohibited Germán's exhibition in the provinces. They said no and that's it. Besides, you cannot argue with them because they are in charge of everything.... They only accept naïve or official artists, or the ones that pass for modern but don't say or invent anything. They are mere decoration.... But don't think I kept quiet.)

NANCY: ¿Qué dijiste?
(What did you say?)

DIEGO: Lo que me dio la gana. Que en socialismo no hay libertad, que los burócratas lo controlan todo, que....
(What I felt like. That in socialism there is no freedom, that bureaucrats control everything, that....)

NANCY: ¡No digas esas cosas sin música, Diego!
(Don't say those things without music, Diego!)

At the same time as she recognizes the omnipresence of vigilance, Nancy responds in recognition of an environment hostile to the expression of dissident personal opinion. Both Nancy and David attempt to censor him, discouraging him from sending the letters. In confirmation of an environment hostile to freedom of expression, having sent the letter, Diego loses his job and ultimately sees himself obliged to leave the island.

From the moment Vivian and David enter the seedy hotel room, from the moment Vivian asks if there wasn't another place, from the moment David fumbles with the faulty light switch, the viewer knows that the film is about the fact that in Cuba **there is no** (No hay...). An essential part of the matrix for reading the film is the insistence of the fact that there is a lack of material comfort. Immediately following the opening sequences, this theme is followed further even as the theme of homosexuality begins to be further developed. In Coppelia, Diego, sitting across the table from David, self-identifies as homosexual through his choice of strawberry ice cream and his overdetermined verbal and physical affect. As he effeminately savors his strawberry ice cream and the "fresa" he has luckily encountered, he twice alludes to material lack in Cuba. "Es lo único bueno que hacen en este país" (It's the only good thing they make in this country), he says, referring at once to his ice cream and to an overall lack of things. And, quickly in the conversation he returns to the theme when he says to David, "Volemos en alas de la imaginación porque en otra cosa no se puede" (Let's fly on the wings of imagination because we can't fly on anything else), or, in other words, given the lack of the material, the only option left is to fly on the wings of the immaterial.

This theme of material penury is further developed in sequences when Diego and David go to or get together in the former's apartment. Comic relief is offered in the "character" of Rocco, Diego's blue refrigerator. An appliance from the 1950's, it leaks water and sometimes seems only to function when its owner lovingly taps it. Though Diego had assured David that his house would be full of family, they arrive to a small empty, though cluttered, *guarida*, and Diego explains the absence of non-existent family speculating as to their having gone out to "hacer cola" (to stand in line). In this way, Diego ironically indexes the lack of material goods by referring to Cubans' need to stand in line even for the most basic of needs.

There is a lack of material comfort, and the filmic discourse further indexes that lack through a documentation of a black market. Diego attributes his having Johnny Walker Red, the "bebida del enemigo" (the enemy's drink), or his having books to friends. Because of a lack of material goods, Cubans spend much of their time and effort "resolviendo" (solving), doing what it takes to get by. And, a black market helps solve ("resolver") material problems for those who can afford it, as in the case of the young woman that the viewer sees buying black market dye and deodorant.

The lack of material goods and the need for a black market to obtain them overlaps with the vigilance motif in the film in the character of Nancy. On two other occasions during the film, material lack is the direct focus through open consideration of a black market. In Nancy's apartment, the viewer sees a female character, the black market customer, for the first and only time. She has just purchased some goods from Nancy, who tells her that she will have some other goods the following week. Later on, Nancy gives some cash to Diego, telling him, and revealing to the viewer, that she has sold his watch in the street.

The possession of goods, especially books, creates suspicion for David, who feels the obligation to report it, again indexing the vigilance motif and tying it not only to consumerism, but, as he does in his exchange with Miguel, to homosexuality, religion, art, and politics. In a revealing conversation with Miguel, David describes Diego and his first encounter with him:

> ... un tipo raro ... un maricocho.... Uno se da cuenta enseguida. Mira, había chocolate y pidió fresa.... Es que el tipo además empezó a decir ironías de la Revolución.... Es que tenía algo que a mí me hizo sospechar. Entonces, dejé que se sentara y que hablara de lo que quisiera.... Terminó invitándome a la casa.... Chico, esto es serio. Primero me enseñó unos libros extranjeros, imposibles de conseguir en la calle. Y con el pretexto de los libros, me invitó a la casa ... tenía que saber si estaba en algo, ¿no? ... El tipo tiene la casa llena de cosas raras. Tiene unas esculturas allí rarísimas. Yo no sé mucho de eso, pero a mí me parece que hay algo en eso. Fíjate que allí había una con una onda medio religiosa.... No son de él, son de un amigo. Quieren hacer una exposición y una embajada los va a ayudar.
>
> (... a weird guy ... a faggot.... One can tell it immediately. Look, there was chocolate and he ordered strawberry ... besides, the guy started talking ironically about the Revolution.... There was something about him that made me suspicious.... So, I

let him sit down and talk about whatever he wanted.... He ended up inviting me to his house.... Man, this is serious. First he showed me some foreign books, impossible to get on the street. And, with the pretext of the books, he invited me to his house.... I had to know if I was onto something, right? ... The guy has a house full of weird stuff. He has some really strange sculptures. I don't know much about that stuff, but I think there is something to it. Look, there was one sculpture that was kind of religious.... They're not his; they're his friend's. They want to have an exhibition, and an embassy is going to help them.)

In an environment in which there is a general lack, Diego's possession of a few material goods, beginning with foreign books, makes him suspicious. Indexing lack, the implication is that a lack of material goods would make him more like everyone else, and therefore, less suspicious. David's suspicions are only confirmed by other "weird stuff," but this only masks the underlying prejudice, since, as he confesses, he realized immediately that Diego was a homosexual.

This conversation with Miguel is important for at least two reasons. First of all, it links the idea of being antirevolutionary or counterrevolutionary to themes of homosexuality, religion, art, and association. Miguel's reactions to David's revelations move from amusement to serious concern, and he insists that David must follow up on this, thus creating a structural function for this conversation. The filmic narrative has a motivation for David to return to Diego's apartment, and he has a justification for building a relationship with Diego. Essentially, David sets out to spy on Diego.

While *Fresa y chocolate* is not a homosexual film, homosexuality is one of its important themes or motifs, and as mentioned, it has been the object of study of most of the critical bibliography dealing with the work. As the ample bibliography on the topic attests, though, because of the centrality of the character of Diego, homosexuality must be dealt with. In fact, though *Fresa y chocolate* is not a homosexual film, most readings of the film would have it be a film about homosexuality in Cuba and/or the relationship of homosexuality to the theme of intolerance in Cuba. Interestingly, as we have seen, homosexuality has only a minor place in the first few interpretation-orienting minutes of the film, and this would speak strongly against the almost singular importance granted it by most studies of the film.

Having received an orientation to look for or to read the film as the expression of lack (No hay...), the scholar-viewer finds lack associated with and expressed in two of the film's central motifs or themes: homosexuality and art. And, with respect to these two socio-cultural elements, the filmic discourse shows how Cuba entering the third decade of its Revolution lacks tolerance.

That there is intolerance for homosexuality in 1979 Cuba of the Revolution there can be no doubt. This intolerance is tied (rightly or wrongly) to the Revolution, and it is Miguel who most stridently makes this clear on two occasions. In his conversation with David alluded to earlier, Miguel substantiates an intolerance for gays when he equates them to antirevolutionary, shouting "...porque la Revolución no entra por el culo, chico!" (...because the Revolution does not enter through the ass, man!). Less graphic, yet equally strident and equally revelatory of a homophobic intolerance is Miguel's later remark about not trusting homosexuals because they cannot even be true or loyal to their own gender.

Diego makes this intolerance for homosexuality evident when he reveals that he has had troubles with the system and that they don't leave him alone at work. His current disaffection with the Revolution seems in large part to be a product of intolerance. Late in the film he explains,

> ¿Quién te dijo a tí que no soy revolucionario? ... Yo también tuve ilusiones, David. A los catorce años me fui a alfabetizar porque yo quise. Fui para las lomas a recoger café, quise estudiar para maestro. ¿Y qué pasó? Que esto es una cabeza pensante, y a Uds. al que no dice sí a todo o tiene ideas diferentes, enseguida lo miran mal y lo quieren apartar....
>
> (Who told you that I am not a revolutionary? ... I, too, had dreams, David. When I was 14, I went to teach literacy because I wanted to. I went to the mountains to pick coffee, and I tried to study to become a teacher. And what happened? Well, this is a thinking brain, but you guys immediately look down on and try to ostracize anyone who doesn't say yes to everything or has different ideas....)

He indicates that the intolerance and repression of homosexuals put an end to dreams that he had for his life's trajectory. Indexing Miguel's crude homophobic remark, Diego holds on to his claim to belonging,

> Rianse de mí, ríanse.... Yo también me río de Uds.... Formo parte de este país aunque no les guste y tengo el derecho de hacer cosas por él. De aquí no me voy aunque me den candela por el culo. Sin mí le faltaría un pedazo de la tierra para que te enteres. ¡Comemierda!
>
> (Laugh at me, laugh.... I laugh at you too.... Whether you like it or not, I am part of this country and I have the right to do things for it. I'm not leaving here even if they set fire to my ass. Without me there would be a piece of this land missing, just so you know, you stupid shit!)

That intolerance for homosexuality exists is explained also in David's trajectory. Again, *Fresa y chocolate* is not a homosexual film. Though one of its protagonists is homosexual, rarely is he the focus of a scene. The focus of the filmic discourse is David's development. David moves from being a naïve intellectually/ideologically-challenged, homophobic peasant scholarship student to a more tolerant, slightly less naïve, somewhat less intellectually changed, less homophobic revolutionary militant capable of establishing a friendship with a gay man. In direct relationship to and beginning with attitudes of intolerance for gays, part of David's development has to do with his coming to terms with the Revolution's repression of homosexuals. Thus, alluding to intolerance, he is finally able to tell Diego,

> DAVID: Lo que quiero decir es que es lamentable pero comprensible que se cometan errores, como mandar a Pablito para UMAP pero...
> (What I mean is that it's regrettable but understandable that mistakes are made, like sending little Pablo to the UMAP but...)
> DIEGO: A Pablito solamente, no y a todos los demás, las locas que no cantaban ... pero ¿qué manera de educar es ésa, David?
> (Not just little Pablo, but all the others, the crazy ones who wouldn't agree ... but what kind of way is that to educate, David?)
> DAVID: Los errores no son la Revolución. Son la parte de la Revolución que no es la Revolución. ¿Entiendes?
> (The mistakes are not the Revolution. They are the part of the Revolution that is not the Revolution. Get it?)
> DIEGO: ¿Y la cuenta, a quién va, eh? ¿Quién va a responder por ellos?
> (And the debt, who is going to pay it, huh? Who is going to stick up for them?)

This recognition of mistakes could be read simply as a catharsis that allows the directors and their film to gloss over abuses of the Cuban Revolution in its treatment of homosexuals. Or, rather, it could be seen as a catharsis that aptly indexes the reading of the film as suggested by the first few minutes. Moving on from the particular case of singer/songwriter Pablo Milanés, David refers to "the mistakes of the Revolution." He refers to a bigger picture than intolerance for homosexuals, to that bigger picture of lack for which the viewer is prompted to look in the film's early establishing moments.

In the final analysis, it is not his homosexuality that puts Diego in a position of having to leave the island. It is his insistence on writing to the authorities to complain about the censoring of the art exhibition. The artist, Germán, who is more flamboyant and camp in his homosexuality than Diego, will be rewarded with a trip to Mexico to exhibit some of his sculptures because he accepts the censorship. Diego, who is unwilling to accept restriction placed on the exhibition, again will suffer life-altering consequences because of intolerance. Overlapping with the intolerance for expression of discordant opinion, what is revealed is a lack of tolerance, an intolerance for artistic expression outside the bounds of the Revolution.

The list of what is lacking in Cuba is obviously long, and Diego's commentary, sometimes lighthearted, is sprinkled with allusions to the island's lacking in cultural capital. On occasion, David displays an ignorance or innocence that indexes a lack in the preparation of the Communist Youth. A scholarship student at the university, David is ignorant or unaware of John Donne, Kavafis, or Lezama Lima. His innocence allows for a few of the film's lighter moments when, for example, he asks Diego if John Donne is a friend of his and if they write to each other; or, seeing the photograph of Lezama, he asks if it is Diego's father. Even funnier, perhaps, is David's *lapsus linguae* when, in the heat of a political discussion, he attributes the dropping of the atomic bomb to Truman Capote. Though humorous, these moments point to a lack of academic/educational preparation, especially considering David's expressed interest in literature.

During the first visit to the *guarida*, Diego plays music, as much for David's edification and for his own enjoyment as to cover up their conversations so that they are not overheard. He plays María Callas, and as he gushes about her voice, he laments the island's inability to produce such a voice. He laments this lack, averring that Cuba lacks for or needs another voice. While it is easy to classify this commentary as related to the thematics of lack, there are studies that have wanted to read the statement as even more subversive. With support in statements by the film's directors, Shields (2004), for example, has read Diego's comment as referring to a need for another voice alternative to that of Fidel.

The lack of freedom of expression and the lack of privacy that are indexed by events and dialogue are underscored cinematographically by the film's preference for interiors. In the film's editing, only a limited number of scenes that are not interior shots are included. The prevalence of interiors creates a feeling of claustrophobia that contributes markedly to the thematics of lack. The prevalence of interiors that are predominantly small spaces suggests that the characters' movements are limited, a sensation that contributes further to the reading of the film in terms of its thematics of lack.

Among the exteriors, there are two "bookend" scenes in Coppelia, the Ice Cream Cathedral. One scene occurs right after the identification of the directors near the beginning of the film; and the other is the film's penultimate scene just before the film-ending hug between Diego and David. These two exteriors function structurally to open and close the topic of homosexuality. The first of the two scenes begins with David in the street, first at a sidewalk bar, then walking, but the sequence consists primarily of the table conversation between Diego and David. The tight shots on David provide only a few descriptive images of surrounding Havana, and the tight shots of the faces of two principles in the Coppelia portion of this sequence, like the similar tight shots in Coppelia in the next-to-last scene, do little to describe surrounding context. In fact, the predominance here of tight shots only serves to underscore the overall claustrophobic feeling consistent with the film's expression of lack.

There are seven street scenes. Four of them are quite brief: David walks, an ambulance passes, and they take Nancy to the hospital; Diego and Germán walk, talk, and turn heads to look at a passing gay; Diego crosses a street to mail letters and the camera focuses on a José Martí quote ("Los débiles respe-

5. For the Lack of

ten; los grandes adelante: ésta es una tarea de grandes"/Respect the weak; the great come forward: this is a task for the great); and, David takes shelter from the rain, and sees Diego get out of a Cadillac embassy vehicle. Though the scenes are brief, they offer enough images to produce impressions. In these exterior scenes, the viewer sees scant vehicular traffic, instead most everyone is walking; a bride and groom are carried in a 1950's Oldsmobile; a 1950's Ford taxi is overloaded; people are standing or sitting in doorways, in a city of underlying beauty but badly worn and in need of paint and repair.

> Vivimos en una de las ciudades más maravillosas del mundo. Todavía estás a tiempo de ver algunas cosas antes de que se derrumbe...
> (We live in one of the most marvelous cities in the world. You are still in time to see something before it all comes down...)

So Diego tells David as they look out on the city from his apartment, and below they see clothes hanging to dry, buildings in disrepair, a rusted barrel. Because film is a graphic medium, the viewer must always ask what is it that the films shows him, what it is that he sees. Though the number of exteriors is limited, the images that they present are a factor in reading the film. The exterior shots present images of the city of Havana through its streets and the port of Havana. Two longer exterior sequences offer views of the city. At Diego's suggestion ("Todavía estás a tiempo...." / You are still in time...) and under his tutelage, David tours the streets. He sees colonial architecture, an interior garden, and stained glass. What the viewer sees with him also are buildings strewn with clothes hanging to dry, chipped paint and plaster, buildings in disrepair, and rubble from a destroyed building. The view of the city outside only confirms what the film's first few minutes had shown the viewer about the inside. Inside, in the hotel, in the apartments, in the interior of Diego's building; and outside, Havana is seen in terms of decay, in terms of physical material lack.

During the exterior sequence in which David and Nancy spend the day in the city, they take a ferry ride. As they pass through the port, the image is one of rusted boats and little or no movement, contributing to the impression of decay and stagnation.

The last exterior is the sequence with Diego and David on the bluff overlooking Havana to the south and west from the Cristo de la Habana. The ambient sound is of the wind, not of street or maritime traffic, suggesting solitude. The view of the city and port is one of parked boats and a few solitary vehicles transiting the portside avenue. While the overall view is beautiful, there is no suggestion of a high level of activity. This only corroborates the sensation of lack of movement, an impression of stagnation and decay.

The images offered by the brief and longer street scenes are ones of people walking, a few old parked cars, and even fewer moving vehicles. The people are not carrying anything in their hands and they seem not to be in a hurry, suggesting a lack of material wealth and a lack of economic, consumer activity.

The sum of the impressions from the visuals presented in the film's limited exteriors contributes to the overall reading of the film in terms of lack. There is a lack of movement, there is a lack of attention to buildings, there is a lack of modern, up-to-date building, transportation, etc. And, according to Diego, there is a lack of will to stop the decay and to preserve "one of the most marvelous cities in the world."

As already mentioned, within the bibliography dealing with *Fresa y chocolate*, critical attention focuses predominantly on the presence of homosexuality in the filmic discourse. The need to make the filmic discourse fit with expectations for an examination of the topic of homosexuality or to fit with homosexuality's relationship to Cuban identity or Cuban socio-political history can and has led to some extreme positions, and even to outright misstatements. A few examples are illustrative.

In an essay comparing *Fresa y chocolate* with *Máscaras*, a novel by Cuba's Leonardo Padura Fuentes, Stephen Wilkinson's (2006) almost singular focus on "moral double standards" leads him to assert that "the film explicitly asks if in the future sexual difference and intellectual dissidence will be openly acknowledged and valued" (135). He needs for the film to ask this question, because for him, Padura Fuentes' 1997 novel provides an answer to it. A reading of the film suggested by its first few minutes discovers that here is a lack of tolerance for homosexuality and for the expression of dissident opinion. But, the orientation for reading the film would not seem to include asking questions. More precisely, at no point does the film "explicitly" ask any question, and to suggest that it does also would seem to contradict at the same time the essay's insistence on both works being national allegories.

Among the studies that focus on the homosexuality theme, perhaps the most critical and controversial is that of Paul Julian Smith (1996) in his *Vision Machines*. Smith bemoans that

> the film's fatal fascination with bourgeois decadence (its heavy-handed weakness for the guided tour of cosmopolitan cultural capital) betrays a further denial: it is not that Diego loves David because he (Diego) is decadent, but rather quite the reverse: the proletarian comes to love opera and supper parties, tea and literature. Neglecting the troublesome dirt and putrefaction of the disturbingly material social world outside ... Gutiérrez Alea delights with his alter ego-witness in the elite pleasures of high culture [95].

A reading of the film following the orientation provided by its first few minutes herein has led to seeing very clearly a presentation of "troublesome dirt and putrefaction" outside. But a focus centered very closely on the homosexual motif, seems to lead Smith to assert negligence in this respect. Disappointed with "the unusual timidity of its mode of representation" (82), he takes Gutiérrez Alea to task for an impoverished aesthetic of overemphasis and demonstrativity. This disappointment seems to stem from wanting the film to have been more daring in its treatment of the Revolution *vis-à-vis* homosexuality, for he states that

> The challenge then (for cinema, for Cuba) is to operate a genealogy of the image which does not simply demystify it as the old Marxian dogmas of *Cahiers* and Gutiérrez Alea would suggest; rather it would initiate a productive and historical slippage, free of the aestheticism and academicism of the guided tour and based not on the visuals of cultural tourism, served up for the art houses worldwide, but on the vision of a newly democratized civil society... [97].

This critical opinion seems to judge *Fresa y chocolate* for the film it could have or should have been (Smith 1994 32). While the film's aesthetics do, perhaps, open up the possibility for a discussion of film aesthetics within the Revolution or within the overall genetic context of Gutiérrez Alea's production, it is a discussion that should have little to do with an evaluation of the film itself. While responding to some sort of challenge may have been an admirable goal that Gutiérrez Alea could have set for himself, it is not how his film asks to be read. With the matrix it establishes for its reading in the establishing minutes, *Fresa y chocolate* asks to be read as an expression of what there is not (lack) in Cuba of 1979. And, it is on that basis should be judged.

Though much of the existing bibliography on *Fresa y chocolate* centers on homosexuality, and the current chapter agues for a reading of the film in terms of the expression of lack, the two positions are not necessarily mutually exclusive. Many, if not most, of the essays examining homosexuality deal with the lack of tolerance, which is, of course, an important but not the sole focus of the reading of the film called for by its first few minutes. Stephen Wilkinson (2000), though, recognizes this linkage of the homosexuality theme to the film's larger thematic concerns when he writes

> ... it is the cultured "bourgeois" homosexual who educates the ideologically-challenged peasant student. He not only raises his consciousness regarding his homophobia but also educates him about his own national history. Diego bestows upon his young friend a sense of his *Cubanidad* beyond the crude Marxist-Leninist revolutionary theory... [303].

This recognition allows Wilkinson to arrive at a judgment of the film's significance that would seem to be consistent with the present chapter's insistence on reading it in terms of lack not limited to homophobic intolerance. While for him it is read within Cuba as an attempt to address past mistreatment of homosexuals, he finally posits that

Outside the island, rather than a diversion from a "repression that cannot be acknowledged" [Smith, 1996], the film should be seen as part of a process of change, brought on in some measure as a consequence of the collapse of the Soviet Union yet also as a result of a new generation coming to terms with the Revolution it has inherited [305].

Some studies have suggested that *Fresa y chocolate*'s discourse and characters allow for viewing the film as a national allegory. In allegorical terms, for example, a suicide-prone Nancy could be viewed as an "about to self-destruct" Cuba (Davies 179), Diego speaks for the oppressed (Bejel 67), and Miguel is the repressive revolutionary (Bejel 71). Though the first few minutes do not explicitly create a matrix for an allegorical reading of the film, the reference to CDR and Havana vieja does activate attention to a specific national period.

What is clear is that the reading of the film in terms of lack produces a none-to-flattering impression of the island nation. And, this leads to a question as to how to interpret this expression. Whether or not *Fresa y chocolate*'s reading in terms of lack is received as a sincere questioning of the state of affairs, is a matter of reception. There are those, particularly some exiled Cubans, who have viewed the film's portrayal of lack as falsely signifying that the regime through the ICAIC demonstrates a tolerance for criticism or critical reflection. For this view, the implied criticism in the expression of lack is too tame, and it turns out only to be some kind of sell out, attempting to convince the viewer of a tolerance for criticism that does not really exist. Alternatively, and less cynically perhaps, the criticism implied in presenting Cuba in terms of lack could be viewed as, if not mildly subversive, evidence of more tolerance in 1993 when the film was made, than in 1979, the period the film purports to represent. In this case, the film is reflective of what Humberto Solás famously reminds us, when he says in a 1978 interview "...whenever you make a historical film, whether it's set two decades or two centuries ago, you are referring to the present."[5]

The film's references to popular cultural features, like syncretism, to national cultural icons like Lecuona, Che, and Lezama, and to national history have less to do with being a cinema for art house consumption, where the bourgeois viewer can reconcile sympathies for Cuba's political experiment and for gay romance; and such references have more to do with redefining the revolutionary project in terms of the nation rather than a socialist revolution.

Seeing *Fresa y chocolate* as a political failure (especially as compared to Gutiérrez Alea's 1968 *Memorias del subdesarrollo*), Paul Julian Smith (1996) asks, "Is there a structural connection, then, between the unprecedented subject matter of this film and the unusual timidity of its mode of representation?" (82). Without entering into a discussion of use of terms like "unprecedented" and "timidity," a reading of the film from the establishing matrix offered by the film itself allows the viewer to answer "Yes, there is a connection." And, that 'structural connection' is found in the film's first few minutes, where the viewer is primed to read the film not only in terms of an 'unprecedented subject matter' but also in terms of a not-so-timid view of **lack** ("no hay") in the Cuban nation that goes beyond just a lack of tolerance for that subject matter.

In this volume, *Fresa y chocolate* is not the only film analyzed in which controversial subject matter has led analysis to limit its focus on that subject matter and to ignore a film's larger message. As will be seen, the fact that the subject matter of a film yet to be analyzed, 2002's *El crimen del Padre Amaro*, resonated with current events distracted readings of the film from its larger panoramic implications in order to focus on the timely subject of questionable behaviors by Catholic priests. Released at a time when the Catholic Church had been shaken by sex scandals and just after a visit from Pope John Paul II, it was easy to focus analysis, and publicity, on a young priest's love affair with an underage girl. Similarly, *Fresa y chocolate* taps into ongoing debates, unleashed nearly a decade earlier by another film, *Mauvaise conduite (Conducta impropia)* (Néstor Almendros and Orlando Jiménez Leal, 1984), regarding human rights abuses of political dissidents, homosexuals, and poets accused of improper or "extravagant" behavior. While the controversial subject matter in both films certainly needs to be addressed, both films, *Fresa y chocolate* and *El crimen del Padre Amaro*, prime the scholar-viewer for wider readings, one in terms of "lack" and the other in terms of a panoply of ills, that ought not be ignored because the readerly matrix is established by the films themselves in their first few minutes.

♦ 6 ♦

DREAM STORY
Alejandro Amenábar's 1996
Abre los ojos (Open Your Eyes)

> ... I must nevertheless here consider that I am a man, and that, consequently, I am in the habit of sleeping, and representing to myself in dreams those same things, or even sometimes others less probable, which the insane think are presented to them in their waking moments. How often have I dreamt that I was in these familiar circumstances, that I was dressed, and occupied this place by the fire, when I was lying undressed in bed? At the present moment, however, I certainly look upon this paper with eyes wide awake; the head which I now move is not asleep; I extend this hand consciously and with express purpose, and I perceive it; the occurrences in sleep are not so distinct as all this. But I cannot forget that, at other times I have been deceived in sleep by similar illusions; and, attentively considering those cases, I perceive so clearly that there exist no certain marks by which the state of waking can ever be distinguished from sleep, that I feel greatly astonished; and in amazement I almost persuade myself that I am now dreaming.
>
> Descartes, *Meditations* (I, 5)[1]

There are few films in which the importance of the matrix-establishing first few minutes to the reading of the film is as clear as in the case of *Abre los ojos*. If viewers occupy themselves with popcorn and conversation until the sound volume comes up and visual images flash on screen, they will have begun the film too late. If viewers postpone paying attention, if they postpone activating their reading skills, until they see opening credits or opening visual narrative, an essential part of the film's orienting matrix will be lost to them.

Following some opening credits, superimposed on a black screen (0:58), in absolute darkness and with a blank screen, softly, almost imperceptibly a female voice begins to repeat, progressively more loudly, "Abre los ojos" (Open your eyes). She repeats the exhortation ten times as the screen hazily begins to show visual images. As the picture comes into focus, the viewer sees a hand slap an alarm clock. The camera then shows a young man lying facedown in bed. The female voice had continued to whisper "abre los ojos," while the screen began to discover contours that became sheets and the young man who is sleeping and who is awakened by his alarm. He shuts off his alarm at 9:03 with a certain discontent. The young man is first seen lying in his bed. The apparently waking young man abruptly sits up in bed, and the sunlight shows how much daylight there already is.

In front of a mirror, the young man clears the sleep from his eyes, and he showers in very hot water. He gets dressed, and he goes downstairs to leave; and the viewer sees surroundings that speak of a large, rather upscale apartment. He gets in his car and starts it. The automatic door opener of his garage slowly rises to discover the bright light of day. A close-up of the license plate reveals it to be from Málaga, and it is a cool white VW beetle convertible that exits the garage turning left down a bright, clean, yet unpopulated street. He goes out of his garage into what appears to be a strange city. There are few cars parked along the streets, but there are no people. Confounded, the young man looks at his watch, 10:03, and he looks around. He stops his car in mid-turn to the right, and he gets out. Looking up, confused he sees a traffic light showing green. He looks down the six-lane street; he is the middle of Madrid's Gran Vía.[2] There is no traffic; there are no cars or buses; there are no people. The city is totally empty. As if not understanding, he begins to run down the empty street, stopping and turning to look around as he goes. On the right side of the screen, the traffic light changes to yellow, then to red. (2:37)

The screen goes once more to black, and the female voice returns whispering "abre los ojos," this time repeating two and a half times. And, the hand again slaps the alarm off, and the clock reads 9:00. Then, while the young man lies thrown across his bed, a voiceover conversation begins to be heard with one man who asks why the other is telling about a dream he had and if there is anything else he wishes to tell. He explains that it is the same dream as always, and that he has explained to a friend before. He explains this as he explains also that he is about to be 25 years old, and that he likes to eat, sleep, and make love, like everybody. And, that he does the same thing as everybody when he gets up.

At that point, elements of the earlier sequence are repeated. He gets up sleepily and looks at himself in the mirror; he showers and gets dressed. As he dresses in front of a mirror, behind him the viewer can see the bed that appears positioned opposite of the way it appears when the young man sits up in bed as he awakes. A half-naked woman wrapped in the sheets watches him from the bed, and she asks him where he is going. He tells her he is going out and tells her not to do that to the alarm again. When she asks why, he curtly responds just because (because I say so). As he turns to leave and walks towards the bed, a reverse shot shows the bed and the woman lying in it in the position in which it was originally seen. He grabs his coat and gets in his car. The automatic garage door slowly opens, and he leaves in his car, a cool, white VW beetle. As the music becomes louder/more intense, thousands of people and cars transit the city, people doing everything, a guy sleeping, women talking, police working, people filming a movie, a woman begging, and another person doing mime to earn money. The young man driving the VW fixates on the mime as he turns the corner.

At this point, the viewer is about five and a half minutes into the filmic narrative. And, by this point the orientation provided for the viewer as to how to read this film is clear. To awaken to a Madrid whose streets are empty is not to awaken; it is to continue dreaming. If the young man did not open his eyes the first time, or the second time as the viewer listens to the voiceover conversation, what is there to indicate he has them open for the third of these sequences contiguous to the first few minutes? Recurrent scenes and motifs between the sequences underscore the oneiric quality of the narrative. The recurrent mirror and the reflections in it serve to highlight the idea of a narrative composed not of reality but of appearances or reflections of reality, and they serve to highlight the pliability of perceptions.

As if the idea of an empty city were not enough to let the viewer know that what he is about to "read" is a dream, the first few minutes continue with an unequivocal identification of the narration as dream.[3] And it is immediately, in the second sequence, where there is a direct reference to telling a dream, when what later the viewer learns is the psychiatrist's voice, asks in a voiceover "Why are you telling me this dream?" This question makes it clear that viewers are being told a dream. The viewers, then, have been oriented towards reading this film as dream.

At the level of filmic narrative, the first time César responds to the imperative to "open his eyes" and his hand slaps the alarm to shut if off, the clock reads 9:03. And, the second time his hand moves to shut off the alarm's "abre los ojos" invitation, the clock reads 9:00. A matrix for reading the film needs to account for the fact that a forward advance in the narrative represents a move backwards in time. After shutting off the alarm at 9:00, the voiceover male voice, which the viewer later will identify as that of Antonio, the psychiatrist, asks "¿Por qué me cuentas este sueño?" (Why are you telling me that dream?). Here "dream" cannot refer to the Gran Vía scene since the scene occurs after 9:03 and the dream content told seems to index the 25th birthday. More important, though, is the chronology itself. Again, the viewer must ask: if it is clear that César did not wake up at 9:03 because the wake up sequence is obviously a dream, why or how should it be that he awakens three minutes earlier?

6. Dream Story

While most of the extant bibliography on *Abre los ojos* would probably not argue with the idea that the whole film can be read as dream, the present chapter is unique in actually asserting that all but some 45 seconds of the film narrative is dream. Even after what is approaching twenty years of scholarship on the film, the present essay is the first to call specific, interpretative attention to the 9:03 → 9:00 temporal shift in the film's establishing minutes. It is unique in observing this narrative advancement-backwards movement in time. The essay is distinct in its emphasis on this disconnect and its relationship to an insistence on reading the entire narrative as dream. The opening minutes demonstrate the filmic discourse's intention to disorient. Ironic is an establishing orientation towards disorientation, a willful orienting of the viewer towards the disorientation that can be experienced in dream. Further, the disconnect between waking times underscores pliability, a temporal pliability proper to dreams, not to realistic narratives. This becomes a further establishing cue orienting the viewer to read this film as dream.[4]

The chronological order of the two times aside, the three-minute differential between them speaks to César having a Philips recordable alarm clock radio with snooze setting. Since it seems the snooze pause is set at three minutes, it would place at 9:06 the last time the viewer hears the recorded alarm ("Tranquilo, tranquilo.... Abre los ojos" [Easy, easy.... Open your eyes.]) in the female voiceover heard over the blank black screen that ends the film, interrupting César's fall. In the six minutes apparently elapsed, the viewer has witnessed narratives spanning an hour and fifty minutes or so of real time, and 150+ years of narrated time.

In order to adequately deal with narratives presenting this sort of complication, modern narratological theory has offered different helpful approaches, as well as useful critical concepts, beginning with *fabula* and *syuzhet*, originated and employed by the Russian Formalists. In an effort to overcome the limitations of the conceptualization of *fabula* and *sujet* as well as the limitations of the binary, other theorists have offered several tripartite variations upon the distinction between *fabula* and *sujet*. One of these[5] is Gérard Genette, whose terms "histoire," "récit," and "narration" can be useful in approaching *Abre los ojos*' narrative complexities. He proposed

> [...] to use the word story [histoire] for the signified or narrative content [...] to use the word narrative [récit] for the *signifier*, statement, discourse or narrative text itself, and to use the word narrating [narration] for the producing narrative action and, by extension, the whole of the real or fictional situation in which that action takes place [27].

It is at this last level, narrating/narration or producing narrative action, where blank, black screens[6] with voiceovers and the shutting off of alarm clock occur. This level in *Abre los ojos* describes a semi-waking, semi-conscious

124 **The First Few Minutes of Spanish Language Films**

state, on which even more complicated dream narrative histoires and récits depend. The narration lasts 115 minutes, the running time of the film, which equates horizontally to the 6 minutes, which could be represented thus, reordering the actual narrating sequence (9:03 → 9:00 → 9:06) into chronological order (9:00 → 9:03 → 9:06) on the horizontal axis:

Abre los ojos (1996). Reproduced with permission obtained through EGEDA (Entidad de Gestión de los Productores Audiovisuales) [Spain].

6. Dream Story

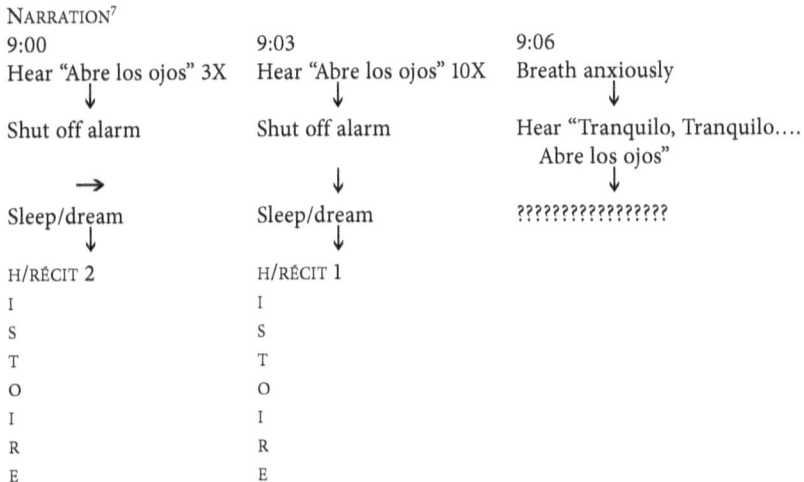

The 6 minutes of the narrating action, in fact, occupy only 45 seconds of "real" time elapsed within the 115 minutes of the film's running time.[8]

On vertical axes corresponding to the 9:03 and 9:00 narration sequences, there are two histoire/récit (story/narrative) wholes, which themselves can be articulated vertically and horizontally. Born obviously from the Sausurrean binary signified/signifier, the histoire is an underlying story, and récit is the way in which the story is told. In very general terms, histoire would be a "natural," non-fictionalized, logical ordering of events. Under the normal reading process of abstraction, the scholar-viewer/reader arrives at a temporal-causal understanding of the order of events. And, récit is the actual rendering of those events or the form that the rendering of those events takes.

In the case following the 9:03 "Abre los ojos" black blank screen voiceover sequence, there is little or no variation between what the viewer can extract as story and the telling of it. The vertical/horizontal axes of histoire/récit 1 could be represented as:

wake up/sit up → look in mirror → shower → dress → go out in VW → run down empty Gran Vía
↓ look in mirror
↓ shower
↓ dress
↓ go out in VW
↓ run down empty Gran Vía

Near the end of the sequence, César looks at his watch, which reads 10:03. If the viewer accepts the earlier reported time on the alarm clock of 9:03, the elapsed diegetic time, the elapsed time of the histoire is one hour. Though there is seemingly no alteration between the order of occurrence and telling, the telling of these events (récit) lasts the 2 minutes and 23 seconds that it takes for the viewer to watch them.

Histoire/récit 2 is the long, complicated dream narrative[9] that corresponds to another axis vertical to the 9:00 "Abre los ojos" black blank screen voiceover sequence. It is numbered histoire/récit 2 because it is narrated second, even though it is narrated immediately subsequent to the camera identifying the hour as 9:00, three minutes earlier than the time associated with the beginning of histoire/récit 1. In the histoire/récit 2 (story/narrative) whole, which also can be articulated vertically and horizontally, there is quite a variation between what the viewer can extract as story and the telling of it. The relationship between the story and the telling of it is further complicated by the existence of the technology-induced dream within the dream. The vertical histoire (story) axis of histoire/récit 1 could be represented as:

Wakeup/sit up
  Look in mirror ⎫
  Shower   ⎬ Repeats sequence outline from historie/récit 1
  Dress
  Nuria
  Go out in VW ⎭
  Drive down busy Gran Vía
Pelayo and frontón
  Conversation about "ugly"
Birthday party
Sofía's apartment
  drawings
  Duvernois on TV
Car crash + Nuria
Surgery + disfigured, ugly result
Sofía in the park
Visit with doctors
Night club + Sofía, Pelayo
Passing out on the street (watch reads 9:00)
Suicide
LE (Life Extension)
  Contract
  Special clause
"Splicing"—"Abre los ojos" (watch reads 6:05)
  Nuria → Sofía "Te quiero" (I love you)
In the park
Visit to doctors
  Successful surgery

Removal of bandages + sex
Restaurant + Sofía + Pelayo
   photo, Duvernois
In bed with Sofía
   Nightmare
         Sofía ⟶ Nuria
Police + Pelayo
Sofía's apartment
   killing
   disfigured—mirror
Psychiatric Penitentiary
   2 months
   drawing
   "happiness"
   Eli?
   Duvernois on TV
   Computer search
Life Extension
   Explanation
   Disfigured, ugly in mirror
   Killing of guard
   Guard shoots Antonio
   Conversation with Duvernois
   Sofía, Antonio, Pelayo ⟶ mirages/holographs
   Jump and fall[10]

From the time references given during the telling of these events, they occur over a time frame that spans some 150 years, bringing the viewer to midtwenty second century times. In order to view the telling of these events, the scholar-viewer invests about 112 minutes of "real time," viewing time.

In its first few minutes, *Abre los ojos* orients the viewer towards reading it as dream, and the whole of this manipulation of time contributes to the film's offering itself to be read as such, as dream.[11] Time periods varying from 6 minutes to over 150 years, the internal shifts in temporal linearity (i.e. telling of a dream to the psychiatrist before the car crash is ever narrated), and the alternate compression and expansion of temporal equivalents produce a relativization of time explainable in terms of dream. These elements provide keys to reading the film in terms of style, organization, and structure; it is to be read as dream or dreams, but what about its/their content? Or, as Antonio, the psychiatrist asks in the voiceover, "¿Por qué me cuentas este sueño?" (Why are you telling me this dream?).

As mentioned, the opening sequence ends with the young man that the viewer will come to know as César, running down the empty Gran Vía, stopping and turning as he does to scrutinize the empty surroundings.[12] César, in his disorientation, questions the eerily empty surroundings, he questions the void of what he could only know consciously as a location filled the life, activity and movement, which the viewer will see in a soon-to-follow sequence. In a questioning that in fact began showing in his facial expressions as he exited his garage and peered into the city and then turned onto the thoroughfare, César continues on foot down the middle of the street as he seems to seek explanations for his sudden, unexpected sense of foreignness.

With this, the viewer knows that the filmic narrative seeks to question. In this regard, *Abre los ojos* is characteristic of Amenábar's other productions, and it is reflective of the cinematographic approach that is distinctive to him. In an interview with Oti Rodríguez Marchante, Amenábar, now famously in multiple venues and in different forms,[13] said

> ... La postura moral en el cine siempre me ha interesado. Esto no quiere decir que en las películas tenga que plantar una moraleja o "moralina" cerrada, sin espacio para que el espectador piense por sí mismo y saque sus propias conclusiones. Por eso digo que mi cine no es un cine de respuestas, sino de preguntas. Yo no voy a decirle al espectador si la crionización es buena o mala, pero sí quiero que reflexione sobre lo que ha visto. Lo que sí debe existir, creo, es cierta inclinación o posicionamiento por parte del autor. Como espectador me gusta saber qué me cuenta la película, dónde me ha situado y adónde me quiere llevar el director. (87–88)

> (... In film, the moral position has always interested me. This does not mean that in movies it is necessary to pose a moral or enclosed moral lesson, with no room for the viewer to think for himself and reach his own conclusions. That is why I say that my films are not films of answers but rather of questions. I am not going to tell the viewer if cryonization is good or bad, but I do want him to reflect on what he has seen. What should exist, I believe, is a certain inclination or positioning by the author. As a viewer, I like to know what the film is telling me, where it has located me, and where the director wants to take me.)

Consistent with Amenábar's confessed characterization of his own films, *Abre los ojos* does not offer the viewer answers to questions or solutions to problems. But, it does, from its very first few minutes, orient the viewer to the fact that it will pose questions and that it will scrutinize its surroundings.

Structuring the entire filmic narrative as dream not only invokes canonical moments of Hispanic culture,[14] it suggests questions inherent in the human condition. Form and content in *Abre los ojos* combine, for example, to enquire as to what is real, what is appearance, what is a dream; and, as they do, they index a thematics frequent in Spanish canon. In this regard, Amenábar's film gives form to Segismundo's often-referenced monologue from a classic of Spanish Golden Age theater, Calderón de Barca's *La vida es sueño*:

¿Qué es la vida? Un frenesí.	(What is this life? A frenzy.
¿Qué es la vida? Una ilusión,	What is this life? An illusion,
una sombra, una ficción,	A shadow, a fiction,
y el mayor bien es pequeño;	And the greatest good is small;
que toda la vida es sueño,	All of life is but a dream,
y los sueños, sueños son. (II, 1)	And dreams are only dreams.)

This philosophical-psychological wondering is a feature of many other literary texts from Spanish literature, and it just as easily could have been pronounced by César at any number of junctures throughout *Abre los ojos*, instead of lines that he does speak like "soñar es una mierda" (dreaming is shit), "lo demás es mentira" (everything else is a lie), or "odio soñar" (I hate dreaming); or instead of César wondering whether he has lived a certain moment before.

If Amenábar's filmic content and organization ask questions as to what is life, what is a dream, so, too, does the film directly ask the question "What is happiness?" Waiting for César after he has spent the night with Sofía, Nuria coaxes him to go with her in her Alfa Romeo. As she drives, she asks César two questions that are central to the overall philosophical musings of the filmic discourse, the second of which will come up to later. She asks her sleepy, disinterested passenger if he is happy: "César, ¿qué es para tí la felicidad?" (César, what is happiness for you?). Answering her own question first, she tells him that this is happiness, being there with him. César, a rich good-looking young man, with three cars, many love interests/conquests, etc., does not answer, saying only that he is not up for such transcendental questions. Later, the topic of happiness comes up again, this time in conjunction with Antonio. Jokingly, the suggestion is that he is married with two kids and that this could be happiness. But, the consideration does not go beyond the level of suggestion or joke. The question of happiness is left open, though it is clear that because of the anguish and anxiety that César suffers, a lifestyle based on material wealth, good looks, eating, sleeping, and having sex is not necessarily the answer.

A repeated presence in the filmic narrative is that of cryogenics, a branch of physics that studies the production of low temperatures and their effects. More precisely *Abre los ojos* invokes cryonics, which is medical technology applying cryopreservation to humans (and animals) for future revival. In its employment of this seemingly futuristic theme, the film poses questions as to what are the limits of technology, what are the implications of technology applied to human existence, and, joining this and the previous consideration, what is the value of perpetuating an empty life.

Given the thematics and the story told, another of the important questions that Amenábar asks through *Abre los ojos* is: What are the limits of medicine? Tied to the previous question regarding technology's limits and implications, doctors and the state of medicine are called into question as César seeks to remedy a situation caused by the car crash. From the repeated scenes of looking in the mirror, from Sofía's reaction, from the comments of club patrons in the bathroom, from discussions with Pelayo and Antonio, etc., it is obvious that César places great importance on his physical appearance, and with a desire to restore his good looks, doctors are twice offered up as a solution. In the first case, believing his wealth and their skill can fulfill his wishes, César seeks aesthetic surgery help from a panel of experts, who explain to him that the state of the art is not yet equipped to respond to what it would take to correct the damage done to his face. In addition to frustrating César's desires, this response has two important functions: it creates the need to wait until medical science is ready (thus, the need for cryonics), and it exacerbates the wish-fulfillment desire that can work as "day residue," overdetermining dreams induced under "Clause 14: Artificial Perception." There, in that virtual reality, a dream induced by Life Extension, César's wishes come true; Sofía loves him, and medical science and his doctors have achieved the ability return to him his good looks.

But, as César himself asks "¿Qué pasaría si hubiera errores?" (What would happen if there were mistakes?). In fact, there are errors, and César's dream within in a dream is not all wish fulfillment virtual reality. It takes on the quality of a nightmare in which he is imprisoned for a crime that he does not remember, in which a supposedly dead Nuria reappears assuming Sofía's place, in which what he sees is alternatively a handsome or disfigured face. Though technology promises "Viva Ud. sin límites" (life without limits), "devolverles la vida" (to restore life), or "seguir viviendo su vida actual" (continue to live your current life), it all turns out to be, in the words of the Life Extension salesman, "una posibilidad más que todavía no tenemos muy desarrollada" (a possibility that we still have not fully developed). Though technology promises a virtual reality in which you decide at all times, that promise does not count on the subconscious. So, *Abre los ojos* asks, what are the limits of technology?

It is, perhaps, this questioning of the limits of technology what takes the scholar-viewer back to the days of Calderón de la Barca and debates about *libre albedrío* (free will). In a scenario in which Life Extension assumes a *deus ex machina* role of predetermining or predestining César's reality, the free will of his subconscious seems to triumph. Technology cannot control it, but neither can a conscious (though conscious within a dream) César.

The very structure of the dream, and the film's dream narrative, is the questioning and the search for answers, as the film's first few minutes establish with César running down an empty Gran Vía visually scouring the cityscape. The questioning motif is confirmed when with his first, and discourse-structuring, question "¿Por qué me cuentas este sueño?" (Why are you telling me this dream?), psychiatrist Antonio asks César questions,[15] and the latter deflects, rejects, or skirts the answers. And, so it is that Amenábar's film is not a film of answers, but rather a film of questions, a common denominator of which seems to be an interest in what is important in life. César is anxious about friendship and being alone, his wealth, his good looks, finding the woman of his dreams, death and dying, being in control, etc. And, the anxieties play themselves out in his dreams, in the induced virtual reality dreams.

Because the first few minutes cue the reading of the film as dream/dreams, the scholar-viewer must bring to bear some understanding of dreams in order to inform his reading. It is understood, for example, that memories formed throughout the waking day play a role in dreaming.[16] These remembrances leave impressions for the unconscious to deal with during REM sleep, when the ego is at rest. The unconscious mind re-enacts these remembrances of the past in dreams. These triggering memories are called "day residue." In recurring dreams, remembrances repeatedly surface demanding the dreamer's attention to a perhaps unresolved or obsessive issue related to the dream. Dreams, of course, are often forged of symbols or images that index issues latent in the unconscious.

Sigmund Freud posited that the motivation of dream content is wish-fulfillment. He further posited that the instigation of a dream is often to be found in the events of the day prior to the dream ("day residue"). Particularly in adults, dream material may be subject to condensation, displacement and distortion in which "manifest content" masks, yet derives from, "latent content" present in the unconscious. Because of distortion and disguise, the real meaning of a dream is concealed. Censorship is part of the disguising process as well, as it works to filter any images that might express latent material too directly because such material might evoke anxiety in the dreamer and threaten to awaken him.

Dreams select dreamwork material from any part of the dreamer's recent experience. In the case of *Abre los ojos*, where "day" would be located in an extra-diegetic time recently prior to the viewer's hearing "abre los ojos," the film's dreamer brings issues of anxieties that range from the existential to the very personal. Throughout the filmic narrative, Amenábar sprinkles enough visual, verbal, conceptual, and wish-fulfillment "day residue" triggers so as to ably create a layered narrative, where at one level "day" becomes dream containing those triggers for another dream and induced virtual reality dreaming at another level. Mimicking the difference between waking life and dream, the layered narrative, with its movements between layers, serves the film's overall oneiric quality.

In *Abre los ojos*, there are multiple examples of "day residues" that would seem to work as apparent triggers of dreams or dream sequences within the filmic discourse. And the most obvious and the most important of these day residues or dream triggers is the interview segment of a TV talk show.

Leaving his birthday party, César takes Sofía home, and later with her having fallen asleep on the couch, he watches television. Half waking up, Sofía explains to him that what he is watching was run on TV before, and that it is about cryogenics, where they freeze your body, like Walt Disney. The impact of this as day residue is obvious. It is repeated several times in the rest of the filmic narrative. Cryogenics and cryonization is the structuring principle for the dream within a dream, and it explains the outcome of it. The man seen interviewed on the TV talk show, Serge Duvernois, emerges as a character in that same dream within a dream. The image of Duvernois being interviewed on TV reappears during the sequence in which a disfigured César, Pelayo and Sofía go out to a club on a Friday night, and in the scene in the common room in the psychiatric hospital. Prior to his appearance in the final sequences at Life Extension, Duvernois appears in person at the café where César, Sofía and Pelayo go, and the latter takes a photograph that will later resurface; and Duvernois appears in the dream flashback in which César signs the contract with LE. The day residue or triggering image of Duvernois, thus, is important not only to the structure of the film's dream and induced dream virtual reality in its appearance and reappearances; it is also the source of the film's questioning regarding the limits of technology.

Other dream triggers are not necessarily visual residue but rather verbal traces. Sentences, questions, and words are the stuff of which dream within a dream is made, and they trigger flashbacks and flashforwards.

As he and Pelayo practice on a frontón court, César invokes God when he misses a shot. The sequence is followed by a flashforward (the first) to Antonio and César in his cell in the psychiatric penitentiary. As César and Pelayo continue racquet practice, the psychiatrist asks César, "¿Crees en Dios?" (Do you believe in God?), in a sound bridge heard before the cut to the scene in the cell. Nuria asks the same question, just before she purposely crashes the car. She says to César, "Dime una cosa: ¿Crees en Dios?" (Tell me something: Do you believe in God?). As the conceptual works as a trigger in the dreamwork, so, too, does the conceptual pose another of the film's many questions,[17] as it also links the levels of *Abre los ojos*' dreamwork.

The scene with the two friends practicing on the frontón court provides another "day residue" that ties one dream to another, one level to another. Pelayo complains that César is successful with the girls but that he himself is not because of his looks, his appearance. This exchange follows:

> CÉSAR: ... pero no eres feo. Mucha gente cambiaría su cara por la tuya. Eres completamente normal.
> (... but you're not ugly. A lot of people would exchange their face for yours. You're completely normal.)
> PELAYO: Allí está. Soy normal, lo que no quiere decir que soy guapo.
> (That's it. I'm normal, which doesn't mean that I'm good looking.)

6. Dream Story

CÉSAR: Eres guapo.
   (You're good looking.)
PELAYO: Soy aceptable cuando no estás tú al lado.
   (I'm OK, when you're not along side.)

Some of these same words later lose their playfulness. In the film's final scenes at Life Extension's offices, César escapes into a restroom, where he sees himself in the mirror as disfigured. Catching up to him, Antonio enters the restroom, and confronting César, he repeats a request he has made earlier ("Muéstrame tu cara"/Show me your face) (another trigger or link between dreams and/or dream segments). Though César initially refuses, saying he does not have to or want to, and that it is his dream, he finally removes the mask. He sees himself in the mirror as disfigured, but Antonio tells him, "Mucha gente cambiaría su cara por la tuya. Eres completamente normal. ¡Qué coño normal! Eres guapo" (Many people would exchange their face for yours. You are completely normal. Fuck normal, you are handsome.), repeating the exact words César had used with Pelayo.

Images captured in photographs are used as triggers to great advantage by Amenábar in the structuring of *Abre los ojos*' dreamworks. Already mentioned, for example, was the photograph that Pelayo takes of Sofía and César in the café. The image of this photograph reappears later with Nuria replacing Sofía, a symptom of César's nightmare within a dream. The anxiety-producing substitution of subjects in photographs is a repeated trigger used in this nightmare. The day residue or remembrance of photographs viewed in his first visit to Sofía's apartment resurfaces when César goes to the apartment in search of her after denouncing her disappearance to the police. Again, Nuria's visage occupies the place of Sofía in the re-invoked photographs.

Once again, the viewer remembers the end of the film's second sequence where Antonio's voiceover question ("¿Por qué me cuentas este sueño?"/Why are you telling me this dream?) to César is heard before the cut to the penitentiary cell, and the viewer can pose the same question. So, why is he telling me this dream?

In the extant bibliography on *Abre los ojos* there are many studies that are fully or partially dedicated to interpretations and analyses of the dream aspect in the film. Generally, the studies are less about the function of dream, and all imply a certain relationship between dream and waking life. But, what the current chapter proposes it that, with the exception of the 45 seconds of real time (film's running time/viewer-invested time) or the 6 minutes of represented time at the level of "narration" (9:00 → 9:06), everything in *Abre los ojos* is dream. Since everything is dream, any perceived relationship between waking life and dream is an illusion. This illusion is created by the establishment of two levels of dream that are separated in such a way that the difference between them appears to the scholar-viewer to be similar to the difference between waking life and dreaming.

The presence of day residue triggers that mimic dreamwork production and that link one narrative level to another is but one of the ways in which this film manages to convince the viewer of a waking life/dream dichotomy. At the same time, such triggers help carry out the read-me-as-dream matrix that the film establishes for itself in the first few minutes.

The repetition of scenes or scenarios also aids in the creation the two-level illusion. Repeated three times, for example, is the scenario in which César is in bed facing the need to wake up. On two occasions, it seems that he sits up in bed and proceeds to his daily routine. A third time, though, he remains face down in bed, while in voiceover he talks with Antonio.

As part of his wakeup routine, César looks in the mirror, sometimes seeing a handsome visage, others a disfigured one. Just as dreams are a reflection of the dreamer's feelings, desires, anxieties, etc., mirrors are reflections. The reflection motif present in mirrors in *Abre los ojos* contributes to the establishment of the two levels of dream within dream.

The already mentioned relativization of time is key to the creation of dream effect. But, condensation and expansion of time are not the only elements at play. Flashforwards and flashbacks are equally important factors. These elements combine with scene repetition in the creation of the two levels. The filmic narrative flashes back or forward more than a half a dozen times to César and Antonio in the former's cell in the psychiatric penitentiary. Beyond the conveyance of an obsessive quality proper to dream, the non-temporal/causal movement implicit in these flashes speaks to a transrational, not rational, motivation distinctive to the implied level separation.

The subject matter of the conversations between Antonio and César is nearly always dream or the difference between reality and dream (Why are you telling me this dream?, I only remember fragments, Dreams are like that, and sometimes the mind acts as if you were in a dream, etc.) The fact that Antonio and César are trying to sort out the difference between dream and reality is a major contributing factor in creating the illusion of that very difference for the viewer.

In a similar conversation, this time with Serge Duvernois in a bar after César's visit to the police and an argument with Pelayo, Duvernois confirms for César, and for the viewer, the key to reading film. He reinforces the matrix for that reading established in the film's first few minutes as he says:

> ¿Qué pasaría si te dijera que estás soñando? ... Los sueños no se descubren hasta que uno se despierta.... No hay sueño simple.
>
> (What would happen, if I told you that you are dreaming? ... One does not realize he's dreaming until he wakes up.... There is no simple dream.)

César, and perhaps the oriented-to-disorientation viewer too, refuses to believe this, until dream-like wish fulfillment causes the bar patrons to go silent and come to a freeze action standstill.

This is not the only use of cinematographic technique employed in the creation of an illusion of difference between waking life and dreaming. When Antonio tells César, "A ver si me dices ese sueño" (Let's see if you can tell me that dream), there is a cut to a blurred, out-of-focus vision of a park and the rain; and when he asks about "that office," there is another jump to an out-of-focus sequence in an office and paper work. At one level there is clarity of focus, and at another there is not, and this technique suggests the two levels of dream narrative, which in turn are reflective of the difference between waking life and dream.

If the transrational quality of some of the editing in flashbacks and flash-forwards contributes to creating two levels of dream that seek to parallel the separation between waking life and dream, there is another cinematographic editing technique effectively used by Amenábar in *Abre los ojos*: match cut. Linking two shots metaphorically, match cut easily suggests two different levels to, and a separation of, narrative levels. After showering, César sits smoking, leaning against a wall, arm bent, and hand on knee in a left profile shot. There is a cut and match to another left profile shot. César, now with mask, sits on the floor of his cell, leaning against the wall, hand on knee. The similarity of physical position motivates the match. The differences in surroundings and appearance suggest the separation of dream levels.

Also, the movement between levels can be reversed. Having asked Antonio for a pencil and block of paper, César draws, attempting to re-create Sofía's visage. After a couple of failed attempts, her faced begins to take shape in the grays and whites of the paper, when there is a cut to Sofía's face as she poses in the park. Though the direction of the movement between levels is different, the effect of suggesting those levels and the separation between them is the same.

If there is any doubt as to whether or not entire the film is or has been a dream, the viewer has only to pay attention to the film's ending. César has thrown himself off of the Picasso Tower, and as he hurtles downward, he is screaming. Suddenly, the screen goes to black and there is silence. Has César splattered himself on the pavement? The silence is brief, and over the blank black screen, a female voice in a voiceover repeats "Tranquilo, tranquilo. Abre los ojos" (Easy, easy. Open your eyes.). After 115 minutes of viewing time, the viewer is sent back to the beginning, realizing, but not surprised, that what has been narrated is only a dream/dreams, and that César has not yet awakened. And the viewer realizes that the questioning of reality vs. appearance is played out as well on the level of time. What are the 115 minutes invested in viewing the film, in which ostensibly there are at least 150 years of snippets of narrated dreams, are compressed into what are a few minutes of sleep in which the narrated/narrating action has been dreamed. Which of these different times is real?

Has César dreamed his own death? Contrary to some popular belief, dream specialists assert that it is possible to dream one's own death. It appears, though, that César twice has opted not to dream his death. In the first instance, he consciously (again though, it is consciousness within a dream, choosing dream within a dream) chooses LE's Clause 14, which allows him to forget his death and splice onto his life a dream of pleasant virtual reality. In the second instance, this falling scene, perhaps out of an instinct for self-preservation, César (his unconscious desires) ends the dream just in time.[18] If the wish-fulfillment motive of the entire dream to this point has been life extension or life preservation, waking up at the instant that the *Abre los ojos* dreamer is about to splatter on the pavement is wholly consistent.

Published readings of *Abre los ojos* focus on the text in its psychological/psycho-analytical dimension (Frechilla, García, Perri, Thakkar) or in its ability to question appearance versus reality (Laraway, Knollmueller, Juan Carlos Martín, Marina Martín). Paradigmatic among them is the 2004 essay by Chris Perriam, which highlights key moments, motifs, and themes, as it also contextualizes the film in terms of Amenábar, Noriega, and its links with other films.

As some readings of the film analyze it, they ignore the importance of the first few minutes, or they seem to miss the point of them, and they seem to reflect how the viewer is disoriented by *Abre los ojos*' opening sequences. Perriam, for example, states

> Voices-over in the second awakening scene bring the psychoanalytical implications to the fore and troubles [sic] the linearity of the narrative and the coherence of the protagonist in what should be the film's real establishing moments, redressing the balance after the shocking false start [210–211].

Whether the viewer thinks the film's sequencing "should be" other than it is, or whether the film's initial sequencing is effective or not, the first few minutes are an integral part of the filmic text, and they are an essential key to prompting its reading. Where the disorientation felt is an intentional product of, among other things, a narrative advancement and a backwards movement in time, rather than symptoms of an unreal or out-of-balance "false start," the opening scenes are the establishing moments, and their "troubled linearity" establishes that the film "should be" read as dream.

In their analyses of a lull/choque/lull rhythm in the film and Freudian dreamwork implications or of links with Spanish aesthetic tradition, Amit Thakkar (2011) and Marit Knollmueller (2009) come closest to recognizing the whole film as dream and César's never having awakened,[19] as the following quotes with my emphasis reveal:

... in the dénouement where loose ends are tied up and meaning restored, especially after a tense climax. In *Abre los ojos*, we have a false secondary revision: the dénouement appears to comfort the viewer with a conclusion but the final cut to black, accompanied by the echoing "Abre los ojos," fails to reveal whether César will **wake up in another dream or in the future** [Thakkar 32].

We never see him look into his new reality ... leading to the possibility that he is just awaking from a nightmare the way he seemed to awake from sleep in the beginning of the film. Amenábar **suggests (but never confirms) that the entirety of the film is a dream** [Knollmueller 212].

But, in the film's first few minutes, Amenábar does "confirm" that the entirety of the film is to be read as dream (not merely "a dream," but dream and dream/virtual reality within it), and he willfully orients the viewer towards the disorientation felt by César in his dreamwork. The 9:03 → 9:00 movement in time displayed by the brief close-ups of the alarm clock clearly confirms that César never awakens and, thus, orients the scholar-viewer towards reading the entirety of the film as dream. This three-minute displacement further suggests that the alarm was not shut off but rather paused, and that the diegetic time is now 9:06.

With the exception of 45 seconds of narrating time, everything in *Abre los ojos* is dream. Other readings within the bibliography studying *Abre los ojos* are either fully or partially dedicated to interpretations and analyses of the dream aspect of the film, but none go so far as to posit this extent of the dreamwork nor its levels. The establishing minutes of the film presage a dream narrative, and with the matrix established there, the scholar-viewer's eyes are opened to the realization that he should read everything, with the exception of the 45 seconds (6 minutes of voice-over darkness at the narrating alarm clock level) as dream. The articulation of dreamwork levels is facilitated by the Freudian concept of "day residue," where images, events, and words from one level trigger manifest content on the other. Some dream content is, of course, induced Life Extension virtual reality dream/nightmare within a dream. But, with the initially disorienting orientation from the film's first few minutes, the scholar-viewer is prompted to the film being read as dream, where the separation between different levels of dreams resembles the difference between waking life and dream.

Like all good artists, Amenábar leaves enough clues along the way to remind the reader/viewer of the dream character and the separation of levels of dreams, as he carries out a narrative whose structure is made clear in the opening sequences. In the scene in which they see each other in the park after his having spent the night in her apartment, César tells Sofía of his "horrible dream" in which Nuria wrecks the car, dies, and he ends up looking like a "monster."

"¿Qué tal encontraste tu casa?" (What kind of shape was your house in?), asks Sofía of César in that same conversation, and the viewer supposes that she is wondering whether the place was a mess after the birthday party there. But, César seems to have no idea what she is talking about; so, for him, either the birthday party was a dream, or this scene is a dream with no antecedent residue (it could be spliced Clause 14 virtual reality without memory), or it is all a dream (César is telling this dream to Antonio). But the scholar-viewer understands Sofía's question, and thanks to the orientation provided by the first few minutes, he realizes that this is one more moment of the overall dream material (*histoires* and *récits* 1 and 2) in which the separation between dream levels is indexed.

Like many of the films analyzed in this volume, *Abre los ojos*' first few minutes offer the viewer a motif matrix. If, for example, we saw Carlos Saura's *Carmen* establish flamenco and performativity as motifs in its opening minutes, Amenábar's film makes dream a clear motif for its discourse. Here, though, the opening minutes do more than identify motif, and their matrix-establishing potential is unique because the first few minutes provide an orientation as to the film's structure. The temporal disconnect on the alarm clock in the opening two sequences points to a deixis- and diegesis-centering subject who never awakens, who continues to dream. From this, the scholar-viewer is programmed to read the film as dream, dream that ultimately folds over on itself.

◆ 7 ◆

SINS OF OUR FATHERS
Carlos Carrera's 2002
El crimen del Padre Amaro
(The Crime of Father Amaro)

> The individual is no doubt the fictitious atom of an "ideological" representation of society; but he is also a reality fabricated by this specific technology of power ... "discipline." We must cease once and for all to describe the effects of power in negative terms: it "excludes," it "represses," it "censors," it "abstracts," it "masks," it "conceals." In fact, power produces; it produces reality; it produces domains of objects and rituals of truth. The individual and the knowledge that may be gained of him belong to this production.
>
> Michel Foucault, *Discipline and Punish*

"Un conflicto entre la ambición y el amor" (A conflict between ambition and love), that is what the viewer reads on the movie posters and on the cover of the DVD for 2002's *El crimen del Padre Amaro* from Mexican director Carlos Carrera. That is the way publicists want to sell the film, the way they want to program viewers to read the film. And, it would seem that, judging from controversies that surrounded the film on its release, early readings of the film were limited to this conflict centered on the person of the title character. But, should this be the canonical reading of this film, which, given its blockbuster success, almost immediately entered the canon of New Mexican Cinema?

El crimen del Padre Amaro premiered in Mexico in November of 2002 at a time when Pope John Paul II's July-August visit to Canada, Guatemala and Mexico, where the canonization of Juan Diego was featured, was still fresh in people's minds. Also on people's minds was the attention again being focused on scandals surrounding Catholic priests and sexual abuse of children under the age of consent. Like *Fresa y chocolate* in Cuba almost a decade earlier, *El crimen del Padre Amaro* seems to actualize elements of public concern that in turn appear to frame critical readings of the film. If the ongoing intellectual debate over the Castro regime's treatment of homosexuals helped to frame critical debate and readings of Gutiérrez Alea's 1993 film, contemporaneous attention focused on the Catholic Church certainly had the effect of framing the reception of Carlos Carrera's work. The result is, perhaps, somewhat impoverished readings of the two films, with their focus limited to a single theme. However, the filmic discourses of both films offer more ample analytical possibilities as suggested by their matrix-preparing openings. For example, the establishing opening minutes of *El crimen del Padre Amaro* prepare the scholar-viewer to read the film in terms that go well beyond the story of a young priest crossing the line between temptation and sin.

Initial credits indicate co-production participation (Alfredo Ripstein, Alameda Films, Wanda Vision, Blu Films, Fondo para la Producción Cinematográfica de Calidad, Instituto Mexicano de Cinematografía, Cinecolor México, Cinecolor Argentina, Videocolor Argentina, Artcam Francia, Daniel Birman Ripstein, Gobierno del Estado de Veracruz-Llave, Ibermedia).[1] Other credits inform of the film's title and the Eça de Queirós 1875 novel by the same name as subtext. These few credits appear over a black background, as the viewer begins to hear a faint sound of traffic. Still over that black background, an intertitle appears, identifying place and time as Aldama Mexico, 2002.

A low-angle shot shows children playing at the side of a road. The right side of the shot is occupied by a cross on its side. A bus passes.

A close-up through the window of the bus identifies a young man who is looking out. A reverse shot looks out of the bus window. The next 40+ seconds move from a close-up of sparse, dry trees to a panoramic view of the countryside. Viewed are trees, fields, fences, cattle, gathered hay, a partly cloudy blue sky, and mountains on the horizon. There is a shot of large electric towers sustaining many cables. And, then, a foggy view where trees seem denser and it is cloudy and rainy.

Again, the camera looks into the bus, where an old man seated beside the young man offers the latter some food. He asks if he is going to Santa María, and the young man indicates that he will stay in Los Reyes. The old man goes on to tell of his plans: with money given to him for his land, he will start a store. If the store does not work out, he says "Yo me largo para el otro lado. Tengo una hija por allá" (I'll leave for the other side. I have a daughter over there).

The camera again looks outside the bus, revealing tress and the sun that is lower in the sky. Inside, the young man is pensive. The image offers shadows, then, it cuts to night.

Alongside the road sits a car with its hood up, and a woman wearing a

7. Sins of Our Fathers   141

tan wool poncho leans against the car. She looks back down the road. The camera moves to the right to discover an oncoming bus. The woman steps out to flag the bus down. It stops, and she taps of the bus door window for the driver to open.

The woman rushes onto the bus with gun in hand and she threatens the bus driver. Two armed bandits, guns drawn, follow her onto the bus, and they push down the center aisle. Passengers are frightened as the bandits shine flashlights in their eyes and demand money and possessions. Taking the old man's money, one bandit strikes him on the head with his gun. The young man tends to him as the robbers leave, wishing all a good evening and a good trip. The robbers speed away in the car.

Three minutes and thirty-four seconds into the film, the reader has a matrix with which to begin to read the film. And, the matrix has nothing to do with the ambition and love that the publicists seem to have wanted to suggest for the film.

With the opening intertitle, the viewer knows that the film is to be read in terms of its relationship with or its presentation of Mexico.

With all of the visual attention paid to the views from the bus window as it travels the provincial roads of Mexico, the viewer knows that the film is to be read in terms of it potential to portray a panoramic of Mexico, a wide-angle view of the country.

With the opening low-angle shot, the scholar-viewer knows that the filmic discourse will work to include him within or to invite him to identify with the film.

With the eruption in the night by the road robbers who quickly strike in the darkness of the bus's journey, the viewer knows that his reading of the film must account for crime. Of course, this confirms a readerly expectation already created by the film's title. But, as the viewer will see, because of the establishing invitation to read the film as panorama, there will be more than one crime.

The robbers demand money and possessions from the anonymous bus riders, and the old man loses everything. Though all are merely threatened by the intruders, one robber strikes the old man on the head with the butt of his pistol. With this scene, the victims of crime(s) are identified. With this, the reading of the film is oriented towards a concretization of the filmic narrative in which it is the Mexican people (el pueblo) that lose; it is the Mexican people that are beaten up.

With all of the attention paid to the young man on the bus through the use of close-up, the viewer intuits that narrative attention will coalesce around him. But, the viewer does not yet know who this young man is.

Given this fact, given that characters have yet to be identified, it might be argued that the matrix-establishing "first few minutes" need to be extended.

Another low-angle shot identifies a road entering a small town with a church having two bell towers and many crisscrossing electric wires; it is morning. The bus enters the town, passes down a narrow, stone street and approaches a bus station where people are waiting. Inside the bus, the young man has changed seats. He is no longer beside the window; the old man is. The young man stands up to retrieve his backpack from above. As the old man watches, he opens the bag, takes out some money and gives it to the old man. Passengers exit the bus, but the old man stays. Having taken down another bag, the young man also exits the bus and looks around.

There is a cut to a tree-lined, fence-lined sidewalk down which a girl is briskly walking towards the camera. With children jumping rope in the background, there is a close-up of the girl as she walks. There is a young man leaning on a car as he waits for the girl; the two greet and kiss. She asks him what he is doing there and why he is not in Aldama looking for a job. He tells her he got the job with *El Independiente*, and now they can be married. She tells him that she cannot see him at that moment because she must teach catechism to the children. They plan to see each other the following day at 8:00 a.m. mass.

Interrupting children playing with a ball in the church courtyard outside area, she tries to get the ball from them so that she can begin catechism. The ball rolls away, and the young man from the bus picks it up. Bringing the ball to the girl, and surrounded by the children, he asks for Father Benito. She points to where he can be found; and she and another young woman look somewhat longingly at the young man as he walks away. The first young woman asks who he is.

Another low-angle shot comes from inside a church looking from the altar towards the entryway. In the light of the entryway the dwarfed figure of the young man appears. He enters, and there is a close-up of him as he looks at the various statues lining the sides of the church. In the background a raspy voice is singing "Bendito sea Dios" (Blessed be the Lord). There is close-up of the not-so-attractive woman singing as she turns to look at the arriving young man, who returns her gaze looking almost frightened. He walks right up to and past the altar.

After a cut to a pair of hands unfolding a letter, the camera draws back to discover the young man standing respectfully in front of an older man with glasses who reads the letter, nods approvingly, and says, "Así que tú eres el padre Amaro" (So, you are Father Amaro).

With this, the viewer learns that this young man he has met on the bus is the new priest for Los Reyes, Father Amaro. At almost the same time, he learns, too, that the publicists' appeal to "ambition," has to be questioned. As Father Benito welcomes the young priest, he predicts a bright future for him, including being sent to Rome to study canonical law. With the innocent face of youth and eyes that seem to avoid direct contact, Amaro responds "Yo sólo quiero servir a Dios, padre" (I only want to serve God, Father). However, the viewer must remember that the first few minutes have oriented a reading of the film in which this young man, now known to him as Father Amaro, may change positions, as he had changed seats on the bus.

The first few minutes of *El crimen del padre Amaro* are somewhat unique in that they offer very little information as to film credits. Most films normally, at some point in their first few minutes, provide the viewer with information as to director, producer, cinematographer, actors, and so on; and quite often the end of the presentation of that filmographic information signals at the same time the end of the establishing moments. *El crimen del padre Amaro*, however, indicates the coproduction details, the film's title as well the subtext before beginning the filmic narrative, and it postpones all other filmographic information until the film's closing credits. But, eight minutes into the film, the matrix for reading the film is set; and, along with having an orientation as to how to read the film, the viewer has met not only Father Amaro, but the other principle characters, too.

Already the viewer has met Amelia. With her hair pulled tight to her head and combed like a young girl, with her inclination to ask questions (from the most mundane [What are you doing here?, the first words out of her mouth, or What would you like to drink?] to the most transcendent [What do you think about love, Father?]), with her custom of using little or no makeup, with her giving catechism, with her adolescent style of dressing, the viewer knows that Amelia is a virginal, devout girl, serious in her dedication and curiosity.

Now also identified for the viewer is the older, long-time village priest, Father Benito. With his Spanish (Castilian) accent, with his quick smile, the viewer knows that Father Benito originates from Spain.

The views of the first few minutes feature many utility poles and electrical towers, whose cruciform suggests an omnipresence of religion. The first cross viewed, though, seems to have fallen as it lies on its side. These images contribute to the configuration of a matrix for reading the filmic narrative. Through the panoramic view offered by and throughout the film, the viewer is above all made aware of the ills affecting the Catholic Church as an institution.

In this regard, first and foremost for the filmic narrative is the violation of the vow of celibacy. The first night he spends in Los Reyes, Amaro is awake and he sees a woman leave Father Benito's bedroom and go to the bathroom. Benito has had a years-long relationship with Sanjuanera, the owner of village restaurant. This relationship is then reproduced in the romance that the new priest Amaro and Amelia, Sanjuanera's daughter, will live. The first of many of the narrative's ironies, since Benito seems to boast that Amaro has been sent to be trained by him, the repetition of romantic/sexual involvement clearly serves the purpose of conveying a sense of the impossibility for change. The viewer sees an acceptance of this situation at one of the film's most transcendent moments. Men of the church are presented as flesh and blood, and Father Benito, overcome with guilt, declares that he will go to hell for his sins. Comforting him, and in her own way absolving him, Sanjuanera, though, answers this by saying, "El único infierno es la soledad" (The only hell is

El crimen del padre Amaro (2002). Reproduced with permission obtained through Daniel Birman Ripstein, Alameda Films (Mexico).

loneliness). Sanjuanera reminds Benito that these are the words he had used with her when he first "comforted" her.

Another ill affecting the Church as an institution is its association with certain powers or powerful groups. Specifically, what the viewer sees is an unhealthy association with drug kingpins and with politicians. Father Benito gets money from Chato Aguilar, one of the strongmen from that area, and with part of the money, a hospital is being built for the community. In exchange the Church remains passive in the face of expropriation of land by the drug barons at the expense of campesinos. At first, Amaro appears shocked by this situation, which Father Benito justifies with the rather undignified doctrine of the ends justifying the means.

A further questioning of the health of the Church is found in characters situating themselves on the margins, challenging the Church's limits and its conventions as an institution. There are two characters in *El crimen del Padre Amaro* who play this role, each with different tonalities. They are Father Natalio and the excentric parishoner, Dionisia. Father Natalio represents the connection with "guerrillas," campesino groups who oppose the forces of the drug traffickers. An indicant of liberation theology, this idealist priest tempts the young Amaro, inviting him to join with him in a kind of mountain utopia. Instead, it is Amaro who, inexorably, must give Natialio the news of his excommunication from the Church. Natalio indexes one more symptom, then, of a Church that is unable to control itself from within and whose power is exercised in order to hold on to power rather than to aid the people who are the Church.

Dionisia, on the other hand, is a symptom of the Church's inability to control from without. She exemplifies the syncretic believes and practices that are so prevalent in many parts of Mexico. She is the typical "bruja" (witch) who exists in the imaginary of every small Mexican town. She is fervently devout, she steals from the offering basket, she makes off with communion hosts to feed them to her (black) cat as though it were taking communion (she says to it, "El cuerpo del Señor" [the body of Christ]). Her house is filled with dolls and doll parts as well as numerous other amulets that index a spirituality built of pagan, folkloric, and Catholic parts. Physically and psychologically repulsive, she functions as a sort of anti-go-between who, rather than arranging for lovers to get together, orchestrates their final undoing.

The filmic narrative directly faces these ills. Father Benito and Father Amaro have a heated discussion regarding each's violation of celibacy. At another point, Amaro speculates that the Church would be better off allowing priests to marry. Gathered together as a group, the priests question the morality of accepting money donated by drug lord Chato Aguilar. During the first mass celebrated by the new, young priest, the other parishioners shush and shun Dionisia in her comments. In its ideological content, then, *El crimen del Padre Amaro* is rather clear. In an understated way, a spirit of criticism and denunciation pervades the film. What is uncovered is so obvious that the film, however, does little to invite deeper critical reflection regarding problems that affect the Catholic Church in Mexico and in Latin America.

Though Father Amaro initially convinces the viewer that he is not ambitious when he tells Father Benito that he only wishes to serve God, it is only a matter of time until his rhetoric and his behaviors reveal that his desires evolve into something much more akin to the publicist-perceived "ambition." At one hour and seventeen minutes into the filmic discourse, Amaro's "ambition" becomes manifest, taking on an overt, confessional form. Slowly, he has experienced, even begun to exercise, the power adherent to those of his vocation. In meetings with the bishop, he has received confirmation of a future that awaits him, that future that Father Benito had foreseen for him. After having visited and "speaking in confidence" with the bishop, the filmic narrative cuts to Amaro and Amelia playfully kissing, but their conversation is serious.

> AMELIA: Me gustaría amarte sin escondernos ... frente a todos.
> (I wish I could love you without having to hide ... in front of everyone.)
> AMARO: No, que eso no se puede. Nuestro amor es distinto.
> (No, that cannot be. Our love is different.)
> ...
> AMELIA: Hay muchos sacerdotes que cuelgan la sotana y se casan.
> (There a lots of priests who hang up the cassock and get married.)
> AMARO: No, pues, yo no. (Mirada de pánico)
> (No, but, not me. [With a look of panic])
> AMELIA: ¿Por qué no? ... Podríamos ir lejos.
> (Why not? ... We could go far away.)
> AMARO: ¿A dónde?
> (To where?)
> AMELIA: A donde sea.
> (Anywhere.)
> AMARO: ¿Para qué? ¿Qué? ¿Terminar como un profesor de civismo? ... Todo lo que estudié, ¿qué?
> (For what? What? And end up as some civics teacher? ... Everything I studied, what about that?)
> AMELIA: Pues, no es lo importante.
> (Well, that's not the important thing.)
> AMARO: No, lo importante es mi vocación.... Además un sacerdote puede hacer mucho por la gente.
> (No, the important thing is my vocation.... Besides, a priest can do a lot for people.)

In a conversation in the middle of which their "different love" is labeled as "carnal," Amaro's personal plans clearly take precedence over "carnal" concerns. In accordance with an analysis for which the viewer has been prompted to read in terms of panorama and crime, Amaro commits two "crimes" at the same time. Not only does he practice here his lust, but his response to Amelia's sweet speculation about a future together reeks of a pride that did not seem so visible in the films' establishing moments. The matrix established in those first few minutes does, however, orient towards a reading in which this character will change positions, and this would appear to be a change from the taciturn, generous young man from the bus.

With the road robbers whose crime confirms a readerly expectation created by the film's title, the viewer is oriented towards reading this film in search of crime. What the viewer finds is not a crime, but many crimes. What the viewer finds is not just crime in the strictly criminally illegal or civil sense, but also, crime in the sense of violation of the most traditional of moral principles. In this latter sense, "crimes" fall into the categories of the seven deadly or capital sins, or violations of the Ten Commandments.

In the first case, *superbia*, *hubris*, *soberbia* or pride, is most always considered as the original and most serious of the capital sins, and the source of other sins. As in the example of Amaro's pride alluded to above, his "crime" is believing that he is essentially better and more important than Amelia and others. Not only Amaro, but Benito and the bishop, too, as ministers of the Church continually fail to acknowledge the accomplishments of others, and they demonstrate an excessive valuation of their personal selves, as self is held out of proper position toward the God they purport to want to serve.

Pridefulness is not limited to Amaro; in fact, he has models for his behaviors in his two superiors. Father Benito's routine treatment of Amelia and Sanjuanera reveals that he thinks of them as servile and somehow beneath him. The way in which he speaks to them, failing always to thank them for their service, demonstrates an excessive admiration of his own self and station with respect to them. This same sense of self-importance comes through as well in Benito's dealings with the younger priests.

Very prideful, too, is the bishop. The filmic narrative punctuates the bishop's excessive admiration of his personal self and station in a verbal expression that is unexpected from a person in his position. Naked and overweight (perhaps indexing gluttony) the bishop takes a sits bath in his scrupulously clean, all-tile bathroom. As he does, he speaks on the cell phone with Amaro. The conversation has to do with the two scandals, but primarily it is about the problem of Father Natalio; and the bishop explains his plan, which Amaro will need to carry out. They will offer Natalio assignment to another diocese, and if he does not accept, excommunication. Succinctly and pridefully put in the bishop's words: "O se dobla o se chinga" (Either he bends or he's fucked).

In what for this viewer is the most shocking scene of the film, another "crime" of Amaro is his commission of the mortal sin of wrath. In the conversation in which he suggests to Amelia that she go away for nine months to then have the baby and then give it up for adoption, she reacts with extreme disappointment. When Amelia pledges to stay in Los Reyes and let everyone know Amaro is the father, he loses control, and he assaults her verbally ("No digas pendejadas. Cállate, pendeja." [Don't say that shit. Shut up, bitch.]) and physically, Amaro hits her in the face, strikes her repeatedly, and pushes her against the wall. While this attack certainly classifies as criminal assault, coming from an agent of the Church, its visual impact is one of sinful wrath, in which the young priest holds himself out of proper position toward the pregnant Amelia.

If the wrathful physical assault of Amelia is the most shocking of the sinful "crimes," in the panorama of the Church's ills, another capital sin is seen as less offensive. Presented within the mosaic of this institution's sins is gluttony. This lacking of virtue is indexed in the visual image of the corpulent bathing bishop to be discussed later. In terms of the filmic narrative, it is the figure (in two senses of the word) of Father Galván that is invested with conveying this aspect of the Church's frailties. At the meeting of the priests, Galván's function seems to be limited to preparing an abundance of food and consuming an excessive amount of alcohol. In fact, at the end of the evening, the other priests must awaken the overly imbibed priest and help him stand up to go off to bed. Undoubtedly, this is a minor detail within the film's narrative flow, and it is the least of the Church's mortal failings. But, it does contribute to an overall view, to the called for panoramic interpretation of the institution, especially as it contrasts with the image of hungry parish children outside the church scarfing down communion hosts with a cacao spread.

Within the panorama of ills that *El crimen del padre Amaro* presents to the viewer is the unreliability of the press. Rubén, Amelia's boyfriend, gets a job with the local newspaper, and with the zeal of a new reporter, the help of his father who provides him with important information, and photographs of Father Benito socializing with Chato Aguilar at the baptism, he is able to print an exposé implicating the Church with drug trafficker Chato. The headline in *El Independiente* reads "IGLESIA ALIADA AL NARCO Y GUERRILLA" (Church linked to drug traffic and guerrillas), and the exposé targets both Benito, for officiating the baptism of Aguilar's child, and Natalio, for arming the guerrillas. The bishop is very bothered by the scandal this creates for the Church, and he calls for Amaro, not Benito.

When they meet to "address Heaven's issues here on Earth," the bishop demonstrates only interest in Benito's desire to build too large a hospital and in the activities of Father Natalio. When Amaro suggests to him the link with the drug lord, the bishop's response only adds more brush strokes to the profile of the Church's ills of complicity:

7. Sins of Our Fathers

> Donde abunda el pecado, sobreabundará la gracia, hijo.... Hasta los santos cometen errores. Lo importante es reconocerlos.... Pero, no pongas esa cara de chupamirtos, pues, para Dios todo tiene remedio....
>
> (Where there is much sin, grace will be even more plentiful, my son.... Even saints make mistakes.... The important thing is to recognize them.... But, don't make that sour face, then, for God all things can be remedied.)

Following this official turning a blind eye, this official self-absolution, a "crime" of omission, the bishop tells the young priest that he has spoken with the editor of the newspaper and that the plan is to publish a rebuttal. The bishop instructs Amaro to take care of it.

To do so, Amaro prepares a rebuttal statement to be run in the newspaper, but the editor initially is reticent to print it. To the editor the rebuttal statement is excessive, and to Rubén, it is lies.

> GALARZA (editor): Los lectores nos tienen confianza desde hace muchos años. Siempre publicamos la verdad.
> AMARO: ¿Y la verdad se sostiene de los lectores? ¿O de los anuncios? ... Se lo digo porque al señor obispo le bastaría una llamada para acabar con la publicidad.
>
> (GALARZA [editor]: Our readers have trusted us for years. We always print the truth.
> AMARO: And the truth is paid for by the readers? Or by the ads? ... I tell you this because it would take the bishop only one phone call to put an end to your advertising.)

As a result of prideful blackmail, commandment-breaking lies are published, as a statement by the mayor is published, and Rubén loses his job. The editor must cave to the self-interests of the Church and politicians, and thus, part of the panoramic view of Mexico is the insinuation of a corrupt or corruptible press.

The fact that a statement from the mayor also will be published highlights another piece of the film's panoramic mosaic of Mexico, the self-interested union of Church and politics. The bishop ends his conversation with Amaro as a nun brings him a telephone. As the filmic editing cuts from bishop to mayor, the telephone link metonymically indexing their self-serving relationship, the viewer ascertains that both are involved in the financing of the hospital and money laundering, and that between the two of them, they will create an explanation for the story reported by the newspaper. Their prideful self-interested lies are offered at the expense of truth and in benefit of criminal activity. As part of the reading of the film as a panoramic view of Mexico, it is necessary to include a toxic, mutually self-serving alliance between Church and elements of the government.

Among the ills plaguing contemporary Mexico is criminal activity. Reflective of economic disparities, lack of employment, underdevelopment, and so on, criminally illegal activity takes the form of kidnapping, robbery, drug trafficking, and murder. Many of these illegal acts are presented or represented in the panorama of Mexico that *El crimen del padre Amaro* presents for viewer to read.

Centrally represented, though never presented, is the illegal activity of drug trafficking, without which no panoramic profile of contemporary Mexico would be complete. While the viewer never sees drugs being transported, sold, or even consumed, he reads a panoramic view of Mexico in which illegal drug traffic is never more than a few degrees separated.

Rather than being present in action and deed within the filmic discourse, drug traffic is indexed. So much a part of the panoramic view of Mexico is this phenomenon that it appears to be an accepted fact of life. Everyone, from the newspaper editor to the bishop, knows who Chato Aguilar is. As in the case of the newspaper headline, to reference him is to reference drugs. In the first meeting of the five local priests, Natalio defends his own activities by alluding to the noxious presence of narcocommerce:

> Y yo le estoy hablando de narcos ... de los que invaden las parcelas de los campesinos, de los que les obligan a la gente a sembrar amapola o los amenazan o los matan si se niegan a trabajar para ellos ... pistoleros y narcos.... Y no me digas que el señor obispo no sabe que el Chato Aguilar lava dinero con limosnas, limosnas para su pinche centro.
>
> (And I'm talking to you about narcos ... the kind who invade the land of the campesinos, the kind who forces them to plant poppies or they threaten them or they kill them if they refuse to work for them ... gunmen and narcos.... And don't tell me that the bishop doesn't know that Chato Aguilar launders money with his offerings, offerings for his damned hospital center.)

In their second meeting, the one following the publication of the newspaper exposé, the three younger priests seem to know very well that the money that comes to/through the church is drug money, but Benito defends his actions with a "criminal" defense:

> MAURO: ¿Y del Chato Aguilar, Padre?
> (What about Chato Aguilar, Father?)
>
> BENITO: Una cosa es una cosa y otra cosa es otra cosa. Yo siempre pensé ... he pensado que al dinero para las buenas obras que ... no hay que ... no hay que ponerle peros.
> (One thing is one thing and another thing is another [That's entirely different.] I always thought.... I have thought that we shouldn't be too picky about money for good works.)
>
> MAURO: ¿Aunque venga del Chato Aguilar?
> (Even though it comes from Chato Aguilar?)
>
> GALVÁN: Es lavado del dinero narco, Padre.
> (It's laundering drug money, Father.)

BENITO: El verdadero lavado es ante Dios.... Es dinero malo que se hace bueno.
(The true cleansing is before God.... It's bad money that becomes good.)

The priests refer to the illegal activity by name, and with each mention of Chato Aguilar, drug trafficking is further indexed. Illegal drug activity is metonymically indexed as well by the Chevy Suburban with the tinted windows, the bodyguards with machine guns, Chato's gated estate, and the narcocorrido music ("Soy el chingón de chingones").

After the baptism ceremony at Chato Aguilar's, two men stand at urinals in a bathroom. A close-up focuses on the man on the right who turns to the other man, the photographer for the event. From underneath his cowboy hat and through a wry smile, the first man asks the photographer if he can buy a few of the photos, and then he asks for film of all the photographs he has taken. When the photographer refuses, the first man pulls out a big knife and stabs the photographer to death. He takes the photographer's film, and leaves him bleeding and slumped on a toilet. He has taken the photos because he appears in a number of them, but a few of them featuring Father Benito and Chato Aguilar arrive anonymously to the hands of the newspaper editor.

Not only does this cold-blooded, criminally murderous act index levels of violence in Mexico, it serves as well to profile corruption in Mexico at all levels. The guy who kills photographer and a guy who works with Father Natalio are the same man. The viewer realizes this later when he recognizes this murderer working among the campesinos with Father Natalio in the mountains. Initially dressed as one of Chato's men and present at the baptism, and later dressed as a campesino and working to raise a building, this man is working two different ethical sides. If, as it would appear, he is responsible for the photos being leaked to the press, it is not the drug lord whose interests are served. On the other hand, the exposé could serve to reduce the pressure Benito is exerting on Natalio to conform.

And, the circle of violence is complete when this same man is found murdered in a ditch outside of town. In the mountains, Natalio celebrates the man's funeral just as Amaro arrives to give him the news of his excommunication.

The filmic narrative's other death is not strictly speaking a murder, but it is the result of illegal activity. The culmination of the melodramatic discourse is, of course, Amelia's tragic death. She bleeds to death as the result of an illegal abortion gone wrong. This death indexes several aspects of the film's panoramic profile of Mexico. The first of those is abortion.[2] In a context in which women's rights lag behind and in which the Catholic Church continues to hold influence, a woman seeking an abortion must turn to illegal, backstreet practitioners.

For these reasons, Amelia commits the "crime" of having an illegal abortion. In her case, this is a crime of last resort, and it is the result of other "crimes" that have led to this tragic filmic climax. When Amelia first tells Amaro that she is pregnant, his unfeeling response comes from a prideful place. Unable to take her feelings into account, his only reaction is to ask her if she is certain about being pregnant. Thinking only of himself, he later suggests to Amelia that she go to Aldama until the baby is born and give it up for adoption. When she rejects the idea, the prideful priest is immediately on board with the idea that she could marry her former boyfriend, Rubén; thus solving Amaro's problem and giving the baby a family. Even though she openly confesses that she hates Rubén and he has now moved on to have Amelia's friend as his new girlfriend, Amelia humiliates herself by seeking out her old boyfriend and suggesting that they marry.

During the opening bus ride, with the old man's reference to "el otro lado" (the other side) as he speaks of his economic plans to Father Amaro, the film's first few minutes index the precarious economic situation of many Mexicans as part of its panoramic view of the country. This "otro lado" is, of course, the United States; and as the old man references it, the filmic narrative indexes the escape valve that the U.S. has been and continues to be for Mexicans unable to thrive within their own country's economy.

The film's first few minutes index an economic situation that later visual images only serve to underscore as part of the panoramic view of Mexico as it enters the twenty-first century. Throughout the film, visual images constantly offer contrasts between extreme poverty of many and the comfort of the priests and politicians and a kitsch opulence of the narcos. At one end of the spectrum, the church's sacristan lives in a hovel that does not even have doors, and his constant preoccupation seems to be keeping the parish's rusty, old pickup truck running. Both he and Amaro recognize that the truck should be replaced, but it never is, and it ends up being the place of Amelia's miserable and tragic death. Further overdetermination of misery is found the in the sights and sounds of the sacristan's daughter, Getsemení. Obviously born with birth defects, she is bedridden, subject to physical spasms, and does not speak. She does seem to be aware, though, and her pitiful groans and grunts punctuate the visual images of misery, as she seems to react not only to religious imagery but to what goes on (Amaro and Amelia's trysts) in the space adjacent to where she lies. A spastic witness, Getsemení is perhaps the film's only character who is not guilty of some "crime."

When Father Amaro seeks out Dionisia to enlist her help in solving the problem of Amelia's pregnancy, he goes to where the old woman lives. A shack among shacks one on top of the other, her home is a cramped collection of cats, idols, amulets, and candles that speaks to poverty almost as much as do Dionisia's clothes and rotting teeth.

The priests on the other hand, with the exception of Natalio, who lives in the mountains with the campesinos, do not seem to want for material comforts. When they gather as a group, they are well stocked with beer, and they eat very well. Both Benito and Amaro eat well at Sanjuanera's restaurant, where they are waited on with reverence and respect. Their living space is very comfortable, and while it is not overly spacious or opulent, it is attractive and relatively modern with abundant foliage and television so that the priests can watch soccer matches and the news. Images of Amaro sleeping in a bed with obviously ironed sheets speak to a considerable level of comfort.

These two material levels pale in the face of the images of narco opulence. When Father Benito agrees to go to Chato Aguliar's estate to perform the baptism of his daughter, the viewer accompanies the priest through the guarded gates into a world as equally overdetermined as that of the poor spastic sexton's daughter and of the "bruja" Dionisia. If the name Getsemaní indexes garden, her real situation is anything but a garden. Benito's arrival up a winding drive through well-manicured, stately gardens indexes that other Gethsemane/Getsemaní bringing into contrast disparate realities in Mexico as it brings the father to buildings mixing baroque and neoclassical styles. Here, Father Benito is greeted by Chato himself, wearing the requisite gold chains and other jewelry and surrounded by bodyguards. Music is being played live, and numerous well-dressed guests wander through the balloon-decorated estate sipping drinks.

At the very end of what have been posited here as the film's first few minutes, the viewer meets Father Benito, whose Castilian Spanish accent is noticeable. The presence of Spaniards within the panorama of Mexico presented by the film is further determined by the presence of another character, Rubén's father, disliked and disconnected from the town's people because of his anticlericalism. As if the accent of the two Spaniards were not enough to confirm the Spanish presence, both offer further evidence in their utterances. At one point, for example, Benito invokes the presence of Spaniards as he employs the very Spanish epithet "gilipollas" (assholes), and Don Paco makes a direct, even historical, reference to Spain, "Como en el Franquismo, coño!" (Like during Franco, damn it!). The somewhat overdetermined presence of Spaniards indexes thoughts of colonization that in turn suggest subalternity. Within the reading of a panoramic view of the country, the suggestive presence of this element helps to emphasize the portrayal of a situation in which the Mexican people have little voice or agency.

From the sum of visual images in the mosaic of a panoramic view of Mexico programmed by the film's establishing moments, the viewer must read worrisome, sweeping contrasts between the best and the worst of material situations the country has to offer.

With the children at play in the film's opening shot, the reading of the film is set up for an element of playfulness. And, while the bulk of the filmic discourse is very serious stuff, even melodramatically so, there are humorous moments. The humor is normally either caused by a tongue-in-cheek editing, or it is intentionally black or slightly sacrilegious. In the scene immediately following a sexual encounter between Amaro and Amelia, she is found with her friend in the church drilling catechism with some children. As they chant the Ten Commandments, one little boy interrupts to ask, mispronouncing as he does, "¿Qué es formicar?" (What does formicate mean?), to which he receives an incongruous answer, "Quiere decir que no vas a comer carne en Semana Santa, Chente (It means you cannot eat meat during Holy week, Chente).

"No quiero más escándalos pues…. Imagínate si los periódicos nos armaran otro numerito" (I don't want any more scandals, then…. Imagine if the newspapers were to do another number on us). So says the bishop to Amaro during one of the latter's visits to him. Of course, the specific reference at the time is to Father Natalio and his operations outside of Church sanctions. But, the words are pronounced immediately contiguous to a cut from the tryst in which Amaro shrouds a nearly naked Amelia in an altar cloth and tells her she is more beautiful than the Virgin. The ironic juxtaposition of the scene he has just witnessed with the bishop's reference to scandal is not lost on the viewer, who must see this humor in the editing as further evidence of the Church's "criminal" obliviousness.

Ironic, too, is the scolding that the children outside the church receive from Dionisia. As they huddle eating communion hosts spread with a syrupy concoction, Dionisia disperses them shouting "La hostia es sagrada. Se van a condenar, mocosos" (The host is sacred. You will be damned, you brats!). The irony is patent as the source of the recrimination is a witch who feeds hosts to her cat as though offering it communion. But, while humorous, the other irony here serves as a highlighting contrast to the "crime" that the viewer has witnesses immediately prior. The preceding scene between Benito and Amaro in the chapel seems to involve desire to atone for their transgressive behaviors *vis-à-vis* celibacy. But, the prideful discussion and argument between the two priest ends in a threat of blackmail. The "crimes" (fornication, pride, blackmail) of the priests seem even more criminal when the viewer considers them juxtaposed with the thought of damnation for children eating.

If, as suggested, Getsemení is the only innocent among the film's characters, her father, the sacristan, is nearly so. But, his innocence and servitude become victims of Amaro's prideful wrath. After Martín innocently (or not so innocently?) lets Father Benito know that Amaro is giving special instruction to Amelia in the empty room at his house, Benito checks up on them, realizing the nature of the two young people's meetings. When, due to Benito's heart attack, Amaro takes over, he fires the sexton. Having packed all his belongings onto a horse-drawn cart, her father places Getsemaní on the cart among some blankets. She clutches in her wrenching hand the crumpled page of a religious pamphlet that Amelia had given her. A close-up of the wrinkled paper shows an image of Christ and the words "Ven y sígueme" (Come and follow me). The association of paths to be followed is darkly humorous here. Surely, the last thing the viewer wants to do is to follow Getsemaní, but the contrast adds to the overdetermination of the Church's, through Amaro, decisions that always seem to be on the wrong side of "right."

The Church's disconnect is emphasized by a visual image repeated twice[3] in the filmic editing. There are multiple extreme long shots of the Los Reyes church, white and with its two bell towers, ensconced amid the trees of the mountainside. These visuals are doubly expressive. On the one hand, their extreme long shot form reinforces the imperative to give a reading of the filmic narrative as panorama. And, on the other, their figurative value suggests the Church's (institution) isolation, since, in these shots, the church (building) is the only human vestige visible among the lush green foliage.

These are not the only visual images of church or churches to index a less than favorable relationship of Church to the institution's faithful. Among medium range exterior shots of the church or church towers of the church, there is a shot that features the long run of steps that rise to the church's entrance.[4] A low angle medium shot looks up the steps to the church above. In the foreground sit old men as other people descend, and the camera looks up towards the church above. A standard use of this kind of low angle shot is to convey a sense of powerlessness, and this would seem to be an appropriate significance to attach to this technique's use in this case. It suggests the common people's powerlessness in the face of institutions.

These visual images work to emphasize one of the elements in the narrative, that of the role of the Church within a panoramic view of Mexico. In that narrative, one thread involves Father Natalio and his supposed adhesion to liberation theology. Because this is an ideology unwelcomed by Church hierarchy, and because it brings with it accusations as well as the appearance of non-conformity, Natalio is punished. Though Amaro would seem to sympathize and empathize with Natalio's dedication, it is he who first threatens and later delivers the news of excommunication. This action highlights the Church's being on the wrong side of "right." The filmic narrative shows a Church that favors drug lords but persecutes Natalio, who seems to be an agent of good for the people. This is a disconnect between institution and those it should serve, and visual images are of use in underscoring that disconnect.

If there are visual images that offer an interpretation of the Church as isolated from the concerns of its parishioners, there is another detail in the filmic narrative that supports a negative view of the institution's connection to the people. In this case, however, instead of offering a cue as to physical-spatial disconnect in the isolated church building, the figurative reference is auditory. In addition to the described images of the church with its bell towers, the filmic discourse also focuses occasionally[5] upon the bell towers. The tolling of bells, of course, is a connecting medium between the church and its faithful. Yet, the filmic discourse discovers for the viewer that the sexton puts in a cassette tape into a cassette player in order to play the sounds of tolling bells that are sent out through speakers attached to the bell towers. The figurative suggestion seems clear. The Church's connection to the people is not natural; it is false, fake.

It is only in Amelia's funeral that the Church displays a more natural relationship to the people. The filmic discourse initiates the funeral sequence with a brief shot of a bell tower and, then, cuts to the new sexton pulling on the ropes to ring the bells. The natural sound of bells tolling fills the soundscape, and there is a suggestion of at least a temporary establishment of a natural connection with the people's pain.

Though a simplistic reading of *El crimen del padre Amaro*, might have the viewer see the "crime" as choosing ambition over love and the consequences of it, the reading produced by the matrix established in the film's first few minutes points to a plural and polysemic understanding of the film's title "crime." The reading of the film discovers not just one crime, but also multiple "crimes." And, as it does, it uncovers "crime" understood in multiple ways. Crime is illegal activity in terms of violation of legal codes, as in the case of banditry, drug traffic, murder, and abortion. Crime is immoral activity in terms of violation of the Ten Commandments, as in the case of murder, lying, idolatry, and fornication. Crime is immoral or unethical activity in terms of capital or mortal sins, as in the case of pride, lust, gluttony, and wrath.

If one of the effects sought by this volume is to raise the consciousness of the film viewer as to the importance of a film's first few minutes in creating an orientation for interpretation, *El crimen del padre Amaro* also offers to that same viewer a lesson in the importance of a film's last few minutes. If a film's first few minutes are important in the establishing of a matrix with which to read the film, the last few minutes often provide the final key to that reading. If it is important for the viewer to pay close attention from the very beginning, it is just as important to pay attention to the very end of the film.

This film's final moving, yet ironic, images are of the funeral mass for "nuestra querida hermana" (our beloved sister) Amelia, presided over by Father Amaro. To the right of the casket, a small choir accompanied by a guitar sings, ending the mass by entrusting Amelia's soul to heaven, as the camera zooms back to a wide angle shot of the church. As the choir finishes its hymn, the screen goes to black, and quickly film credits begin to appear. At that point, the soundtrack changes to extra- or non-diegetic music. First, heard is a classical choir accompanied by orchestral violin music. As the choir sings its "Amen," at two minutes into the closing credits, narcocorrido music, accordion and all, takes over the soundtrack. It is the music of Los Cardenales de Nuevo León singing the "Corrido del padre Amaro" (The Ballad of Father Amaro). The content of this narcocorrido reinforces the reading of the film, not merely as a story of ambition, seduction, and tragedy, but rather as a panoramic view of Mexico. Referring to the function of sound and image, Frederick Luis Aldama, in his 2013 book, supports the same conclusion when he writes:

> The soundscape reinforces the film's message: the tragedy rests not only on the shoulders of Amaro, who seduces a young girl and indirectly causes her death by coercing her to have an abortion, but also on a corrupt and decrepit social tissue herein the church, the state, and a drug economy all nest together [41].

While the film's publicists seemed to want to insist on a conflict between ambition and love, most of the reactions to and studies of *El crimen del padre Amaro* focus on the film as an exposé of the "ethical turpitude within the Catholic Church" (Blackwelder), or as a "crushing critique of corruption and criminal behavior in the Catholic Church" (Aldama 85). Some studies and other reviews seem to repeat or perpetuate the reaction of the *New York Times* on the film's 2002 release in that city:

> "El Crimen del Padre Amaro," a suds-filled political melodrama that bashes the Roman Catholic Church in Mexico with a contempt that verges on hysteria, could be accused of many things, but timidity is not one of them.

At least one of the earliest reactions to the film, though, did not ignore that *El crimen del padre Amaro* itself suggests to the viewer a much wider reading. In a review written only a month after the film's release, Agnes Poirier suggests the film's panoramic signifying potential, when she writes that "Carlos Carrera's fifth feature is a compelling, multi-textured social drama that fires some hard questions at the role of the Catholic Church amid the extremes of wealth and poverty." Not much of the critical bibliography on the film follows up on the "hard questions" or the "multi-textured" nature of the filmic narrative.

El crimen del padre Amaro can pretend to canonical status for several reasons. As its very intertextual/intermedial genesis would suggest, being born of a nineteenth century novel, its story traverses temporal boundaries. With its Oscar, Golden Globe, and Goya nominations as Best Foreign Film, its many international awards, and its many Ariel awards, this film has the resumé to claim interest and attention. Much initial attention to the film came from surrounding circumstances and its ability to index them. In the

U.S., for example, the film was released at a time when pedophile priests captured headlines, and in Mexico, the Church and other groups protested the film's content. The controversy itself obviously contributes to the film's status. With the controversy that surrounded the film upon its release well behind, it is freer to be the object of a growing analytical bibliography.

The DVD jacket for the English-language version of *El crimen del padre Amaro* orients the viewer as follows:

> A recently ordained priest ... is sent to help an aging priest run a small parish church in rural Mexico. Upon arriving at his new post, he meets a beautiful young woman with a religious passion that borders on obsession. Quickly, her passion for her faith becomes helplessly entangled in a growing attraction to the new priest. But when the handsome priest crosses the line that separates temptation from sin, he finds himself torn between the divine and the carnal, the righteous and the unjust.

This orientation reads as if the film has been misnamed, and that it perhaps should have been more properly titled "the crime of Amelia." Such an orientation reveals a machismo that ascribes a responsibility to Amelia for the narrative events far beyond a level that is reasonably visible in the filmic discourse. And, this not only misplaces guilt, but it also blinds the viewer to all of the film's semantic potential. While the romantic entanglement between Amaro and Amelia does form a central narrative thread, it is not the only narrative thread. In fact, even though some studies would like to reduce the complexity of the narrative in *El crimen del padre Amaro* to that of a telenovela (soap opera), it is more complicated than that.[6] It is a weaving of multiple threads (for example, Benito's story, Rubén's story, and Natalio's story) into a panoramic tapestry of Mexico. An orientation as provided by the DVD sets the viewer up to miss not only the significance of the film but also significant portions and the richness of the filmic narrative. The fact that the story of the two young people's relationship is a primary element in the structure of the film's discourse does not mean that a reading of the film should begin and end in the melodrama that is their tragedy.

In *El crimen del padre Amaro*, the establishing moments do not even suggest love story. So, the viewer should know that the story of a "priest [who] crosses the line" is but part of a larger meaningful whole. This film's first few minutes provide a matrix for the reading of this film in terms of a panoramic view of Mexico, and reading the film in this way leads to viewer to a richer reading experience and an understanding of many "crimes."

◆ 8 ◆

THE NEED TO SEE AND BE SEEN
Icíar Bollaín's 2003 *Te doy mis ojos (Take My Eyes)*

> Duele el dolor. Te amo.
> Duele, duele, Te amo.
> Duele la tierra o uña,
> Espejo en que estas letras se reflejan.
> —Vicente Aleixandre, "Humana voz,"
> *La destrucción o el amor*

The very title, *Te doy mis ojos*, suggests the importance that deixis might play in the reading of this film. In linguistic terms, the viewer is called to think about identifying the interlocutors, the "tú" (you) and the "yo" (I) invoked by the indirect object "te" the verb "doy" (implying "yo" [I]), and the possessive determinant "mis" (my), respectively.

Deixis and deictic interplay take on a great importance in the understanding and analysis of the Spanish film *Te doy mis ojos*. Textual evidence offers a couple of possibilities upon which there is a potential base for the deictic organization in *Te doy mis ojos*.

Deixis is a language modeling system by means of which relationships of person, place, time, deference and discourse are organized. Deictics are those linguistic elements that make reference to or substitute for persons, things, places, time or concepts; and their interpretation depends upon or assumes the existence of another element within the same discourse or within the context of this discourse. Deictics indicate relationships between participants and the content of a message, and they contribute to the discourse's internal cohesiveness and its external links.

Deixis is also a human activity, and as such, functions can be attributed to it, depending upon what deixis is trying to achieve, beyond its strictly linguistic aspects. There are, then, a personal deixis, a spatial deixis, a temporal deixis, as well as a social deixis and a discourse deixis. Additionally, there is an empathetic deixis.[1]

This last kind of deixis, empathetic deixis, has to do with the metaphorical use of some deictic in order to indicate distance or proximity or intimacy between the speaker and a referent. It is often the use of a demonstrative or other deictic in order to underscore the emotional distance or closeness of the speaker. For example, the speaker can employ "this" in order to show that he feels an emotional closeness to a referent; on the other hand, he might employ "that" to show an emotional distance from a referent. In literature, the effect created by deixis can impact the degree of closeness that a receiver-reader feels to a text. Lesley Jeffries (2008) has shown that the movement, change, or shift from one deictic to another [deictic shifting] can create a situation in which the reader feels more involved or identifies more with a text. To the degree that such involvement or identification [reader-involvement] resembles or invokes empathy on the part of the receiver-reader, it is possible, in these cases, to think in terms of deixis invoking the empathetic function.

Within this modeling system, deictics are those elements of language that lack their own meaning. They are those linguistic elements, words, or expressions that only take on a specific meaning when they are used in a specific communication. Deictics cannot be described without recurring to aspects of the speech act, to aspects of the enunciation's context. As such, deictics are references whose interpretation depends on the extralinguistic context of the enunciation; their interpretation, their ultimate meaning depends on the communication situation. Central to this system of relationships is the speaker, since everything is organized as a function of the speaker. Additionally, it must be understood that the speaker and the deictic organization that flows from him implies the moment at which he speaks, the place where he speaks, his gestures, and his place within the discourse. A full deictic reference not only establishes relationships with the rest of the elements within the enunciation, it further depends on the participants being aware of its constituents. Information about time, place, and the roles of participants are all related to the referent of a deictic.

Deixis is a universal phenomenon, and, as a modeling system, it is situated between Semantics and Pragmatics. Although deixis does not lend itself to a verification of semantic-truth and giving an enunciation meaning or determining its denotative value on the basis of a deictic expression is problematic, a deictic clearly creates a referential meaning. When a deictic is used, the speaker is referring to a specific entity.

Deixis must be studied at the level of discourse, and its study necessarily has an empirical component, though perception and cognition also must be kept in mind. In order to identify the referent, the receiver's attention must be oriented and guided toward the referent. Not only is it necessary to know what the elements of the enunciation are, but also how they are perceived. A component of that orientation can be gesture. The gestural function can complement the invocation of deictic function in as much as it can refer the situation to a particular referent, orienting as to the who, the what, the when, and the where of the deictic field.

A deictic expression creates a mental space in which sender and receiver are equally present at a specific moment. That mental space evoked by the deictic expression implies a shared understanding of the deictic center, understood as the perspective from which events are viewed. As has been mentioned, deictic organization most commonly revolves around the speaking-I, but it is also possible to think in terms of a "de-subjectivisation" in which the deictic center is diverted from the subject-sender towards the receiver or the referent (Adamson 2008). A de-subjectivisation or re-centering of the deictic center on a "non-speaker" (non subject-sender) clearly has implications for a possible empathetic function.

Deriving, then, from the Greek δεῖξις (to signal, reference) and being part of Pragmatics, deixis is manifest in different deictic expressions that can refer to people, objects, places, or spatial-temporal spaces, and it should be studied not only in internal linguistic terms but also within the context in which it is found. In examining deixis in *Te doy mis ojos*, it will be necessary to keep in mind not only the characters' enunciations in their diegetic time and space, but also deictic shifts with their implications for the deictic center, for (real as well as metaphorical) gestures, and for the context in which they achieve their reference. Not only will it be necessary to describe the implications of deictics for the organization of the filmic discourse, but also, and more importantly, their function as an invitation to empathize.

Deixis and a deictic gambit are very important to the understanding and interpretation of the heroic film *Te doy mis ojos* from Spain. Released in 2003 and the winner of seven Goya awards,[2] *Te doy mis ojos* is a heroic film because it takes on the taboo theme of marital violence. But, it is heroic not just because it takes on this touchy topic but also because of the way in which it does it. Contrary to much of contemporary international film that seems to live off of violence, the filmic discourse of *Te doy mis ojos* does not spend its time showing explicit violence. Rather, the filmic discourse is based on metonymy; the film's director, Icíar Bollaín, has the intelligence to show the effects of gender violence, forcing the viewer to tie up loose ends, as her film ably expresses how deep and lasting the trauma associated with the phenomenon is. Heroic, too, is the film's willingness to present different perspectives. It would have been easier and safer, perhaps, to create a story that would make the viewer completely and blindly take the side of the victim. Heroically, though, the narrative discourse dedicates almost as much narrative space to the victimizing husband, who, in spite of his efforts, is depicted as falling deeper and deeper into the tragic reality that his violence has created.

In this way, *Te doy mis ojos* contrasts with another Spanish film that premiered just two years previous, *Sólo mía* (Javier Balaguer, 2001), whose thematics is also centered on gender violence. The title of this film, director Javier Balaguer's *opera prima*, could offer the possibility of a deictic gambit of the kind that will be analyzed in this chapter on *Te doy mis ojos*, but here the director of *Sólo mía* decides to go in a more conventional direction.

Sólo mía begins with a black screen over which are heard a couple's angry shouting and screaming ("Cállate," "Suéltame," "Eres la culpable," "Eres una fracasada," etc.["Shut up," "Let go of me," "It's your fault," "You're a failure."]). Suddenly, a gurney explodes through the swinging doors of a hospital hallway; doctors and nurses frenetically tend to a bleeding patient. The scene flashes to transport the viewer to an apartment whose floor shows drops of blood and sweat, and the signs of a struggle. Ángela, smoking and with an exhausted, angry air, gets up among the shadows and moves towards the center of the shot. Looking more and more closely into the camera, which assumes the perspective of Joaquín, who labors to breathe, Ángela says to him:

> Mírame, eh, mírame ... ¿Sabes quién soy? ... ¿Me conoces? [...] ¿Has intentado mirar una, una sola vez, ponerte en mi lugar? ... Ahora, te toca a ti. [...] Se acabó, pero, se acabó para siempre.... Y no vuelvas a levantarme la voz.
>
> (Look at me, huh, look at me.... Do you know who I am? ... Do you know me? [...] Have you once tried to look, just once, to put yourself in my place? ... Now it's your turn ... [...] It's over, but it's over forever.... And don't every raise your voice at me again.)

From the first few minutes of *Sólo mía*, it is clear that deixis and perspectivism combine to invoke revenge, and *Sólo mía* is about revenge like that seen, for example, in *Kill Bill* (Quentin Tarantino, 2001). Using flashbacks, this is a film that explains the reasons for that revenge with several scenes of abuse, physical as well as psychological, as it follows the couple's evolution, from the moment of their wedding, to parenthood, through reproaches, insults, and excuses on through to divorce, followed by harassment and court fights, all the while showing how defenseless, impotent, and afraid women can feel as victims of marital violence.

It is possible to refer to this topic as "taboo" because of the place this thematics holds within the historical flow of contemporary Spanish film, which cannot be fully understood without looking back and contextualizing in view of what the Franco dictatorship and the Francoist censorship practices were.

The Francoist dictatorship tried to impose a model for an organic society with a gender politics that denied women any sort of individual autonomy.[3] Given the complexity and variety of the phenomenon of gender violence, it is very difficult to understand in its many dimensions. Yet, it does seem plausible to suggest that any environment in which one person is deemed as inferior, less valued, or demeaned is an environment that creates conditions for the abuse of that person. The Francoist dictatorship institutionalized a mentality that conceived of woman as a passive subject with respect to her husband as the active subject. This became an engraved model with an enduring sediment of many dimensions in Spanish society where only slowly does it appear to fade away. The subjugation of women was legitimized, creating a situation that undoubtedly could contribute to gender violence, if not as causative, as an attitude making it seem tolerable. A reflection and evidence of this type of "tolerant" attitude is seen in several of the characters in *Te doy mis ojos*. In the film, several of the men in the therapy group, Pilar's mother, and the policeman who takes Pilar's statement (Chapter 36)[4] seem to view a certain level of violence in couples as normal, and they seem to be inclined to tolerate it.

This is one of the ways in which violence is represented in *Te doy mis ojos*, a film that prefers not to present violence directly in favor of offering to the viewer "eyes" to see marital violence's causes and effects. In this case, the viewer does not have to see the actual violence, but he knows it is there because he sees how many people are willing to tolerate it.

During the almost four decades of the Francoist dictatorship, an official censorship apparatus did not tolerate any semiotic material which could undermine confidence in the regime. It was a censorship apparatus that took care of any text that might attack the Regime or its policies, the Church, or morality. Beginning in 1963 there was an "aperturista" (relaxing) movement in censorship, but it was not until 1966, when under the direction of Manuel Fraga Iribarne, the Ministry of Information promulgated a law which gave specificity to censorship norms, which let artists know what they were facing. For example, clear cinematographic norms were published, specifying a list of taboo themes that included divorce, abortion, euthanasia, and the use of birth control.

In this way, with the publication of a specific list of proscribed topics, what was created was a kind of "to do" list for later Spanish films. In theory, the idea of a "to do" list for Spanish film had been started by the Conversaciones Cinematográficas de Salamanca (Salamanca Conversations on Cinema) (1955),[5] for later films, for films of the last years of the dictatorship, for the films of the "transition," and for films even further on. These "to do's" have been progressively addressed; the taboo themes have been taken on one by one, and among the last taboos to fall were the problem of unemployment in *Los lunes al sol* (León de Aranoa, 2002), gender violence in *Te doy mis ojos* (2003), and euthanasia in *Mar adentro* (Amenábar, 2004).

Te doy mis ojos tells the viewer the story of Pilar, a victim of mistreatment within her marriage, who tries to re-make her life. She begins to work as a cashier at the tourist visitor area in the Iglesia de Santo Tomé which houses El Greco's famous painting *El entierro del Conde Orgaz* in Toledo,[6] and through her new job she begins relationships with other women. Antonio, her husband, sets out on his own self-search and recovery, promises to change, and seeks the help of a therapist. In the words of the film's director:

> *Te doy mis ojos* cuenta la historia de Pilar y Antonio pero también de quienes los rodean, una madre que consiente, una hermana que no entiende, un hijo que mira y calla, unas amigas, una sociedad y una ciudad como Toledo que añade con su esplendor artístico y su peso histórico y religioso una dimensión más a esta historia de amor, de miedo, de control y de poder. ("Escribe")
>
> (*Te doy mis ojos* tells the story of Pilar and Antonio, and also of those who surround them, a mother who acquiesces, a sister who doesn't understand, a child who watches and is silent, some girlfriends, a society and a city like Toledo which adds, with its artistic splendor and its historical and religious weight, one more dimension to this story of love, of fear, of control, and of power.)

Te doy mis ojos is the work of Icíar Bollaín, who is known for being a socially committed director. With this, her third feature film,[7] her ability to tell stories, as a director as well as a scriptwriter,[8] is once again confirmed. Hers are stories where even the titles provoke interest and offer keys for the reading of the films.

The title itself, *Te doy mis ojos*, as it foregrounds the earlier delineated deictic modeling system, suggests the importance of personal deictics/deixis to the understanding of the film's true meaning (meanings) and to the structural aspects of this acclaimed work of Spanish cinema. The presence in this title of "te" (to you) and "mis" (my) (besides the implicit "yo" [I] in "doy" [I give])[9] actualizes the personal deictic system and immediately poses the need to clarify who is the speaker around whom a series of precise meanings should coalesce.

In fact, within *Te doy mis ojos*, deixis must be analyzed on two different levels, those levels corresponding to two different communication situations. The first of these two levels has to do with the construction of the filmic discourse, and it is the communication of the director-scriptwriter (sender of the message) with her public, the viewer (receiver of the message). On the other hand, deixis also must be analyzed within the diegetic space. That is, deixis must be examined at the level of the enunciations between and among the characters that populate the narrated/narrative world. These enunciations possess their own internal meaning in that same discourse, a meaning created by the communication situation between and among characters.

8. *The Need to See and Be Seen* 165

On that other level, at the level of the construction of the filmic discourse itself, there is other textual evidence upon which it is possible to base another deictic organization in *Te doy mis ojos*. This level concerns the communication established between the director and the viewer.

Te doy mis ojos (2003). Reproduced with permission from Producciones La Iguana S.L.

The repeated premise is this volume has been that in its first few minutes, every film declares itself in the face of reality. It is in those first few minutes where films present the viewer with a matrix for their interpretation. The first few minutes are crucial because it is there that viewers are given an orientation as to how they are to read the film. *Te doy mis ojos* is not an exception.

In its first three minutes *Te doy mis ojos* provides the viewer with a matrix for its own deictic organization, a first key for how it is to be read. It is nighttime and, after a brief pan of an apartment building, the camera allows the viewer to enter one of those apartments where he meets a woman (Pilar played by Laia Marull), who frenetically is filling a suitcase, and then wakes her son. She leaves with him in search of a taxi. Since none will stop for them, they take a bus. The viewer sees them walk across a plaza in the historical old section of Toledo. During these introductory scenes, the film credits periodically begin to appear. Pilar knocks at the door of her sister's house, and, in an emotional welcoming scene, Pilar discovers she has gone out in slippers. It is at this instant that there appears the last of the credits, all of which have been shown superimposed upon the images narrating the flight the viewer is witnessing. This last of the credits is, of course, the one that identifies the director, Icíar Bollaín. Immediately the screen goes to black in order to move on to a *fade-in* of the film's title *Te doy mis ojos*. In other words, the credits end with the identification of the director, which is followed by a metaphorical closing and opening of the eye of the camera.

Metonymically, then, in the filmic discourse, through the intimate association of continuity in the film editing, director Icíar Bollaín appears as the one who "pronounces," the one who enunciates the phrase "Te doy mis ojos." This fact is emphasized by the very difference in the credits themselves. The credits, until the title appears, are presented superimposed upon the images that are happening in the world that these images are creating. As soon as the credit identifying the director disappears, though, that narrated world is momentarily left behind by the blank screen upon which appears the title "TE DOY MIS OJOS" (I GIVE YOU MY EYES) (yes, all of the title is in emphatic capital letters). This leaving behind the events of the narrated world is important because it reinforces the attempt to underline the communication that exists between sender and receiver, between director and viewer.

Because of the intimate association of contiguity between the name in the credits and the enunciation "Te doy mis ojos," the director is identified not only as the one responsible for organizing perspective of the filmic discourse, but also as the "I-sender" of the message (the film), organizer of the communication. If the director is the speaking/sending "I" around whom deictic relationships are organized, the "you," receiver of the message, is the viewer. With the film being the message sent, what is emphasized is a communication situation that always exists in film in which director and viewing public are enjoined in a sender-receiver relationship.

In this communicative situation the same dual deictic quality is seen as will be observed later in the intimate conversation between Pilar and Antonio. On the one hand, the sender chooses "tú" (you, familiar) in order to refer to the person with whom she is communicating: the receiver-viewer is referred to as "tú." In terms of social deixis, the choice of "tú" in order to refer to the receiver-viewer with whom she speaks through the "te" in "Te doy mis ojos" establishes a relationship of closeness between sender and receiver, and it implies a desubjetivization that changes the deictic center towards a different referent. Although this might seem strange at a level of familiarity where there is a lack of acquaintance (for which "usted," [you, formal] referenced in "le," might seem more appropriate), its use seems extremely legitimate given the intimacy of the thematics to be treated. Through personal deixis, the invocation of a close relationship between the "yo" and the "tú" participants in the communication situation, in which *Te doy mis ojos* is the message, works as a foreshadowing of the intimate character of what is to be treated in the 103 minutes that follow. At the same time, the initiation of that communication in a space outside of that intimate narrated world, in that blank screen, also serves to make clear the social, societal character of the message to be sent.

At the beginning of the film, the viewer is witness to the desperate flight from the family domicile of a terrified woman and her son. Beginning with the playing of a solitary piano, then a violin, the camera pans a nighttime suburban scene of "pisos" (apartment complexes). The viewer enters the window of one of them, to find a woman frantically searching for clothes to put in a suitcase, and waking her son to get him dressed. Except for the mother's exhortation to wake up and get dressed, the scenes are wordless. Leaving the building, mother and son cross the parking lot to hail a taxi. No taxi stops for them, and the camera focuses on Pilar's troubled expression. Seated on a bus, Juan stares out into the darkness, and his mother, assuming an almost-fetal position on the bus seat, examines her feet wrapped in red cloth slippers. The bus passes by the old city walls of Toledo; then mother and son cross one of its plazas in the darkness. Climbing one of Toledo's old narrow stone streets, they arrive at a door where Pilar presses the call button, and identifies herself. She waits anxiously until her sister answers the door, asking if Pilar is all right and asking what has happened.

The introductory sequence ends with a desolate disconnect that is all Pilar can manage to say, "¡Que me he venido en zapatillas!" (I came here in my slippers!), while she cries in the arms of her sister. Because of the central value of personal deixis (the implied "yo" [I] re-enforced by the pronoun "me" [my]) in that sentence, the viewer knows that his analytical attention, his readerly mission, has to be focused on Pilar; it establishes her as the subject of the sentence and as the organizing subject of the film. Because Pilar is the "yo" (I), the viewer knows that the movie is about her "doy" (I give) and, given the prevalence of metonymy as an expressive discursive device in the film, it is, quite simply, an intimate portrait, made to stand for the thousands of other cases.

Because of the terror Pilar shows and because of the disconnect of the sentence she utters, the viewer intuits that the film must be read as the search for an explanation as to why she has taken flight. After the first few minutes of viewing the effects of a woman taking flight,[10] the viewer realizes that his readerly mission is to ascertain what has caused her to take flight and where it will lead her. The scholar-reader knows, for example, that he must answer the question: What has caused this woman to go out without shoes?

Because of that introductory sequence and the apparent disconnect with which it ends, the viewer is made aware also of the principal, and powerful, rhetorical device which will inform the film's structure. It is metonymy; it is cause and effect. As *Te doy mis ojos* treats the issue of domestic or gender violence, its rhetorical stance will be to *not* present violence itself, but rather it presents the effects of it, and at times, it even indexes its causes. What would make a woman leave her home this way in the middle of the night wearing only slippers? Rather than show us a horrific violent episode, this film chooses to show the viewer its terrified effects.[11]

A scene from very next day, in the light of day, underscores this metonymical technique of showing effects of violence rather than showing the violence itself. Pilar´s sister goes alone to her sister´s flat to pick up some things for Pilar and her son, Juan. As she moves through the place, she (and the viewer) sees what may well be the aftermath of a domestic battle, complete with broken dishes, food on the floor, and food splattered on the walls. While Ana searches for things to pack, she comes across some papers in a dresser drawer. They are emergency room reports that document visits for physical injuries. Again, it is the effect of violence that which allows the viewer to learn of it, without the violence having to be explicitly played out on screen.

One cannot overstate the value of Laia Marull´s acting in the metonymical representation of violence in *Te doy mis ojos*. Worthy of the Goya Award for Best Actress in a Lead Role, Marull´s performance shines in Pilar´s facial and physical expressions. Her usually makeupless face, is a mirror of the effects of violence as it skillfully reflects the chill of the fear of violence in the presence of an abusive husband, the humiliation of his comments, the frustration of having a mother who does not understand (more metonymy), the doubts about making it on her own, and the apprehension in the face of Antonio´s promises. With Laia Marull´s portrayal, Pilar genuinely looks out-of-control and terrified as her gestures metonymically index violence. They communicate her suffering as the result of past violence and the fear that she could again suffer at the hands of the man she loves. It is not necessary for Bollaín to portray explicit physical violence against Pilar, because Marull´s performance incarnates the ever-present effect of that violence.

From within *Te doy mis ojos*' diegetic world, and from the perspective of the storyline, these words "Te doy mis ojos" are spoken by Pilar. Pilar flees in the middle of the night from her flat, located on the residential outskirts of Toledo[12]; she takes her eight-year-old son with her. In her flight she seeks refuge at the home her sister, who is a restorer of art and who lives a free sort of life with her Scottish boyfriend. One more victim of marital violence, Pilar has set in motion an effort to re-make her life, and she has begun to work. Her husband seeks her out because he loves her and wants to get her back. He has sought the help of a therapist, individual and group therapy. He promises to change. One afternoon, instead of going to eat with her girlfriends, Pilar goes with Antonio, who is waiting for her. They have a romantic (sexual) interlude at her sister's house. Naked in bed, tenderness and passion carry them away and immerse them in the following conversation:

> ANTONIO: (*Acariciándola*) Hace mucho que no me regalas nada ... como esas orejas o esa nariz.
> ([*Caressing her*] It's been a long time since you have given me anything ... like those ears or that nose.)
> PILAR: Di lo que quieres y yo te lo doy.
> (Tell me what you want and I'll give it to you.)
> ANTONIO: Todo, lo quiero todo. Desde allí hasta aquí. (*Señalando con el dedo desde los pies hasta la cabeza.*)
> (Everything, I want everything. From there to here. [*Pointing with this finger from feet to head.*])
> PILAR: Ya lo tienes.
> (You already have it.)
> ANTONIO: No, quiero que me lo des.
> (No, I want you to give it to me.)
> PILAR: (*Reticente*) Te lo doy.
> ([*Reticent*] I'll give it to you.)
> ANTONIO: Pero todo ... lo quiero todo. Todo ... los brazos, las piernas, los dedos.... Me tienes que dar todo. Dímelo.
> (But everything.... I want everything. Everything ... arms, legs, fingers.... You have to give me everything. Say it.)
> PILAR: Te doy mis brazos. (*Se besan.*)
> (I give you my arms. [*They kiss.*])
> ANTONIO: Las piernas ...
> (Legs ...)
> PILAR: Te doy mis piernas. (*La penetra.*)
> (I give you my legs. [*He penetrates her.*])
> ANTONIO: Los dedos ...
> (Fingers ...)

PILAR: Te doy mis dedos.
(I give you my fingers.)
ANTONIO: El cuello ...
(Neck.)
PILAR: Te doy mi ... mi cuello. (*Hay más pasión.*)
(I give you my ... my neck [*There is more passion.*])
ANTONIO: Los pechos ...
(Breasts ...)
PILAR: Te doy mis pechos.
(I give you my breasts.)
ANTONIO: Tu espalda ... tus hombros.... (*Poseyéndola.*)
(Your back ... your shoulders.... [*Possessing her.*])
PILAR: (*Entre suspiros.*) Mi espalda ... mis pies.... Te doy ... te doy mis ojos ... y mi boca ...
([*Sighing*] My back ... my feet.... I give you.... I give you my eyes ... and my mouth ...)[13]

While Pilar surrenders herself physically to her husband, she offers him a precious "gift," "Te doy mis ojos" (I give you my eyes). Deictically, and in conjunction with the personal function, the organizing "yo" (I), Pilar, underscores intimacy by identifying the other as a "tú" (you, familiar). She underscores the intimate, loving nature of a couple. She underscores as well the representational structure of the filmic discourse. The choice of "my eyes" as her "gift" calls attention to the fact that Antonio, and the viewer, must "see," not the violence itself, but rather the effects of violence through the eyes of the victimized.

Others have highlighted the obvious importance of eyes, the feminine gaze, and vision in *Te doy mis ojos*. Their studies of the filmic discourse analyze Pilar's recovering her vision and her ability to see herself as crucial to her slow emancipation, recuperation, or escape (Soliño and Thibaudeau), or to her becoming a feminist model for other women (Blanco García). Both Soliño and Thibaudeau emphasize the role of art (painting) and access to its visual pictorial language as part of the film's insistence on the sense of sight and as important factors in Pilar's progressive recovery.

> No es de extrañar que la emancipación de Pilar pase por la pintura, arte visual por excelencia, en la medida en que su alienación pasa por la entrega de sus ojos a Antonio ... [Thibaudeau 237].
> (It is not strange that Pilar's emancipation comes through painting, visual art *par excellence*, in as much as her alienation comes through her giving her eyes over to Antonio.)

But, these other studies do not recognize Pilar's empathy in recognizing herself or part of herself in paintings.[14] Nor do they recognize her attempts/invitations to get Antonio to "see" or empathize with her as victim.

On the other hand, and again through the metaphorical use of the idea of giving one's eyes, the organizing "I" of the deixis is invoking empathetic deixis. Thus, at that other level, the director invites the viewer to identify mentally and emotionally with the "other," in this case, the characters whose story is being narrated. With her eyes, with her vision, the director will put the viewer in the place of those subjects.

In view of the general tense dynamics of this marital relationship, it would be possible to also interpret the use of "mis" (my) in "Te doy mis ojos" in terms of an empathetic function. Until the point in the conversation at which Pilar offers her precious gift, it is Antonio who sets the pace; he controls the dialogue. Each time he suggests something, Pilar responds offering to Antonio what he has asked for (brazos, piernas, dedos, cuello ... [arms, legs, fingers, neck...]). Before he can ask for more, though, with "te doy mis ojos" (I give you my eyes) it is Pilar who takes the lead. Within the established pattern of asking-and-offering, it is Pilar who now asks, in hopes Antonio will offer. Thus, it is possible to postulate that she momentarily takes charge of the discourse, changing the deictic function. Consistent with the intimacy of the moment, the discourse is deictically marked by the yo-tú (I-you[familiar]) that marks for closeness or intimacy between the two participants in the discourse. But, it is possible to postulate that upon saying "te doy mis ojos," Pilar invokes an empathetic deixis, in which what is requested is the mental and emotional identification of one subject with the state of mind of the other.

Thus, as she uses figurative language ("te doy mis ojos"/I give you my eyes), Pilar asks Antonio to "see," to "look at" the state of affairs of their intimate relationship from the perspective of her state of mind. In an empathetic deixis, "mis ojos" (my eyes) now contrasts with "tus ojos" (your eyes) in order to create an invitation to empathy in which Antonio should identify mentally and emotionally with what Pilar is feeling and going through. It is an invitation for him to look at things from her perspective. It is as if she were saying to Antonio: "Antonio, "mira lo que estás haciéndome," "mira lo que estás haciendo a nuestra familia, a nuestro hijo," "mírate a tí mismo como yo te veo" ("look at what you are doing to me," "look at what you are doing to our family, to our son," "look at yourself like I see you"). In a communication situation in which deixis is organized by Pilar and Antonio as interlocutors, it is an invocation of the empathetic function in which Pilar asks Antonio to assume her place as the organizing "yo" (I) of the deixis so that the linguistic change, the changes in the deictic center, might produce affective understanding.

The invitation/invocation of empathy is a plea for love. The noted psychologist, father of Humanistic Psychology, and a founder of psychotherapy, Carl Rogers consistently maintained that empathy is more than a set of skills. For empathy to be effective there needs to be an attitude or mindset of empathy.

Empathy works, only when it comes from a person who really cares about people and who has a compassionate heart. Love precedes understanding and knowledge. Love heals, even when knowledge fails. Empathy without love can be patronizing and condescending, but empathy with love never fails to build up the other person. Love is a pre-condition for empathy. So, when Pilar calls for empathy, she does so out of love and in a search for love.

It is important to note also that Pilar also gives her mouth to Antonio, without him requesting it. She gives up, then, not only her possible ownership of the discourse but also her ability to denounce and self-define. Her invitation to empathy and her figurative request that Antonio "see" her implies that she be seen as victim. It is a tacit acceptance of herself only as victim. This foreshadows an ending in which Pilar realizes that she must see herself, find herself, know herself; it is an ending in which she also recognizes that she has been unable to speak.

With the presence of a victim, violence is indexed as the cause. There is yet another way in which violence, the central theme of this film, is represented, and it is again, and still, through the representation of its effects, and not through its presentation. Through the metaphorical use of the idea of giving eyes, the organizing "yo" (I) of the deixis invokes empathetic deixis, begging the other to see and feel the effects of his violence. So too, does the director, at that other level, invite the viewer to identify mentally and affectively with the "other," in this case, with the characters whose story is being narrated. With her eyes, with her vision, (metaphors for the camera), Icíar Bollaín puts the viewer in a position to empathize with some of the film's other subjects.

As has already been seen, this invitation to empathy that is extended at the linguistic level of deixis is reinforced at the level of the narrated material in such a way as to seem that the director is proposing empathy as part of the solution to gender violence. There are different contrasting moments of the storyline that clarify this intention for the viewer.

The first of these moments occurs with the men in group therapy. They are there because they abuse their women; and, although Antonio and the other men are supposedly there of their own volition, they seem to form a closed community and to be unreceptive to the psychologist's ideas. With them, the most revealing moment is the session in which the psychologist asks them to do a role-play. In an effort to lead them to an awakening of consciousness of and responsibility for their behaviors,[15] he assigns them the roles of husband and wife in a scene in which the husband comes home after a hard day at work. Of course, none of the men wants to play the role of the woman, and, when they do the role-play, the dialog between them is absurdly reserved and disconnected; it is comical, and it would be even more so if it didn't involve so much tragedy. The "husband" cannot think of any question

8. The Need to See and Be Seen   173

or commentary other than his own preoccupation with being fed. The dialog does not go any further than a series of "¿Qué?" (What?), and "¿Qué de qué?" (What do you mean what?).

This exercise underscores two qualities in these men. The first quality, seen already in the previous scene, is that they are unable to seriously talk about their emotions, not even in a relaxed, artificial scenario like a role-play. But, more importantly, we see that they cannot put themselves in the place of another person, and that they are unwilling to try. They are incapable of empathy. This fact is crucial to understanding their mentality; they abuse their partners because their partners, supposedly, "provoke" them, since they are out "peleando con la vida" (struggling with life), and they have certain expectations of their wives. They cannot imagine the perspective of their wives much less the terror that they inspire in them. They are incapable of identifying mentally or affectively with their partners' state of mind.

There are studies that suggest that a person is better able and more inclined to feel empathy with a person similar to himself or herself. But, in order for that to be possible, it is necessary that the first person knows himself or herself. And, it is clear that Antonio, like the majority of abusers, does not know himself, and he does not feel.

In another group therapy session, the therapist suggests to the men that in the face of the temptation to move towards violence they should seek refuge in a world of tranquility that can calm them down. When he asks them about times when they have felt at peace, two of the men respond with "pesca" (fishing) and "la parra" (the vineyard). But, when he asks Antonio, his only response is "No sé, no me acuerdo" (I don't know, I don't remember). Then the therapist asks the men to write in their notebooks about that place of refuge as if they were writing to a friend. Antonio is unable to write anything, and, following several attempts to put something on paper, he simply lets go of the pen. An even more apparent evidence of Antonio's inability to get in touch with his own feelings is manifest in a meeting with Pilar on the banks of the Tajo River. She arrives with fear written all over her face, and she can only listen as Antonio parrots the things he has heard in the therapy sessions. The blank notebook, thrown into the river, and the couple's final negative shouts ("¡A tomar por culo todo!" [To Hell with everything!]) underscore that there has been no empathetic progress.

This same inability to affectively identify becomes very focused on Antonio. Viewers are witnesses to a one-on-one exchange between Antonio and his therapist that begins with the question of what Antonio misses about Pilar. After much prodding, Antonio comes up with a response, and the conversation continues on to a standstill:

THERAPIST: ... algo, algo de ella que te guste mucho.
   (... something, something that you like about her.)

ANTONIO: El ruido.
(Noise.)
THERAPIST: ¿El ruido?
(Noise?)
ANTONIO: A ver, es que.... O sea, Pilar.... Pilar, Pilar se mueve muy rápido pero hace poquito ruido ... ¿entiendes? ... No sé lo que es, si son las pulseras, la ropa, no sé qué es pero se mueve muy ligerita y hace muy poquito ruido.... Y es como suyo ese ruido, ¿sabes? ... Y cuando está en casa, me quedo como atontado escuchándola.
(Let me see, it's that ... well, Pilar.... Pilar, Pilar moves around really quickly but she makes very little noise.... You understand? ... I don't know what it is, if it's her bracelets, her clothes, I don't know what it is, but she moves about lightly and she makes very little noise.... And, it's like it's hers that noise, you know? ... And when she's at home, I'm like caught up in listening to her.)
THERAPIST: Antonio, ¿tú le has pedido disculpas alguna vez?
(Antonio, have you ever asked her forgiveness?)
ANTONIO: (*Pausa*) ¿Pero cómo?
([*Pause*] But why?)
THERAPIST: Que sí, vamos, ¿si le has pedido perdón?
(Yes, come on, have you asked for her forgiveness?)
ANTONIO: ... (*No responde*)
(... [*No response*])

As the camera focuses on Antonio in expectation of his rejoinder, all he can muster is a furrowed brow and a perplexed look. The perplexity in Antonio's eyes in response to the therapist's question shows the viewer Antonio's, inability to empathize. His vacant stare is as much as to say "I cannot imagine what it is that I should apologize for," as it reveals to the viewer that Antonio is unable to identify with Pilar's feelings.

What is also revealing about this conversation is Antonio's choice of "noise" as that which he likes about Pilar. In fact, it is not the noise Pilar makes that Antonio likes, but rather the lack of it as he confesses that "hace poquito ruido" (she makes very little noise). This is consistent with the image created earlier in which Pilar surrenders her voice, allowing herself to only be viewed as victim. Also, it is imagery that is completed in Pilar's final recognition that she had no voice (in Chapter 39, to Ana, "Tú me escuchaste pero yo ... yo no podía hablar" [You listened to me but I ... I was unable to speak]).

As if to emphasize this lack in the abusive men, the film offers a contrast with them in the form of another community formed of its own volition. It is Pilar and the women with whom she works, but they are very different from the men because they have an inclusive, sharing relationship. They enjoy their time together, and they have an interest in each other's lives (they ask Pilar about her sister and her Scottish boyfriend; they ask about Lola's boyfriend, for example). In contrast with the abusive men who show no ability to imagine the other side of a conversation, these women do it very well. While Lola speaks with Chato outside the bar, two of her friends watch them and they add their own "soundtrack," inventing the dialogue that is taking place outside. It is comical because the two women seem to follow the conversation rather well; they show an aptitude for understanding, for following, even for getting inside another's conversation from different angles. These women show their capacity to "de-subjectivize" and to identify with the "other," and, with this, Icíar Bollaín would seem to postulate empathy as a requisite to responding to the problem of gender violence. With this also, it is again clear that Bollaín prefers to represent violence metonymically, in this case through its causes, in the inability to empathize, rather than to present violence, which might well undermine the call to empathy.

To show empathy is to identify with the feelings of another. It is the mental or affective identification with the state of mind of another person. As the therapist from the film suggests, it is putting oneself in the place of the "other." The capacity for empathy depends directly on being in touch with one's own feelings and identifying them.

Repeatedly the viewer sees Antonio unable to articulate his own feelings. He does not write in his notebook, when he and the other men are asked to write occasions in which they have felt at peace. We see him flounder when he is asked to articulate what he loves about Pilar, what he misses about her. If one has never experienced a certain emotion or a certain sensation, it is difficult to comprehend what another is feeling, whether it is a question of pleasure or pain.

That is why the therapist invites the men in group therapy to try to express what they feel when they abuse their wives, or that they try to express what they have felt at some moment of peace in their lives.

That is why, also, another key moment in the film, the denouement, is marked by another deictic interplay. This key moment occurs after the only episode in the film that openly presents violence, a violence that is brief, but singularly humiliating, lasting only 2 minutes and 37 seconds (Chapter 35). After it, and almost in a state of shock, Pilar realizes, as she repeats almost absent from herself, that Antonio "ha roto todo" (has broken everything). Pilar resolves that she must leave Antonio.

And, what follows that determination, and Antonio's failed suicide attempt, is an intimate conversation between Pilar and her sister Ana in which deixis assumes a revealing role. It is again empathetic deixis invoked by the metaphor of the eyes or seeing.

>   PILAR: No me puedo volver con él. Ya no.... Ana, necesito que te quedes con Juan hasta que lo pueda llevar conmigo.
>   (I cannot go back to him. Never again.... Ana, I need for Juan to stay with you for a while until I can take him with me.)

ANA: Claro.
(Of course.)
PILAR: ¿Lo harás?
(Will you do it?)
ANA: Claro, lo que tú quieras. Vamos, si quieres vivir aquí, si necesitas dinero, lo que quieras.
(Of course, whatever you want. I mean, if you want to live here, if you need money, whatever you want.)
PILAR: Seguro que ... que Lola y Rosa me pueden ayudar.
(Of course.... Lola and Rosa can help me.)
ANA: Tengo la sensación que no he sabido ayudarte.
(I have the sense that I haven't known how to help you.)
PILAR: Tú me escuchaste pero yo ... yo no podía hablar.
(You listened to me but I ... I couldn't speak.)
ANA: ¿Y ahora puedes?
(Can you now?)
PILAR: Tengo que verme.... Tengo que verme.... No sé.... No sé quién soy.... No sé quién soy.... Hace demasiado tiempo que no me veo.
(I have to see myself.... I have to see myself.... I don't know.... I don't know who I am.... I don't know who I am.... I haven't been able to see myself for such a long time.)

With this, with the metaphorical "Tengo que verme" (I have to see myself), and at the level of the storyline (also trauma line), what is again invoked is empathetic deixis. In spite of his efforts to change things, Antonio has been incapable of empathy: he has not been able to put himself mentally and affectively in Pilar's place. His inability to come from a loving place "has broken everything." Since Antonio has been incapable of accepting Pilar's loving, deictic invitation that lends its name to this heroic film, *Te doy mis ojos*, Pilar has to assume the role of subject as well as the role of the "other"; she has to identify her state of mind and identify mentally and affectively with it. Only in that way will she be able to overcome the terror that has had her disconnected from herself.

And so it is that for the final time in the film, violence is represented and not presented. As augured in the film's first few minutes, the overriding metonymical device in the film has been the choice to represent violence through its effects rather than to present it. As the viewer has seen, the effects of domestic violence range from the circumstantial in which one leaves home wearing only slippers to the existential in which what is lost is one's identity.

On two discursive levels of *Te doy mis ojos*, invitations to empathy are extended. At the epic level of the events narrated, Antonio is incapable of mentally and emotionally identifying with Pilar's state of mind. And, at this level, the responsibility for a solution to domestic violence is left to Pilar, who must leave her abusive husband and find the non-victim Pilar.

There is the other level, that meta-level of the construction of the filmic discourse, at which the director openly reveals herself, the level at which she locates herself in the place of the organizing "yo" (I) of the discourse, and she invokes an empathetic deixis through which the receiver-viewer is invited to identify her/himself with what the "others" on screen are feeling and suffering.

It is at this level that *Te doy mis ojos* has been characterized herein as a heroic film. Counter to mainstream cinematic preferences for graphic violence and sex, and consistent with the matrix established in its first few minutes, this film uses metonymy as its discursive choice, where effects index causes. Heroic, too, is the choice to invite the viewer to identify with Antonio's feeling and suffering. It would have been much easier, perhaps to elicit viewer reaction offering up Antonio as a monster not, as the viewer sees him, as apparently normal (Cruz 72).[16]

Along these lines, Begin (2009) asserts that *Te doy mis ojos* "subverts the voyeuristic expectations of mainstream film in order to affirm the cinema's capacity for fostering social discourse and awareness" (32). But, at this level, the response remains open. Bollaín has invited the viewer to empathize, to see the thematics of gender violence through her eyes, through her words, through the images she chooses of its effects indexing latent causes. Is the viewer, unlike Pilar's husband Antonio, capable of enough human empathy so that the response to the director's invocation/invitation in *Te doy mis ojos* is one of understanding and mental/emotional identification?

The empathetic viewer, though, must be capable of enough intelligence to realize that empathy is only a necessary first response to the problem of gender violence; because as Pilar's final determination shows, it is not a solution.[17] The first step is empathy, an identification with the other that will allow recognition of the problem. But, the ultimate solution, as one abused woman, a participant in the video-forum organized to gauge reception of *Te doy mis ojos* put it, "Creo que para solucionar el problema hay que centrarse quizá más en quién provoca esa situación" (I think that, in order to solve the problem, it is necessary perhaps to focus on the one who provokes the situation) (Fernández Romer 287).

In the course of this volume's consideration of some canonical Spanish-language films, on occasions, notably the cases of *La historia oficial*, *Camila*, and *Fresa y chocolate*, critical reception and analysis have included critique of films *vis-à-vis* their daring in presenting controversial or sensitive subject matter. With these three films analyzed earlier, a common critique points to a bourgeois aesthetic employed to allow the films to appeal to a wider viewership. *Te doy mis ojos* is like the other three films in that none of the films creates a readerly matrix asking to be read in terms of its potential as a blueprint for the solution to political or social ills. Each establishes, instead, a film-specific orientation as to how the film itself is to be read. It is on the basis of the project each film sets out for itself that it ought to be analyzed and judged. But, it is from a perspective similar to critiques of the other three films that Duncan Wheeler (2012) levels one of his major criticisms of *Te doy mis ojos*, which, for him, "In spite of its ostensible restraint and social-realist veneer ... essentially places a cultured and distinctly Spanish spin on Hollywood's victim empowerment frame" (478).

All of this notwithstanding, Icíar Bollaín's film (nor any film) cannot and should not be judged on the viability of any solution that a scholar-viewer-critic might want to see proposed there. The film must be judged according to its success in achieving the goals it sets for itself. In its first few minutes, *Te doy mis ojos* sets up a matrix for the invocation of or the invitation to empathy. In its establishing minutes, *Te doy mis ojos* also primes the scholar-viewer for a metonymical discourse that eschews the presentation of domestic violence, representing it instead through its effects. The film has acquired canonical status precisely because it masterfully does both.

FILMOGRAPHY

Entries are in the order of chapters 1 to 8.

1. *El espíritu de la colmena*
(The Spirit of the Beehive)
Víctor Erice, 1973

Production Company	Elias Querejeta Producciones Cinematográficas S.L.
Executive Producer	Elias Querejeta
Production Manager	Primitivo Álvaro
Screenplay	Víctor Erice, Ángel Fernández Santos, Francisco J. Querejeta
Director of Photography	Luis Cuadrado
Editor	Pablo G. del Amo
Art Director	Jaime Chávarri
Set Director	Adolfo Cofiño
Costume Design	Peris
Wardrobe	Angelines Castro
Sound	Luis Castro, Luis Rodríguez, Jean Michel Sire
Music	Luis de Pablo

95 minutes

CAST

Ana	Ana Torrent
Isabel	Isabel Tellería
Fernando	Fernando Fernán Gómez
Teresa	Teresa Gimperra

SYNOPSIS

The year is 1940, and little Ana is a quiet girl who lives in an isolated Spanish village on the Castilian meseta with her parents Fernando and Teresa and her older sister, Isabel. Her father spends his time tending to and writing about his beehives. Ana's mother dreams about a distant person, to whom she writes letters.

A truck brings the movie *Frankenstein* to the village and the two sisters go to see it. Ana is particularly interested in the scene where the monster plays with a little girl, then accidentally kills her. Ana asks her sister why the monster killed the girl. Isabel tells her that the monster did not kill the girl and they are not really dead. She tells Ana that everything in films is a lie. Isabel says that the monster is like a spirit, and Ana can talk to him if she closes her eyes and calls him: "It's me, Ana." Teresa writes and sends a letter to someone she misses.

Ana's closest companion is Isabel, who cannot resist playing tricks on her little sister. Ana's interest increases when Isabel takes her to an abandoned farmhouse, which she claims is the monster's house. Ana returns alone many times to look for him but finds only a large footprint. One day, Isabel screams from a distant part of the house, and when Ana comes to investigate, she lies perfectly still on the floor, pretending to be dead. That night, Ana sneaks out. In the next scene, a fugitive republican soldier leaps from a passing train and limps to the abandoned farmhouse.

Ana finds the soldier hiding in the farmhouse. Unafraid, Ana feeds him and later brings him her father's coat, with his watch in the pocket. This wordless friendship ends when shots in the night kill the soldier. The police connect Ana's father with the fugitive through the coat and watch, and Fernando realizes Ana's complicity from her reaction when he produces the pocket watch. When Ana runs to visit the soldier, she finds only fresh blood on the ground. Fernando confronts her as she gazes at the blood, and she runs away.

Wandering alone that night, Ana finds a poisonous mushroom like those her father previously warned about. Later, Ana has a vision of the monster; like in the 1931 *Frankenstein* film, he gazes sadly at her and kneels beside her as they are reflected in the water. In a voiceover, Teresa reads a letter she wrote, but she burns it unsent, implying the love affair is over or that she will stop communicating with him.

A search party finds Ana unharmed the next morning, but she refuses to speak or eat. The doctor assures Teresa that Ana will gradually forget the shock she's just experienced. Teresa cares for Fernando, who has fallen asleep at his desk. The film ends as Ana recalls what Isabel said about calling the monster, and she stands alone at her bedroom window and she closes her eyes.

2. *Bodas de sangre*
(Blood Wedding)
Carlos Saura, 1981

Production Company	Emiliano Piedra Producciones
Executive Producer	Emiliano Piedra
Coproducer	Ángel Escolano
Production Manager	Gustavo Quintana
Screenplay	Carlos Saura, Antonio Gades, Alfredo Mañas; Federico García Lorca (play)
Director of Photography	Teo Escamilla

Filmography—2. Bodas de sangre

Editor	Pablo G. del Amo
Set director	Rafael Palmero
Wardrobe	Francisco Nieva
Sound	Bernardo Menz
Music	Emilio de Diego
Choreography	Antonio Gades
71 mins	

Cast

Bride	Cristina Hoyos
Groom	Juan Antonio Jiménez
Leonardo	Antonio Gades
The Groom's Mother	Pilar Cárdenas

Synopsis

A black and white, though seemingly aged and tending towards yellow, photo still of an entire dance troupe posing. Credits are superimposed as there is a slow zoom in on principle characters, Bride, Groom, Groom's Mother, etc., in the center of the photograph. Credits end.

Cut to a prop master who enters a dressing room, turning on lights and attending to costumes, etc. Members of the dance troupe begin to enter and situate themselves. Dancers arrange make up and personal items at their individual makeup mirror stations.

After Antonio asks for the photograph (García Lorca and La Barraca), he places it on the mirror. He then puts on his makeup. As he does, in a long voiceover, he tells the story of how he came to be a dancer.

Beginning as a bellhop and trying many things, Gades ended up at a dance school at the suggestion of a neighbor. He was discovered by Harry Flemming, who put him to work dancing mambo in a cabaret. He moved on to work with Pilar López, and later he decided to stay in Paris to study dance and other arts. Discovering similarities with Vicente Escudero, he describes his admiration for and relationship with him. He even ended up living where Escudero had lived in Paris.

His makeup finished, Antonio goes into the rehearsal hall to warm up. Their makeup finished, the other performers also go the rehearsal hall, at one end of which is a mirrored wall; they warm up for a few minutes, and Antonio explains and demonstrates. All leave to put on costumes, and to check props. Antonio paces, gives final instructions (there will be no stopping), and all find their places.

The dance rehearsal portion of the film is divided into six scenes, which flow seamlessly one to the other. In the first, the mother helps the groom to dress. She discovers a knife and takes it away from him. They hear a horse's gallop, an omen.

The second scene begins with the morning of the wedding, and Leonardo's wife, dressed for the wedding, awaiting his late arrival. She rocks the baby and sings a lullaby, but when he enters, she stops. She and Leonardo perform a dance of jealousy and reproach. When he rocks the cradle, she takes the baby away, and Leonardo leaves.

In the third scene, Leonardo is in deep thought. His imagination brings the bride into view. The bride is being prepared for the wedding ceremony. A love dance begins between the bride and Leonardo, joining them in passion and sensuality. A woman attendant comes to dress the bride in her wedding dress, and the dance fades.

Leonardo enters after the wedding ceremony and he sees the whole wedding party. Everyone is celebrating, and the bride and groom dance, while Leonardo broods. There is a brief pause in which the entire group (sans Leonardo) poses for a photograph, the same as the black and white photograph seen behind the film's opening credits. When his wife accepts to dance with another man, Leonardo takes the opportunity to dance with the bride. Leonardo's wife reacts with jealous rage. The bride and groom again dance, but Leonardo seeks her out and the two escape on horseback. The bridegroom looks for his knife, which his mother returns, urging him to redress their honor.

The fifth scene consists of Leonardo and the bride riding on horseback, locked in passion. The bridegroom appears with four other riders, as they follow the escaping couple.

In the final scene, the sixth, the bridegroom's horse approaches Leonardo and the bride, and the two men dismount. She tries to separate them, but they push her aside and open their knives. They perform an intense, agonizing knife fight dance to the death. Leonardo thrusts his knife into the groom's abdomen as the latter thrusts his blade into Leonardo's heart. They fall and die at her feet. The bride walks between them looking at her hands and moving towards the mirror. Wiping her hands on her breasts, blood stains are visible as she stops to look at herself and the scene behind in the mirror.

As the music of the music continues ("Despierte la novia…"/Awaken the bride…), there is a cut to the group photo, again black and white.

2. *Carmen*
Carlos Saura, 1983

Production Company	Emiliano Piedra, Televisión Española (TVE)
Executive Producer	Emiliano Piedra
Production Manager	Gustavo Quintana
Screenplay	Carlos Saura, Antonio Gades; Prosper Mérimée (novella)
Director of Photography	Teo Escamilla
Editor	Pedro del Rey
Set Director	Félix Murcia
Costume Design	Teresa Nieto
Sound	Carlos Fauolo
Music	Paco de Lucía
Choreography	Antonio Gades, Carlos Saura

102 minutes

Cast

Antonio/José	Antonio Gades
Carmen	Laura del Sol
Cristina	Cristina Hoyos
Paco	Paco de Lucía

Synopsis

This is the story of Antonio, the director of a contemporary dance company, who is working with a group of female dancers. The girls are practicing their steps in front of Antonio and on stage in front of a mirrored wall. Rehearsing in a studio near Madrid, Antonio is looking for the perfect Carmen for his flamenco-style version of the Mérimée (and Bizet) work of he same name. He asks Paco if he can look for a Carmen in dance studios in Seville. He plays music from the opera as those present interpret a flamenco version. Credits roll over 19th century engravings.

In Seville, Antonio finds his Carmen (also her name) in a flamenco dance school. She is a strong-willed dancer at a flamenco *tablao*. Carmen captivates Antonio; they fall in love and begin a relationship. Sleeping together in his apartment at the rehearsal studio, Carmen leaves in the middle of the night.

Rehearsals of four key episodes structure narrative attention: the tobacco factory scene where Carmen knifes a co-worker; Carmen's tempting of Don José; Don José's murder of Carmen's husband; the final bullfight sequence.

Carmen has a husband, who is serving a sentence in a Madrid jail for selling illegal drugs. With the instruction of both Antonio and Cristina, Carmen assumes the role of her mythical namesake, but she also demonstrates her destructive character traits. When Antonio learns of the husband, he offers money so that the husband will disappear and Carmen will move in with him. She, however, has other ideas, although she says she loves Antonio.

After rehearsal the day before Antonio's birthday and before the rehearsal of the bullfight number, Antonio catches Carmen *in flagrante* with one of the male dancers. The next day, with the arrival of the bullfighter, Carmen flirts with him. As the entire company dances on stage, Antonio drags Carmen from the scene. And, in the doorway to the dressing room, he takes out a knife and stabs her.

Members of the troupe go on, seemingly oblivious.

2. El amor brujo
(Love, the Magician)
Carlos Saura, 1986

Production Company	Emiliano Piedra
Executive Producer	Emiliano Piedra
Production Manager	Emiliano Otegui
Screenplay	Carlos Saura, Antonio Gades; Gregorio Martínez Serra (libretto)

184   Filmography—2. *El amor brujo*

Director of Photography   Teo Escamilla
Editor   Pedro del Rey
Set Director   Gerardo Vera
Costume Design   Gerardo Vera
Sound   Daniel Goldstein
Music   Manuel de Falla, et alia
Choreography   Antonio Gades

103 minutes

Cast

Carmelo   Antonio Gades
Candela   Cristina Hoyos
José   Juan Antonio Jiménez
Lucía   Laura del Sol

Synopsis

A large garage door, open onto an alley, descends slowly as soundover orchestral music begins the overture from *El amor brujo*, and the door slams closed.

The camera pans right into the interior of a movie soundstage with its flats and braces, catwalks, scaffolds, lighting and so on, as it moves to the set, which is comprised of a group of shanties around three sides of an open dusty area. Children are playing, and adults gather or are seated at tables. Two men are drinking, one of them is singing. They seal a pact with a handshake poured over with wine.

A gypsy girl named Candela is promised in marriage in this gypsy ritual by her father to José, the son of his friend. A third child, a boy, observes concerned from a distance.

Years later, as promised, José and Candela marry, although her affections belong to Carmelo. José's affection belongs to Lucía. The community dances with joy as the wedding is celebrated, carrying the couple on their shoulders. The couple steals away to consummate their union.

During community celebrations for Christmas, José steals away with Lucía. The two dance intimately, but another man arrives with his companions. In a group knife fight precipitated by this newly arrived man who wants to take Lucía away, José is killed as he tries to defend her and his own honor. When the police arrive, Candela and Carmelo are holding the dead body. They arrest him.

The ghost of José continues to haunt Candela. She puts on the clothes she was wearing the night he was killed, and she goes every night to evoke his presence and to dance with him (Danza del terror/Dance of fear).

Four years later, Carmelo returns, determined to win Candela for himself. Candela, now a widow, is desirous of having a relationship with Carmelo, but she is not free because she continues to being haunted by José.

From an old gypsy woman, Carmelo and Candela get advice that fire is the only way to free Candela from the ghost. They organize a ritual dance designed to cast the ghost off (Danza ritual del fuego/Ritual dance of fire), but it does not work.

Carmelo then consults the old gypsy woman again, and she advises that the ghost will only be content if he can have his real love, Lucía.

Carmelo convinces Lucía to go help free Candela from José. Since José died for her and she still loves him, she can be with him, freeing Candela from his obsession. At night, Carmelo and Lucía accompany Candela as she goes to meet José. As Candela's dance with José begins, Carmelo and Lucía join in. During the dance, José and Lucía pair up, and the two finally go away together, leaving Candela and Carmelo.

Dawn breaks, Candela and Carmelo embrace, finally free to enjoy their love.

3. *Camila*
María Luisa Bemberg, 1984

Production Company	GEA Producciones, Impala
Executive Producer	Lita Stantic
Production Manager	Marta Parga
Screenplay	María Luisa Bemberg, Beda Docampo Feijóo, Juan Bautista Stagnaro
Director of Photography	Fernando Arribas
Editor	Luis César D'Angiolillo
Art Director	Miguel Rodríguez
Costume Design	Graciela Galán
Sound	Jorge Stavropulos
Music	Luis María Serra

105 minutes

Cast

Camila O'Gorman	Susú Pecoraro
Ladislao Guitérrez	Inmanol Arias
Adolfo O'Gorman	Héctor Alterio
Joaquina O'Gorman	Elena Tasisto
La Perichona	Mona Maris

Synopsis

In an opening scene, Grandmother O'Gorman, La Perichona, is returned by soldiers to the family estancia to spend the rest of her days under house arrest. She meets the little Camila and asks her if she likes love stories.

The narrative flashes forward to 1847 and Buenos Aires. Camila O'Gorman belongs to a high society family that supports dictator Juan Manuel Rosas. One day, during confession, she is surprised to meet a new, young priest, Father Ladislao Gutiérrez. She has a suitor, Ignacio, with whom she is not in love. Secretly, Camila reads literature critical of the regime, which she obtains from bookseller Mariano. In the dark of night, Camila and her brother Roberto see Rosas' death squads in the street. The following day, Mariano's head is on display in front of the church.

Camila seems to have developed a crush on Father Ladislao, but after hearing him denounce the regime's death squads from the pulpit, she falls deeply in love. She also openly speaks her views, which enrages her father, who sends her from the table during a family meal.

Father Ladislao also begins to show feelings for Camila. He first attempts to beat his feelings for Camila out with a whip, but finally he surrenders to her advances. The two begin a clandestine affair. When her fellow socialites advise her to not let Ignacio get away, she describes her longing for a husband she could love and feel proud of.

Camila and Ladislao escape and take up residence in Corrientes province, where they pose as school teachers, Valentina and Máximo Brandier. While Camila is ecstatic with happiness, Ladislao is torn between his love for Camila and the abandoned duties of his priesthood.

Meanwhile, Camila's father, Adolfo O'Gorman, is enraged by how the family name has been dishonored by Camila's actions. Despite the pleas of his wife and Ignacio, Adolfo writes to the authorities and demands the death penalty for his daughter. The Church hierarchy and Rosas' political allies demand blood, and his exiled opponents use the scandal to critique Rosas' rule.

The two fugitives are recognized, however, by Father Gannon, a priest who knows them both. The village commandant informs Camila that he will not arrest her until morning and advises her and Ladislao to cross into Brazil. Ladislao's troubled conscience pushes him to the village church where he screams to know why God cannot leave him in peace. Camila and Ladislao do not try to escape and the commandant arrests them.

Camila and Father Ladislao are ordered be shot without trial. In a military prison, Camila and Ladislao are forbidden to see each other. Camila learns that she is pregnant. Despite the fact that law forbids the execution of pregnant women, the authorities refuse to delay or commute Camila's sentence.

Although the firing squad shoots Father Ladislao without hesitation, they initially refuse to kill a woman. When their captain threatens them, they shoot Camila. The two bodies are placed into the same coffin. The couple's final words are heard in voiceover:

> Ladislao, are you there?
> By your side, Camila.

4. *La historia oficial*
(The Official Story/Version)
Luis Puenzo, 1985

Production Company	Historias Cinematográficas Cinemania, Progress Communications
Executive Producer	Marcelo Piñeyro
Production Manager	Carlos Latreyte
Screenplay	Aída Bortnik, Luis Puenzo
Director of Photography	Félix Monti

Editor	Juan Carlos Macías
Set Director	Adriana Sforza
Costume Design	Ticky García Estévez
Music	Atilio Stampone

112 minutes

Cast

Alicia	Norma Aleandro
Roberto	Héctor Alterio
Ana	Chunchuna Villafañe
Benítez	Patricio Contreras
Sara	Chela Ruiz

Synopsis

After a patriotic ceremony opening the school year, Alicia, a teacher, tells her class that what they are to study in the history of Argentina.

Set in Argentina in March 1983, Alicia and Roberto, her husband and a businessman, live in Buenos Aires with their adopted daughter, Gaby. On Gaby's fifth birthday, Alicia wonders about Gaby's real parents, a topic her husband has told her to ignore, although he seems to know the story of his daughter's adoption.

Ana, Alicia's longtime friend, returns from exile and tells Alicia about having been held and tortured for having lived with a man labeled as a subversive. When she tells Alicia that she had seen children taken away from their parents in jail, Alicia begins to think that Gaby's parents may have been similarly arrested.

Alicia sets about to learn of Gaby's origin. While searching records at a hospital, Alicia learns about an organization that searches for missing children. A woman there, Sara, believes Gaby may be her granddaughter.

Alicia, like other members of the Argentine middle class, is not aware of how much killing and suffering has gone on in the country. Her views are challenged by a fellow teacher, Benitez, and by some of her students. One student argues that the government-issued history textbooks are written by murderers. Alicia reports the student, but Benítez intervenes to protect him. Alicia and Benítez become friends as her investigation opens her eyes.

Roberto is stressed from work, where some of his colleagues disappear. Ana confronts Roberto, accusing him of denouncing her and causing her arrest. Roberto also has frictions with his father and brother, who dislike his ties to the conservative military elite.

Alicia brings Sara home to meet Roberto, and he becomes furious. Later, Alicia surprises Roberto when she tells him that Gaby is not home, saying, "How does it feel not knowing where your child is?" Roberto becomes enraged and assaults her.

A phone call from Gaby interrupts the violence. As she sings a nursery rhyme to Roberto, Alicia gets her purse and walks out the door, leaving her keys behind.

A final shot shows Gaby sitting in a rocking chair at her adopted grandparents' house, continuing to sing.

5. Fresa y chocolate
(Strawberry and Chocolate)
Tomás Guitérrez Alea and Juan Carlos Tabío, 1993

Production Company	ICAIC, Instituto Mexicano de Cinematografía, Telemadrid, SGEA, Tabasco Film
Executive Producers	Camilo Vives, Frank Cabrera, Georgina Balzaretti
Production Manager	Miguel Mendoza
Screenplay	Senel Paz (based on *El lobo, el bosque y el hombre nuevo* [*The Wolf, the Forest, and the New Man*] by Paz)
Director of Photography	Mario García Joya
Editors	Rolando Martínez, Miriam Talavera, Osvaldo Donatien
Set Director	Orlando Gonzáelz
Costume Design	Miriam Dueñas
Sound	Germinal Hernández
Music	José Javier Vitier

111 minutes

Cast

Diego	Jorge Perugorría
David	Vladimir Cruz
Nancy	Mirta Ibarra
Miguel	Francisco Gattorno
Germán	Joel Angelino
Vivian	Marilyn Solaya

Synopsis

David, a student and ardent Communist, takes his girlfriend to a rundown hotel in hopes of having sex with her, but he ends up promising not to sleep with her until they are married. She marries another man. At a café near a park, he meets Diego, who self-identifies as a homosexual because he's eating strawberry ice cream, even though there is chocolate. David accepts an invitation to Diego's apartment, where he sees religious statues made by Diego's friend Germán. Though David realizes that Diego has seduction on his mind, Diego's lair houses forbidden pleasures. Besides, his friend Miguel sees Diego as a dangerous dissident, and urges David to spy on him.

Vivian suggests to David they could be lovers, but he refuses. He continues to visit Diego, learning of Cuban culture and the finer things, and meeting Nancy. She is Diego's neighbor and the Watch Officer for the block. With her suicide attempt, Diego and David get her to the hospital, the latter donating blood to her. The more time David spends with Diego, the more he is intrigued by this very different man, and what he learns. David also begins to like Nancy. His desire to write is reawakened.

The request for an exhibition of Germán's work is denied, and Diego writes a letter of protest to the authorities. In her attraction to David, Nancy initiates him, following the Lezamian banquet in Diego's apartment. Believing David has been corrupted, Miguel visits Diego, but David intervenes. Under pressure, Diego plans to leave Cuba, and as the two friends say farewell, they embrace.

6. *Abre los ojos*
(Open Your Eyes)
Alejandro Amenábar, 1996

Production Company	Canal + España, Las Producciones del Escorpión, S.L., Les Films Alain Sarde, Lucky Red, Sogetel
Executive Producers	Fernando Bovaira, José Luis Cuerda
Production Manager	Emiliano Otegui
Screenplay	Alejandro Amenábar, Mateo Gil
Director of Photography	Hans Burmann
Editor	María Elena Sáinz de Rozas
Art Director	Wolfgang Burmann
Set Directors	Carola Angulo, Ramón Moya
Costume Design	Concha Solera
Wardrobe	Humberto Cornejo
Sound	Pelayo Gutiérrez
Music	Alejandro Amenábar, Mariano Marín

117 minutes

Cast

César	Eduardo Noriega
Sofía	Penélope Cruz
Nuria	Najwa Nimri
Pelayo	Fele Martínez
Antonio	Chete Lera

Synopsis

An alarm clock awakens a young man to the sound of a woman's voice repeating "Open your eyes." He sits up in bed, looks at himself in the mirror, showers, looks again in the mirror, and dresses. Leaving his garage and driving into the city, he discovers that its main thoroughfare is empty.

After again hearing "Open your eyes," the same waking routine is repeated, though, this time a young women is present. This time the young man drives into a city filled with people.

From a prison cell, César, a 25-year-old in a prosthetic mask, tells his story, his dreams to psychiatrist Antonio. Flashbacks and flashforwards reveal the following events: He is attractive to women. At his birthday party, good-looking César flirts with Sofía, the date of his best friend Pelayo. He takes her home and stays the night, although they don't sleep together. During the night he sees television talk show interview dealing with cryonization. The next morning, César's obsessive lover Nuria pulls up outside Sofía's apartment, and she offers him a ride back to her apartment to have sex. On the way there, however, she intentionally crashes the car, committing suicide, and César is horribly disfigured. Meeting with doctors, he learns that his disfigurement is beyond the help of cosmetic surgery. Sofía can't bear to see him like this and goes back to Pelayo.

After César's disfigurement, he has a series of disorienting experiences. Drunk, César passes out and sleeps in the street. When he awakes, things have changed: Sofía now claims to love him and the doctors are able restore his lost looks. But as he makes love to Sofía one night, she appears to change into Nuria. Horrified, César smothers her with a pillow, yet finds everyone else believes Nuria was indeed the woman everyone else calls Sofía.

While he is confined to the psychiatric prison, fragments return to César as if in a dream. After his disfigurement, César contracted with Life Extension, a company specializing in cryonics, to be cryogenically preserved and to experience extremely lucid and lifelike virtual reality dreams. Returning to the LE offices with Antonio, and under supervision by prison officers, he discovers that he signed a contract including Clause 14, providing "artificial perception" during cryonization. Having committed suicide, César was placed in cryonic suspension, his experiences spliced onto his actual life and replacing his true memories. After escaping, discovering his continued disfigurement, and shooting a guard, followed by a conversation with LE's Serge Duvernois, and encounters with Pelayo and Sofía, César leaps from the roof of the company's high-rise headquarters.

The film ends as it began, with a blank, black screen and a voiceover woman's voice that says "Open your eyes."

7. *El crimen del Padre Amaro*
(The Crime of Father Amaro)
Carlos Carrera, 2002

Production Company	Alameda Films, Artcam International, IMCINE, et alia
Executive Producer	Laura Imperiale
Producers	Daniel Birman Ripstein, Alfredo Ripstein
Co-producer	José María Morales
Production Manager	Fernando Huberman
Screenplay	Vicent Leñero, novel by Eça de Queirós
Director of Photography	Guillermo Granillo
Editor	Óscar Figueroa
Art Director	Carmen Giménez Cacho
Set Director	Ivonne Fuente
Costume Design	María Estela Fernández
Wardrobe	Margarita Lozada
Sound	Santiago Nuñez
Music	Rosino Serrano

118 minutes

Cast

Father Amaro	Gael García Bernal
Sanjuanera	Angélica Aragón
Amelia	Ana Claudia Talancón
Father Natalio	Damián Alcázar
Father Benito	Sancho Gracia
Rubén	Andrés Montiel

Synopsis

Newly ordained Padre Amaro takes a bus ride across Mexico to Los Reyes, a small town in the fictional state of Aldama, to start his life of service in the Church. At night, road bandits stop the bus en route.

Father Amaro is a protégé of a very political bishop, and he discovers that the local priest, Father Benito, has an ongoing affair with local restaurant owner, Sanjuanera. Father Benito is building a large clinic, which is partially funded by money from a drug lord. Another priest in the area, Father Natalio, is under investigation for supporting left-wing insurgents in the secluded rural mountainside.

Amelia, a local 16-year-old girl, teaches catechism to a group of the town's children. She is the daughter of Sanjuanera, and she is contemplating marriage to Rubén, a young journalist. Rubén is a non-believer and Amelia is strongly Catholic.

Amaro becomes infatuated with Amelia, and she is attracted to him. She asks awkward questions about love and sin in the confessional, and later she touches his hand while serving him at the restaurant. The newspaper gets information about Benito baptizing the drug lord's newborn child, and Rubén writes about the scandal. With evidence compiled by his father, an avowed anti-clerical, Ruben publishes a story about the hospital being a front for money laundering. The bishop has Amaro write a denial, and Rubén is fired under pressure from the Church.

Amelia then phones Rubén and breaks up him, berating him with a string of obscenities. Devout Catholics vandalize Rubén's family home, and when he returns to the town, he assaults Padre Amaro. Amaro, though, does not press charges, so Rubén avoids jail time. Father Amaro is plagued with guilt about his feelings for Amelia. With the local press revealing the secrets of the parish, Amaro turns to his superior, Padre Benito, who responds cynically.

Father Amaro and Amelia start an affair, and he recites verses from the "Song of Songs" as he seduces her. During one secret meeting at the sexton's living quarters, he drapes a robe meant for the statue of Virgin Mary over Amelia. Amelia becomes pregnant, and Amaro tries to convince her to leave town to protect him. She decides to attempt keep the baby to by trying to pass off Rubén as the father, proposing to get back with him, but he is no longer interested. When Benito threatens to report Amaro, Amaro threatens to retaliate over Benito's own affair.

Father Amaro arranges for an abortion in the middle of the night. It goes wrong and Amelia begins bleeding uncontrollably. Amaro begins to drive her to a hospital in a large city, but she dies on the way. A false story is circulated, blaming Rubén for impregnating Amelia, and praising Amaro for breaking into the abortion clinic and liberating Amelia in a failed attempt to save her.

Father Amaro presides over Amelia's funeral. With the church packed with mourners, Father Benito, now in a wheelchair, turns and leaves in disgust.

8. *Te doy mis ojos*
(Take My Eyes)
Icíar Bollaín, 2003

Production Company	Alta Producción, Producciones La Iguana S.L.
Executive Producer	Santiago García Leániz
Coproducer	Enrique González Macho
Production Manager	Pizca Gutiérrez
Screenplay	Icíar Bollaín, Alicia Luna
Director of Photography	Carles Gusi
Editor	Ángel Hernández Zoido
Art Director	Víctor Molero
Costume Design	Estíbaliz Markiegi
Wardrobe	Angelines Castro
Sound	Pelayo Gutiérrez
Music	Alberto Iglesias

106 minutes

Cast

Pilar	Laía Marull
Antonio	Luis Tosar
Ana	Candela Peña
Aurora	Rosa María Sardá
Therapist	Sergi Calleja

Synopsis

It is nighttime, and an obviously distraught woman quickly gathers a few belongings and wakes her son, Juan. After getting him dressed, they flee the apartment, which is on the outskirts of Toledo. No taxi will stop, so they take a bus. In old Toledo, they cross a plaza and arrive at her sister's place. Still distraught and embracing her sister, Pilar realizes that she has left wearing slippers.

Pilar and her son find shelter with her sister, Ana, who lives with her Scottish live-in boyfriend, whom she soon will marry. Antonio, Pilar's husband, tries to make her change her mind, but she is tired and fearful of his abusive behavior. Determined to start a new life on her own, Pilar sends her sister to retrieve her belongings from the apartment she shared with her estranged husband. There, Ana discovers medical bills that indicate possible physical abuse by Antonio. When he arrives, the two have a confrontation.

Antonio still loves his wife, but he cannot control his temper outbursts. In an effort to bring Pilar back, he joins a men's anger management group. The male therapist listens to them, guides them, and gives Antonio a notebook in which to express his feelings in order to understand them and control his anger.

Ana, an art restorer, encourages Pilar, and she finds her a job in the gift shop of the church of Santo Tomé, a Toledo tourist attraction. Her newfound economical independence and the camaraderie of her coworkers awaken in Pilar an interest in art. She begins to study on her own in order to become a tourist guide. Pilar initially continues to be fearful of Antonio, but they are brought together when, in spite of Ana's protestations, Gloria, their mother, invites Antonio to Juan's birthday celebration.

Pilar still loves Antonio in spite of his abusive behavior towards her. Juan misses his father, and Pilar's attitude softens towards Antonio. When they have a chance to talk, Antonio explains to her that he wants to change, and that he has enrolled in group therapy. Pilar warms up to Antonio's courtship attempts, and the two begin to sneak away for secret meetings and romantic encounters.

With the encouragement of her mother, Pilar brings Antonio to Ana's wedding. The two sisters have an argument when Pilar tells Ana that she is going back to live with her husband. At first, Pilar and Antonio are happy to be back together. Encouraged by his wife, Antonio still goes to his anger management therapy. However, he also has to deal with his frustration with his low paying job as an appliance salesman. He feels threatened by Pilar's economic independence since she continues working in the gift shop.

Pilar applies for a job as a tourist guide in a museum in Madrid, but they would have to leave Toledo and Antonio wants to stay put, fearing that it would be difficult for him to find a better job in Madrid. Pilar tries to convince him that if she gets the job and they move to Madrid, it would be beneficial. The day in which she has the job interview, just when a coworker is waiting for her outside to take her there, Antonio explodes in anger. He mistreats her, tears off her clothes and locks her naked on the balcony.

Clearly Antonio's attempts to control his outbursts are failing, and he attempts suicide. After all of the abuse and humiliation, Pilar decides she must leave Antonio in order to find herself. Her friends help her retrieve belongings from the couple's apartment, as Antonio can only watch.

Chapter Notes

Introduction

1. Cortázar, Julio. *Hopscotch*. Trans. Gregory Rabassa. New York: Random House, 1966.
2. This term is employed in the general sense of exegesis or seeking a coherent explanation of the texts analyzed. It is not employed with reference to any particular theory.
3. Jan Mukařovský, "Intentionality in Art," *Aesthetic Function, Norm and Value as Social Facts*, trans. Mark E. Suino (Ann Arbor: University of Michigan Press, 1970), 96.
4. Whether or not film, and/or cultural, criticism has spoken about or postulated the existence of a "migration genre," it seems clear that the existence of such a genre should be proposed. It should be obvious that there is sufficient evidence in a sufficient number of texts in multiple media to justify speaking of such a genre. There are so many texts, such a thematic tradition, and so much bibliography over those migration texts to easily be able to insist on a corpus of works that possess the characteristics necessary to qualify as a genre. In Spanish language film, for example, see, Thomas Deveny, *Migration in Contemporary Hispanic Cinema* (Lanham: Scarecrow, 2012).
5. There are corridos that are about love themes, that chronicle natural events, and, of course, that tell stories of historical events running from Independence, through the Mexican Revolution and up to current times. There is even the popular new subgenre of the narcocorrido. With the corrido and through the interpretation of an artist, a people collects, spreads, and perpetuates the news that affect them; this is news sung in assonant rhyme and eight syllable verse and with the accompaniment of a guitar and various other instruments (in the case of Los Tigres del Norte the accordion figures prominently).
6. The lyrics of the whole corrido are as follow: "Aquí estoy establecido / en los Estados Unidos. / Diez años pasaron ya, / En que crucé de mojado, / papeles no he arreglado / sigo siendo un ilegal / tengo a mi esposa y mis hijos / que me los traje muy chicos / y se han olvidado ya / de mi México querido / del que yo nunca me olvido / y no puedo regresar. // De que me sirve el dinero / si estoy como prisionero / dentro de esta gran nación / cuando me acuerdo hasta lloro / y aunque la jaula sea de oro / no deja de ser prisión. // 'Y ESCÚCHAME, HIJO, TE GUSTARÍA QUE REGRESÁRAMOS A VIVIR A MEXICO,' / 'What's you talkin' about, Dad? I don't wanna go back to MEXICO, No way, Dad.' // Mis hijos no hablan conmigo / otro idioma han aprendido / y olvidaron el español / piensan como americanos / niegan que son mexicanos / aunque tengan mi color. // De mi trabajo a mi casa / yo no sé lo que me pasa / aunque soy hombre de hogar / casi no salgo a la calle/ pues tengo miedo que me hallen / y me puedan deportar. // De qué me sirve el dinero / si estoy como prisionero / dentro de esta gran prisión / cuando me acuerdo hasta lloro / y aunque la jaula sea de oro / no deja de ser prisión." (Here I am established in the United States. Ten years have passed since I crossed as a wetback. I haven't fixed my papers; I continue being illegal; I have my wife and kids that I brought very young, and they have forgotten already the dear Mexico that I never forget and where I cannot

return. *Refrain.* Listen to me, son. Would you like for us to return to live in Mexico. 'What's you talkin' about, Dad? I don't wanna go back to MEXICO, No way, Dad.' My kids don't talk to me; they've learned another language, and they forgot Spanish. They think like Americans; they deny they are Mexicans, even though they're the same color as me. *Refrain.*

7. This is not the first study to analogize film and language. The "notion of filmic grammar" is and has been an idea open to debate and ongoing precisions, and it will not be resolved in these pages. For the purposes of this study, it is not necessary to resolve the debate in favor of the existence of some formal grammar of film. What is clear is that film is a communication situation and, as such, it shares properties common to sign systems in general. And, it is those commonalities which allow for a basis upon which to ground notions of grammar. Among others, see "Bibliography": Bazin, Bordwell, Deleuze, Giannetti, Metz, Monaco, Prince, Stanley.

8. Intended to help identify the location or time for the scene and the action that is to follow and to orient the viewer as to the reading of the scene, establishing shots were a more common practice and feature in films of earlier eras than they are in current filmmaking practice. More recent filmmaking tendencies eschew the establishing shot with a view to moving the scene along more quickly. More recent filmmaking is more likely to depend on the orienting value of the images themselves, and in addition, the expositional nature of the shot may be suited to narratives where details are better intentionally omitted or obscured.

9. This said, it is difficult to ignore the centered phallic presence of an erect, fully open stick of red lipstick protruding from its metal tube as the central motif of the nineteenth frame.

10. The scholar-viewer soon will learn that it is specifically the summer of 1936.

11. See, for example, Thomas Deveny's *Cain on Screen* (Scarecrow, 1993).

Chapter 1

1. *The Spirit of the Beehive* shows how a child views History ... the only thing that's left to a child is that there are certain things which are not talked about. That was the approach that interested me, that way of wanting to see reality as a child. That feeling was very well understood, by the public, I think, although in an intuitive, almost unconscious, way.

2. See readings like those by Vicente Molina Foix (1985), Lomillos (1998), and Chris Perriam (2008).

3. Echoing Celestino Deleyto, for example, Perriam (2008) speaks of the film's two prologues (the arrival of the truck and the prologue of *Frankenstein*). Although he does recognize the earlier drawings, for him they are but a supplemental and anticipatory "visual synopsis," while the intertitles have archetypal implications.

4. Moments during which instrumental versions of children's songs comprise the soundtrack are, for example: diegetically, when the children sing ("El farolero" ["Dos y dos son cuatro, cuatro y dos son seis..."]) in school, and non-diegetically, when the girls first go to the abandoned farmhouse, the soundtrack is an instrumentalization of "Ahora que vamos despacio/Vamos a contar mentiras."

5. Juan F. Egea rightly observes how the tension between localization of the story in a precise geographical space and in a historical time, and the earlier "Once upon a time..." together signal a bifurcation and announce bivalence. This allows for a distinction between a concrete, recognizable topography and an arbitrary, mythical geography.

6. See, for example: López, Pablo. "Las mejores películas de la historia del cine: *El espíritu de la colmena*." *Fotogramas*, núm. 1689 (Sept. 1983), 45–52; or "*El espíritu ... is* perhaps the best movie in the history of Spanish cinema" in Deveny, Thomas G. *Cain on Screen: Contemporary Spanish Cinema* (Metuchen & London: Scarecrow, 1993), 118. Additionally, consultation of almost any current website or blog dedicated to "ranking" films, shows that *El espíritu de la colmena*, while not necessarily enjoying the status of #1, continues to be held in high esteem. See, for example: Cineario, theranking.com, cinemaadhoc, cinedor, oscarcine, elblogdecineespanol.com, entre muchos otros.

7. See, for example, the beautiful commemorative DVD which was released in 2003 on the 30th anniversary of the film's release.

8. Quoted in Peter Besas, *Behind the Spanish Lens* (Denver: Arden, 1985), 250.

9. See, for example: E. C. Riley (1984), where one reads, "it is not a particularly easy film to 'read' in a rationally satisfying way."; or Ronald Schwartz (1986), where he speaks of a film "whose style may be characterized as ambiguous and elliptical"; or when the film was re-released in the U.S. in 2007, a film critic for *The New York Times* reviewed the film and praised Erice's direction (A.O. Scott, January 27, 2006, accessible at: http://movies.nytimes.com/2006/01/27/movies/27beeh.html?_r=0) stating that "the story that emerges ... is at once lucid and enigmatic, poised between adult longing and childlike eagerness, sorrowful knowledge and startled innocence."

10. For commentaries on time in *El espíritu de la colmena* and Erice, see Paul Julian Smith (1993 and 2000), Rob Stone (2002), and Jaime Pena (2004).

11. Immediately continuous to asking the girls not to tell their mother, they come across a mushroom which is "...un auténtico demonio ... cuando es joven engaña, pero de vieja ya es otra cosa. Es la peor de todas, la más venenosa." (...a real demon ... when it is young, it deceives; but when it is old, that is something else. It is the worst of all, the most venomous.). See, for example, Deleyto (1999), 48; or Miles (2007), 107.

12. Curiously here, though Juan F. Egea ("El monstruo metafórico en *El espíritu de la colmena*") correctly insists on the importance of metonymy as a rhetorical device throughout *El espíritu de la colmena*, he ignores this, perhaps the most important occurrence of metonymy in the film.

13. In spite of Robert J. Miles' (2007) criticism of my 1996 article where I first proferred this conclusion, I repeat it here. This time not so much as a paternalistic service to the "uninitiated viewer," but rather as a conclusion to which the text's own established matrix and other textual evidence lead. I profer this conclusion aware now, as I was then, of its implications for feminist readings of the film as well as its effects on the production of allegorical-symbolical meanings of a socio-historical inflection.

14. In her 2014 essay, Dolores Tierney seems to allow the need to make the filmic text fit the exigencies of a cultural studies analysis ('transnational political horror') to lead her to mis-view this scene. Needing for the film to "hint at a broader reality beneath this repressed surface" misguides this viewer into seeing the *maquis* ("fighter"), not Fernando, in Ana's imagination of the likeness of the Boris Karloff incarnation of the Whale film's monster.

15. An early recognition of Ana's search for father is that of Alain Mitjaville (1984), who writes, "*l'Esprit de la ruche* décrit la quotidien d'une petite fille de cinq ans que cherche autour d'ell une figure paternelle ... susceptible de répondre à ses exigences psychologiques.," and who sees the search in allegorical terms, "Je pensse que *l'Esprit de la ruche* à travers l'itinéraire de Ana visualise la conscience d'une génération de'espagnols àla recherche d'une identité...." One of the first studies to look at Ana's "search" in a coherent way was E.C. Riley (1984). This seminal article, however, is not completely satisfying because it ends up attributing the cause of the search to a "crisis of identity" (491), without delving into the causes for such a crisis. See also, Marsh Kinder (1983).

16. I echo here Virginia Higginbotham as she writes: "As a metaphor for Spain, Frankenstein is a ghoulish collage, a monstrous figure constructed by a sinister creator whose name sounds very much like 'Franco'" (119).

17. See Carmen Arocena (1996: 88–91), for example, for a cogent explanation of the interpretative value of this imagery in terms of its socio-historical inflection.

18. "Ataca al Régimen y sus instituciones ... [y] califican el contenido total de la obra" See the criteria used by readers in the censorship office during the Franco regime.

Chapter 2

1. "Carlos Saura." *Current Biography Yearbook 1978* (New York: H.W. Wilson, 1979), 360. "Franco era como un muro, una barrera, más allá de la que fue imposible avanzar...."

2. See, for example, Higginbotham (1988).

3. It is important to observe here that in the case of Carlos Saura, this style is born as much out of necessity as out of preference. In an interview with Antonio Castro [*Dirigido por*, 249 (1996): 52–67], the director confides, "Por un lado, es verdad que no

se podía tratar directamente ciertos temas, pero por otro tratar las cosas de una manera indirecta es algo que siempre me ha gustado, usar la interpretación como un juego ... me parece más rico, más interesante, más fértil...." (On the one hand, it is true that certain themes could not be treated directly, but on the other, treating things in an indirect way has always appealed to me, to use interpretation as a game ... seems richer to me, more interesting, more fertile....)

4. The novella's Part 4 does not continue the story. It consists, instead, of commentary on the gypsies, on their appearance, customs, history, and language.

5. Prosper Mérimée, *Carmen* (Paris: Encre, 1984). Although the word order is changed as presented in the film, the quote comes from Chapitre II (54):

> ... ses lévres un peu fortes, mais bien dessinées et laissant voir des dents plus blanches que des amandes sans leur peau. Ses cheveux, peut-être un peu gros, étaient noirs, á reflets bleus comme l'aile d'un corbeau, longs et luisants. C'était expression á la fois voluptueuse et farouche que je n'ai trouvée depuis á aucun regard humain. Oeil de bohémien, oeil de loup, c'est un dicton espanol....

6. Mérimée, *Carmen*, Chapitre III, 67–68.

> Je levai les yeux, et je la vis. C'était un vendredi, et je ne l'oublierai jamais ... Dábord elle ne me plut pas, et je repirs mon ouvrage; mais elle,suivant l'usage des femmes et des chats qui ne viennent pas quand on les appelle pas et qui viennent quand on ne les appelle pas, s'arrête devant moi et m'adressa la parole....

7. Kiril Taranovsky, *Essays on Manel'stam* (Cambridge University Press, 1976), 18.

8. Taranovsky. 18.

9. Consistent and very similar to this idea, yet expressing it in different terms, is Gwynne Edwards (1987) when she writes: "We have, then, a highly concentrated version of the story, one which emphasizes above all its conflicting passions of love, jealousy and rivalry. This simplification, removing all the padding, is itself a step towards a greater universality. To that, in turn the tight discipline of flamenco adds a powerful element of ritual" (145–146).

10. The ultimate conservatism of Saura's direction is revealed here. The dialectical tension is resolved in favor of the way things always have seemed to be. This is disappointing perhaps because of the time when the film was made. The 1980's are a time in which the women's movement was achieving much, but this film eschews an ending that might be more "feminist."

11. See, for example, Colmeiro (2005); Davies (2004); or Simonari (2008).

12. See, for example, Torrecilla (2001).

13. De Falla's 1915 composition, inspired in gypsy flamenco music and commissioned by the famous Pastora Imperio, met with criticism. The composer reworked it, and in 1925 he debuted a ballet version, which is the most well-known version of the work.

14. Reference is made here, of course, to: *Sevillanas* (1992), *Flamenco* (1995), *Salomé* (2002), *Iberia* (2005), and *Flamenco, flamenco* (2010).

15. In the subtext, Candela manages to trick Lucía to come that night, with the excuse of hooking her up with Carmelo. As she turns up, the nightly ritual of Candela's dance with her husband begins, but at the last moment Candela moves away from her husband and Lucía is taken away by her dead lover.

16. Those numbers are: the wedding (with the entire troupe); winter/Christmas (entire troupe); knife fight (two groups of men); Candela and ghost (2X); Lucía dancing surrounded by men; women hanging laundry; Lucía in a 'bar' surrounded by men; Carmelo and Candela courting; dance of fire (entire troupe); Carmelo convincing Lucía; and, dance of the game of love.

17. The film's early successes place it on the road to the canon. Seen by over 400,000 Spaniards, running for months in New York, nominated for an Oscar, winner of two prizes at Cannes and a BAFTA best picture award, *Carmen* began with critical and commercial success. Canonical status is confirmed by a lengthy critical bibliography and inclusion in studies ranging from *Out of the Past. Spanish Cinema after Franco* (Hopewell, 1986), where a photogram from the film serves as the cover art, to *Spanish Cinema: A Student's Guide* (Jordan & Allinson, 2005) to *Great Spanish Films Since 1950* (Schwartz, 2008), and so on.

18. He refers here to the moment in which Antonio listens to the tape of the Bizet opera music while Paco and Marisol attempt to improvise a flamenco equivalent.

The conclusion is that Spanish folk arts struggle to emulate the Bizet score. Interestingly, for the current chapter, this segment forms part of the "first few minutes," those that, including the prior sequences and the following credit sequence, create a matrix for reading the filmic discourse.

Chapter 3

1. This is a claim that is hard to substantiate, of course. Not that it is the definite evidence of such a claim, but Camila has become commonplace (read 'canonical') in U.S. university-level course work. As an example of its canonization in this regard, for example, see: Fabiana Sacchi, Sivlia Pessoa & Luis Martin-Cabrera. *Más allá de la pantalla* (Boston: Thomson Heinle, 2006), a book used for teaching Hispanic culture through film. Undoubtedly, the lengthy bibliography on Bemberg and *Camila* is an even better indicator of the film's canonical status.

2. Theoretically, of course, this is impossible. Reference here is made to the most general of possibilities, in which every attempt is to portray events "objectively."

3. Some studies have focused on the "female gaze" or "woman's gaze." See, for example, Williams (1998) or Kepner (2003). The studies do much to analyze the female structuring presence in *Camila*, although the emphasis on "gaze" may lead to overlooking other elements closely tied to the feminine. Williams, for example, when discussing the scene in which Camila and Ladislao meet face to face at her birthday party, focuses on touch and gaze, ignoring that it is actually through voice (word) that Camila recognizes the young priest even before they "gaze" into each others eyes. His focus on "gaze" leads even to errors, such as positing the birthday party sequence as occurring after the sermon (180), and the emphasis on wanting "woman's gaze" to grant dominion over the discourse leads to misinterpretation of the sermon scene (179–180). In that scene, Williams posits that Camila and other porteñas view from a balcony (an earlier scene). But, the tracking shot elevates to Ladislao's sermon position, and, more importantly, the 20+-seconds-long closeup on Camila's "gaze" shows her looking up as she listens to the priest's words. Kepner does, though, recognize the importance of voice in the founding moments of the relationship in confessional.

4. Here there is a double importance of the *word*. In the first place, it is the *word* (the priest's sermon) that is the basis for this effusive criterion for love. And, it is the *word* (shouting in the streets) that will be the manifestation of that love.

5. The word "curiosity" is used here in the sense of a wanting to know. The feminine perspective is noticeable because it is a scene that probably would not be seen as a "male choice." It reflects a desire to know the male "other" or to make the male "other" known.

6. It is interesting to observe a directorial "wink" to the symbolism here. In the scene in which Camila and her grandmother share love stories (the word), the perceptive scholar-viewer will pick up on the presence of a cat in the grandmother's arms and then on the bed (a reference back to the earlier episode and the maternal instinct indexed there).

7. In her brief essay, Katherine Gatto (2002) approaches "madness" in *Camila*. She sees the relationship to confinement and Foucauldian conceptualizations, but she ignores that it is man who is defining "madness." In fact, Gatto states that "The strictures of church, state, and family, drive both the grandmother and Camila to madness."

8. Stephen Hart (2002) sees in this sentence "an overt allusion to a Romantic notion of post-corporeal love," and in the suggested transcendence he wants to see an expression of hope or political optimism at the birth of a new democratic period in Argentina after the trauma of the Dirty War.

9. Unlike other languages, in Spanish, a confusion of terms here can muddy this consideration. Trying to clarify, for example, "Historia" and "historia," the distinction that exists in English between "history" and "story" is very useful. I have tried herein to highlight the contrast by using capital and lower case letters in this approach to a new kind of historical film. Instead of narrating great Histories (epics), they narrate small "histories"/stories, which index that larger History. Clearly, other narratives and other films could be adduced here.

This is a paradigm shift in historical film, and it may be hard to recognize. When Ruffinelli (1996), for example, disqualifies *Camila* as a historical film, he does so by ironically offering a definition of aspects of this new historical film:

> ... el proyecto de Bemberg no consiste en hacer un film histórico (una reconstrucción perfecta de época, ya fuera en la ambientación como en la ideología y la psicología de los personajes). Toma al pasado para saltar al presente, y hace de sus personajes, Camila especialmente, una joven contemporánea nuestra (21).
>
> (Bemberg's project does not consist of making an historical film [a perfect reconstruction of the period, be it in the setting as well as in the ideology and psychology of the characters]. She takes the past in order to jump to the present, and she makes her characters, especially Camila, a young contemporary of ours.)

10. In this consideration of the idea of historical film, the terms "iconical" and "indexical" are used to classify the signic character of traditional historical film and new historical film. Another terminology might easily prefer "metaphorical" instead of "iconical," and "metonymical" or "synecdochical" instead of "indexical."

11. It is necessary to recognize that the distinction here is more methodological than real. It would be wrong to think, for example, that feminism does not imply an ideological-political viewpoint. Nevertheless, for the purposes of this chapter a somewhat artificial methodological nuance has been made in order to be able to consider elements that, while they might coincide with them, do not necessarily have a strict relationship to feminist principles.

12. As well as support for the historical-political reading cued by the film's first few minutes, further indexing of the period is the omnipresence of Rosas' image in the film. We see his portrait in the church, in offices, in homes; and the red ribbon of support is on everyone's chest.

13. See, for example, Ruffinelli (1996): "Lejos de dar lugar al análisis de la crisis de la pareja o la situación de la mujer independizada ('liberada") del matrimonio, *Camila* contaría ante todo una historia pasional, de 'Romeo y Julieta' de las pampas....'" (Far from offering an analysis of the couple or the situation of the independent [liberated] woman in a marriage, *Camila* tells above all a story of passion, a kind of "Romeo and Juliet" of the Pampas.) (11). This observation notwithstanding, Ruffinelli's article offers the reader an excellent and interesting historical contextualization, within which one can see the historical-political dichotomies to which the filmic discourse alludes; and it recognizes their potential to offer "la oportunidad para 'releer' la historia y hace con ella un discurso del *presente*" (the chance to 're-read' history and it makes it into a discourse about the *present*.) (16).

Chapter 4

1. The remainder of the lyrics would be:

May the laurels be eternal,
the ones we managed to win,
the ones we managed to win.
Let us live crowned in glory ...
or let us swear in glory to die!
Or let us swear in glory to die!
Or let us swear in glory to die!

2. Readings that ignore the importance of the film's first few minutes in orienting a reading of the film fail to recognize the important metonymical aspect of the reading.

3. The viewer must remember that the film's title, before it is torn in half in the first few minutes, appears in light blue letters. This color immediately indexes Argentina. The light blue lettering of a title that includes the word "historia" clearly, then, announces an approach to Argentine national or capital H history, and the tearing of the title in two, augurs, as it orients a reading of the film, a revision of it.

4. In his 1987 essay, Willy Oscar Muñoz first suggests the idea of narrative levels in *La historia oficial* when he writes that the film "intended by director Luis Puenzo as a documentary movie, masterfully blends the fiction and the reality of its content." But, Muñoz never develops the ideas of narrative levels nor documentary qualities, concentrating instead on Alicia's consciousness raising *a la* Paolo Friere,

5. He has removed Costa's file from the principal's office, where Alicia had sent it, complaining of his attitude. Benítez says that Costa deserves another chance and that such a complaint could have lasting, unseen consequences. He returns Costa's file to Alicia.

6. For the critical bibliography on the film, this conclusion is not a certainty. There are those who assert that the film's end signifies the end of the marriage, and there are

others who, recognizing that, yes, Alicia leaves, see an ambiguity in the ending and Alicia's future. Given that the film's first few minutes establish that metonymy is a key device for reading the filmic narrative, the attentive scholar-viewer should experience no ambiguity with the ending. As Alicia leaves, the camera shows the keys to the family's home that remain hanging from the inside of the lock. The viewer realizes that Alicia has no need for the keys because she is not coming back.

7. Though he does not refer to it as metaphor, Mark Szuchman (1991) alludes to another visual metaphor used by the filmic narrative to alert the viewer to this same personal and vital project. It is the metaphor of Alicia's hair, which at the beginning of the film is pulled up tightly into a bun, but later on she sports a freer style, having let her hair down. For Szuchman, "in the same way as the lead actress' hair unravels over the course of the film (in contrast to the tightly controlled bun…), the official history of events in the Argentina of military governments unravels … loosened from the weight of fear and political naïveté" (191).

8. In the conclusion to his treatment of *La historia oficial*, Stephen M. Hart (2004) also recognizes the semiotic value of the doll. For him, the doll is a symbol, the film's best, and a 'free' rather than 'bound' motif within the filmic narrative (123).

9. The omitted third chorus' lyrics are (See translation in note 1):

> Sean eternos los laureles,
> que supimos conseguir,
> que supimos conseguir.
> Coronados de gloria vivamos …
> o juremos con gloria morir
> ¡O juremos con gloria morir!
> ¡O juremos con gloria morir!

10. In the case of these last two, corruption and fraud, the presence of Macci and Roberto's firm's treatment of him are elements that the filmic narrative includes in order to most strongly index these aspects questioning the "official story" of the period of the "proceso."

We know that sacrifices lie ahead of us and that we must pay a price for the heroic fact that we are, as a nation, a vanguard. We, as leaders, know that we have to pay a price for the right to say that we are at the head of a people that is at the head of America. Each and every one of us readily pays his quota of sacrifice, conscious of being rewarded with the satisfaction of fulfilling a duty, conscious of advancing with everyone toward the new man that is glimpsed on the horizon.

2. See, for example, McVey-Gil, Mary; Smalley, Deana, & Haro, María Paz, *Cinema for Spanish Conversation* 1st & 2nd eds. (Newburyport MA: Focus, 2002 & 2006); or Sacchi, Fabiana; Pessoa, Silvia & Martín-Cabrera, Luis, *Más allá de la pantalla. El mundo hispano a través del cine* (Boston: Thomson Heinle, 2006). In the first case, *Fresa y chocolate* figures among the 18 films selected for discussion, including *La historia oficial*, *Como agua para chocolate*, *Danzón*, *Mujeres al borde de un ataque de nervios*, *Belle epoque*, *Todo sobre mi madre*, and *El norte*; and in the second, it is one of 16, which include *El norte*, *La historia oficial*, *Bread and Roses*, *Camila*, *Los olvidados*, *Todo sobre mi madre*, and *Amores perros*.

3. This is not the first study to assert the importance and centrality of David's gaze/focus, as suggested by the film's establishing moments. Among others, see, for example, Enrico Mario Santí's often cited "*Fresa y chocolate*: The Rhetoric of Cuban Reconciliation" (1998), 417; or Jean-Claude Seguin's "Nobody's Perfect" (2006), 217.

4. As most studies would have it, the year is 1979 to be precise. In a scene at the university, students watch the news on a black and white television. The news reports Anastasio Somoza's resigning and fleeing Nicaragua, events corresponding to July 1979.

5. Burton, Julianne and Marta Alvear. "Interview with Humberto Solás. 'Every point of arrival is a point of departure,'" *Jump Cut* 19 (December 1978): 32–33. Web. 15 Oct 2013. http://www.ejumcut.or/archive/online essays/JC19folder/SolasInt.html.

Chapter 5

1. Published March 12, 1965 in the Uruguayan newspaper *Marcha*.

Chapter 6

1. English translation (1901) by John Veitch of Descartes, René, *Meditationes De*

Prima Philosophia (1641), later *Meditations Metaphysiques*, trans. Duc de Luynes (1647). Accessed 6 June 2013 at: *www.wright.edu/~charles.taylor/descartes/meditation*1.html.

2. This thoroughfare, the Gran Vía, is a main artery in Madrid. It is one of the busiest streets in the world. Within Amenábar's penchant to create movies that question, this scene is curious. Not that the film asks the questions here, but most certainly there are viewers who ask how did Amenábar manage to get this shot.

3. Not all readers of the film are attuned to the importance of a film's first few minutes. Nathan Richardson (2003), for example, would seem to short shrift the opening scene when he says "Following the opening scene, *Abre los ojos* temporarily turns conventional…. Amenábar has demonstrated particular skill in many of the classic Hollywood story-telling techniques. So it goes during the following twenty minutes of this film, in which César awakens now from his nightmare on the Gran Vía, follows his same dream course to find this time the geography teaming with life" (333).

4. Some might argue that according to Freud, the unconscious does not recognize time, and thus there might be a question about attention paid by this analysis to particular time scales. For Freud, though, it is not that time is not recognized, but rather that dreams display a lack of a sense of time and/or an independence of space and time. Furthermore, any analysis should not ignore that on all three occasions [most importantly for the moment, the first two, which occur in the matrix-establishing first few minutes of the film], the camera focuses specifically on the clock reporting the exact time to the viewer. As the narrative moves forward, the reported hour has gone backwards, preparing the viewer for a diegetic independence of time.

5. Others include: Emil Volek; Mieke Bal (*Narratology. Introduction to the Theory of Narrative*. Toronto: University of Toronto Press, 1985), who proposes the tripartite division of fabula/story/text, where *text* refers to the signifiers or surface structure of the *story*, which itself refers to the signifiers or surface structure of the *fabula*; and José Ángel García Landa (*Acción, relato, discurso. Estructura de la ficción narrativa*. Salamanca: Universidad de Salamanca, 1988), who distinguishes between three levels of the narrative work: *acción* (plot), *relato* (narrative), and *discurso narrativo* (narrative discourse), where *acción* means the sequence of narrated events, *relato* the presentation of the narrated events, and *discurso* the presentation of the *relato*, its transformation of the into a sign system in conjunction with the act of utterance that is the *narración*.

6. Jacques Terrasa (2007) has an interesting study of Amenábar's use of black screens in his films. In *Abre los ojos*, among other things, this technique underscores "la solitude absolute du cauchemar urbain de César" (41). The times Terrasa gives for the duration of black screens in the film differ slightly from my own.

7. For the sake of a linear presentation, the actual order of the organization of the "narration/narrating," the sequence of the act of narrating, appears as altered. Of course, the producing narrative order is: 9:03→9:00→9:06.

8. The opening black blank screen voiceover sequence lasts 22 seconds; the second lasts only 8 seconds; and the film-ending black blank screen voiceover last 15 seconds before the viewer begins to see film credits and to listen to a non-diegetic musical soundtrack. "Real time" here refers to the amount of time invested by the viewer in viewing.

9. Dream narrative does not work so well with Genette's model because it is based on a realist equivalence in structural logic, and dream facts/events are not necessarily dream meanings. This objection aside, the model is useful for this chapter's analysis, as it allows for a convenient organization of narrated material. Further, it must be remembered that the object of analysis here is an artistic text, not dreams *per se*.

10. This broad stroke rendering of a temporal-causal ordering of events contrasts with the actual order of the telling, which features numerous flashforwards and flashbacks, match cuts, etc. in a dream within a dream structure. The telling/récit 2 could be represented as follows (where bold highlights some interruptions in temporal-causal order):

> Wakeup/sit up (look in mirror, shower, dress, Nuria, go out in VW, drive down busy Gran Vía) → Pelayo and frontón (Conversation about "ugly") → Conversation with Antonio in penitentiary cell (God, 2

months, that night)→ Birthday party→ Sofía's apartment (drawings, Duvernois on TV)→ Nuria + Car crash→ **With Antonio in cell (in the park (Sofía, horrible dream, remember the party?→ dreaming is shit→ wakeup/situp, mirror, disfigured), show me your face)** → Visit with doctors→ With Antonio in cell (difference between dreams and reality, drawing)→ mime Sofía in the park/rain→ Night club + Sofía, Pelayo→ Passing out on the street (watch reads 9:00)→ "Splicing" ("Abre los ojos" [watch reads 6:05] Nuria > Sofía "I love you")→ Sofía in the park (been here before)→ With Antonio in cell (Eli?, fragments, papers)→ Visit to doctors (successful surgery)→ **With Antonio in cell (happiness, dream about memories)**→ Removal of bandages + sex→ Restaurant + Sofía + Pelayo (photo, Duvernois)→ In bed with Sofía (nightmare, Sofía turns into Nuria)→ Police + Pelayo→ **In bar with Duvernois (What if I told you that you were dreaming?)** → With Antonio in cell (hypnosis, suicide, difference between dreams and reality)→ Sofía's apartment (photos changed to Nuria > Sofía > Nuria, killing, disfigured in mirror)→ **With Antonio in cell (dreams are like that, trial)**→ Duvernois on TV→ Computer search→ Visit to Life Extension (explanation, disfigured in mirror, killing of guard, guard shoots Antonio, conversation with Duvernois, Sofía, Antonio, Pelayo > mirages/holographs, jump and free fall).

11. Time and its relationship to narrative are important, and this relationship has been the focus of important theoretical work. See, for example, Paul Ricoeur (*Time and Narrative*. 3 vols. Trans. Kathleen McLaughlin and David Pellauer. Chicago: University of Chicago Press, 1983, 1985), or Meir Sternberg (*Expositional Modes and Temporal Ordering in Fiction*. Bloomington: Indiana University Press, 1993).

12. In this reception/reading of the first few minutes, there are some important differences with other readings of the same. Paul Julian Smith (2004), for example, prefers to see César "roaming a deserted boulevard" of an "evacuated" city. Rather than "evacuated," I prefer a less charged adjective, "empty." And, though Smith correctly concludes that the sequence is a dream, rather than roaming, César's "lone figure on the street," (96) runs, stops, turns, and hesitates; and, the distinction is important.

13. So widespread is the idea of Amenábar's films not giving answers but rather posing questions, that his official website flashes "Mis películas no son de respuestas sino de preguntas" almost immediately when the internaut accesses the site. See, www.clubcultura.com/clubcine/club cineastas/amenabar/intro.htm. Another very illustrative case in Amenábar's filmic *corpus* of this opening up a space for the viewer to think for himself is his Oscar-winning *Mar adentro*. Taking on the socially and morally touchy topic of euthanasia and Ramón Sampedro's publicly well-known fight to die with dignity, the film explores the question from many directions, but it does not take sides. Evading the temptation of falling into a "'moralina' cerrada" is not only characteristic of Amenábar's cinema, but, alongside Javier Bardem's portrayal, it is what contributes to this film's appeal.

14. Seeing parallels between Amenábar's filmic texts and other texts of Hispanic tradition, critics have described various links. See, for example: Marina Martín (2002 and 2004) and Marit Knollmueller (2009).

15. For Laraway (2008), this is really "the central conceit of the film" (67). Given the importance of this "central conceit," the question "Why are you telling me this dream?" could just as easily be asked by the viewer. In this case, the film becomes highly self-reflective, offering up more questions. Only now, the questions respond to a metafilmic level dealing with the relationship between film and viewer.

16. Among many other references, see, for example, Freud's section A on "Recent and Indifferent Material" in Chapter V, "The Material and Sources of Dreams," in *The Interpretation of Dreams*, 210–220.

17. The repetition of the question from these two sequences and its prominence create the potential for another of Amenábar's questions, that of technology (here, cryogenics) trespassing on divine territory.

18. Dreams that involve falling are common. Like most dream motifs, falling indicates anxieties and insecurities. Triggers can be feeling overwhelmed and out of control in a relationship or at work in one's waking life. The loss of control in falling may parallel a waking life situation. Falling dreams can also reflect a sense of failure or inferiority in some waking life circumstance. Freudian interpretation of dreams of falling points towards wishing to succumb to sexual urges. Any one, if not all, of these triggers

could be the operant determinants of César's falling dream.

19. Thakkar, like Richardson (2003), might be criticized, though, for taking the psychological too far in finding implications for all of Spain's youth culture. And, Knollmueller only needs Amenábar to suggest "a waking dream or 'conscious hallucination'" in order to place him in the dreamwork pantheon with Cervantes, Calderón, Buñuel, and Dalí.

Chapter 7

1. For an analysis of the phenomenon of contemporary funding and distribution approaches of major Latin American film industries, see Luisela Alvaray, "National, Regional, and Global: New Waves of Latin American Cinema," *Cinema Journal* 47, No. 3, Spring 2008: 48–65.

2. In Mexico during the years prior to and following the film's release, abortion is a controversial topic. Though the Supreme Court found in 2008 that there was no federal impediment to abortion, it was, in part a states' rights issue. While some states nominally permit abortion in cases of rape, threat to the mother's life, fetal deformities or economic burden, little or no access or assistance is offered to pregnant women, and abortion is, in fact, prohibited in more than half of the country's thirty-one states. On the other hand, in Mexico City, since 2007, a woman can get an abortion on request up to 12 weeks into her pregnancy.

3. The first time this visual is presented, it is between the scene in which Benito and Amaro argue about their celibacy violations and the scene in which Rubén and his dad talk about the evidence the latter has about the priests. The second time the visual of the church ensconced on the mountainside is seen, it is found between the scene in which Amaro put his vocation above Amelia's concerns and the scene in which Martín alerts Benito to Amaro's tutelage of Amelia.

4. This is the church of Santa María Magdalena in Tepetlaoxtoc, Mexico, where many interiors, especially the film-ending funeral mass, are also shot.

5. In these images, the very attentive viewer discovers, perhaps, another disconnect. This time it is technical. While the long shot visuals of the church portray a white church, including its two bell towers, other images just of bell towers display a tower that is not white, rather plain stone.

6. One study would even have this narrative complexity as a defect. Luis García Orso (2007) says, "Carrera's movie has the defect of dealing with so many characters that he cannot go into any of them in detail about their journeys and problems" (100). For him, this is intentional because the Mexican viewership is incapable of greater readerly complexity having "been formed by watching soap operas."

Chapter 8

1. To read more about this concept, see studies like those by Sylvia Adamson, Einav Argaman, Stephen C. Levinson or John Lyons, among others (see bibliography).

2. At the XVIII Goya awards, *Te doy mis ojos* won the following awards: Best Picture, Best Director (Icíar Bollaín), Best Actress in a Lead Role (Laia Marull), Best Actor in a Lead Role (Luis Tosar), Best Supporting Actress (Candela Peña), Best Original Script (Icíar Bollaín and Alicia Luna), and Best Sound (Valiño, Pino, Crespo and Gutiérrez).

3. The regime developed legislation which excluded women from many activities in an attempt to keep them in traditional roles. See, for example, the Fuero de Trabajo from 1938 under which the State "prohibirá el trabajo nocturno de las mujeres y niños, regulará el trabajo a domicilio y liberará a la mujer casada del taller y de la fábrica" [will prohibit women and children from night work, will regulate domestic work, and will free women from workshops and factories]; or the so called 'licencia marital' [marital/marriage license] (Derecho de Familia, artículo 57) which obligated women to obey their husbands, without whose permission [license] she could not work, nor earn a salary, nor do business, nor hold a job, nor open a checking account in the bank, nor get a passport, drivers license, etc. (This idea of 'marital license' held on until the legislative reform of 1975); or an order from 1938 (*Boletín Oficial del Estado*, 31 diciembre) that declared that "la tendencia del Nuevo Estado, es que la mujer dedique su atención al hogar y se separe de los puestos de trabajo" [the tendency of the New State, is that women dedicate their attention to the home

and that they distance themselves from the workplace].

4. Reference here, and elsewhere, to "chapter" is made to "capítulos" (or "chapters") divisions of the film on its commercial DVD.

5. Used here is "in theory," because, although no list of themes to be treated was proposed, what was proposed was film that would become more socially conscience, as film in other countries and that it "concentra su interés en los problemas que la realidad plantea cada día, sirviendo así a una esencial misión de testimonio" [focus its interest on the problems that reality presents every day, serving in that way an essential mission as witness], as the inaugural manifesto of said conference read.

6. Crucial for the understanding of this film is the relationship between the film and art (painting). For a thorough analysis of this relationship, see Jorge González del Pozo, "La liberación a través del arte en *Te doy mis ojos* de Icíar Bollaín," *Ciberletras* 19 (julio 2008).

7. Previously, as a director, Icíar Bollaín had made *Hola, ¿estás sola?* (1995) and *Flores de otro mundo* (1999), both with a thematics that centers on women and the search for identity and happiness.

8. She is scriptwriter or co-scriptwriter on *Hola, ¿estás sola?* (1995), *Flores de otro mundo* (1999), *Te doy mis ojos* (2003), *Mataharis* (2007), and *Katmandú, un espejo en el cielo* (2011); that is, five of her seven films.

9. The semantic potential actualized by the deictics here is lost in a poor translation of the title for the film's distribution in the English-speaking world. *Te doy mis ojos* was rendered as *Take My Eyes*. The change undervalues the deictic interplay as it reduces the number of deictics used, and it cancels the support for an invocation of empathy as it substitutes an offering (I give) for a command (Take).

10. This "flight" can be approached productively as "exile." See, for example, Tobin Stanley (2012).

11. It is not clear what stylistic implications of the centrality of this device are for categorizing this film as "realistic." Begin (2009) and Goss (2008), among others, categorize *Te doy mis ojos* as such. This doubt notwithstanding, the importance of metonymy is certainly consistent with his categorization of it as "a carefully constructed artistic endeavor that affirms the New Spanish Woman's aspirations" (34). For Goss' realism, foreshadowing (for example, throwing the wedding dress off of the roof as auguring the decision to end her marriage), and contrast are key devices.

12. Jaqueline Cruz (2005), Pascale Thibaudeau (2008), and María Elena Soliño (2008) recognize the metaphorical-symbolical value of using Toledo, with its walled old city and peripheral residential areas, and the weight of its "history of repression," as the setting for this story. And, the director herself ("Historia") indexes the metonymical value of Toledo as the choice for the story's setting.

13. Given the importance of this scene, it has received very little critical attention. Zecchi's (2006) interest is in representation of the male body. Begin (2009) feels it does not necessarily fulfil the code of erotic decodification, primarily because of the film's general social context.

14. An important current of scholarship on *Te doy mis ojos* treats the ways in which the film utilizes paintings as supporting intertexts. See, for example, Beltrán Brotons (2003), Gimeno Ugalde (2011), González del Pozo (2008), Gould Levine (2007), Soliño (2008), and Tobin Stanley (2012). There is, though, no unanimity as to the efficacy of the use of the paintings, as both Smith (2004) and Wheeler (2012) see the probably unintended suggestion of equating lovemaking and wife battering in the use of Titian's *Danaë*.

15. For example, and consistent with the film's call to empathy, when the "husband" cannot think of anything to say, the psychologist tells him "Mira, trata de ponerte en su lugar, tú has estado todo el día fuera trabajando; llegas a casa y tendrás ganas de contarle cosas a tu mujer. Ella ha estado todo el día en casa y tendrá cosas que contarte. Pues, venga." (Look. Try to put yourself in her place, you've been out all day working; you get home and you probably feel like telling your wife stuff. She's been at home all day and probably has stuff to tell you. Alright, come on).

16. I would agree, though, with critics who view the behavioral attribution solely to Iberian machismo as simplistic. I do not agree, however, that the film itself, consistent with its own orientation as to how it should be read, limits adscription of Antonio's

psychology to Spanish tradition. For example, the triggers for the most forceful, most humiliating scene in the film have far more to do with Antonio's insecurities than they do with machismo.

17. In fact, the film does not offer a solution or solutions to domestic violence. And, it is with this point that a criticism of the film surfaces, as will be quickly seen below.

BIBLIOGRAPHY

Adamson, Sylvia. "From Empathetic Deixis to Empathetic Narrative and De-subjectivisation as Processes of Language Change." *Transactions of the Philological Society* 92 (1) (March 2008): 55–88.

Aldama, Frederick Luis. *Mex-Ciné: Mexican Filmmaking, Production, and Consumption in the Twenty-first Century*. Ann Arbor: University of Michigan Press, 2013.

Almeida, Ricardo Normanha Ribeiro de. "As Ditaduras Militares no Cinema Argentino e Brasileiro: Uma Análise de *A História Oficial* e *Para Frente Brasil*." *Baleia na Rede: Revista do Grupo de Estudos e Pesquisa en Cinema e Literatura* 6 (2009): 128–145.

Alvaray, Luisela. "National, Regional, and Global: New Waves of Latin American Cinema." *Cinema Journal* 47.3 (Spring 2008): 48–64.

Amenábar, Alejandro, dir. *Abre los ojos*. Perf. Eduardo Noreiga, Penélope Cruz & Chete Lera. Canal + España, et al. 1997. Summit/Artisan DVD, 2001.

Amestoy, Ignacio. "De la 'historia oficial' a la 'historia real.'" *Primer Acto: Cuadernos de Investigación Teatral* 280 (Sept.–Oct. 1999): 15–18.

A'ness, Francine. "A Lesson in Synthesis: Nation Building and Images of a 'New Cuba' in *Fresa y chocolate*." *Lucero: A Journal of Iberian and Latin American Studies* 7 (Spring 1996): 86–98.

Antaolalla, Isabel. *The Cinema of Icíar Bollín*. Manchester: Manchester University Press, 2012.

Arocena, Carmen. "Ana en el cine: El momento esencial." In Pérez Perucha, Julio, Ed. (2005). 307–333.

———. *Víctor Erice*. Madrid: Cátedra, 1996.

Arroyo, Jorge I. "La marginación en *Danzón*, *Fresa y chocolate*, *La guagua aérea* y *Taxi para tres*." *Arenas Blancas: Revista Literaria* 7 (Spring 2007): 10–11.

Ashworth, Peter P. "Silence and Self-Portraits: The Artist as Young Girl, Old Man and Scapegoat in *El espíritu de la colmena* and *El sueño de la razón*." *Estreno: Cuadernos del Teatro Español Contemporáneo* 12.2 (Fall 1986): 66–71.

Aubert, Jean-Paul. "En parcourante la Toile…" *Le Cinéma d´Alejandro Amenábar*. Ed. Nancy Berthier. Toulouse: PY Mirail, 2007. 57–77.

Babel. Dir. Alejando González Iñárritu. Perf. Brad Pitt, Kate Blanchett, Gael García Bernal, and Rinko Kikuchi. Paramount, 2006.

Babovic, Sarah, and Lisa Vollendorf. "Beyond Violence: Defining Justice in New Spain." *Revista Canadiense de Estudios Hispánicos* 34.1 (Fall 2009): 77–98.

Bach, Caleb. "María Luisa Bemberg Tells the Untold." *Americas* March–April 1994: 20–27.

Balaisis, Nicholas. "Cuba, Cinema and the Post-Revolutionary Public Sphere." *Canadian Journal of Film Studies/Revue Canadienne d'Études Cinématographiques* 19.2 (Fall 2010): 26–42.

Barnard, Timothy, ed. *Argentine Cinema*. Toronto: Nightwood, 1986.
_____, and Peter Rist, eds. *South American Cinema: A Critical Filmography 1915–1994*. Austin: University of Texas Press, 1996.
Barquet, Jesús. "Paz, Gutiérrez Alea y Tabío: Felices discrepancias entre un cuento, un guión y un film: *Fresa y chocolate*." *Fe de Erratas* 10 (mayo 1995): 83–86.
Bazin, André. *What Is Cinema?* (Ed. and trans. Hugh Gray). 2 vols. Berkeley: University of California Press, 2005.
Becerra Mayor, David. "Construir la diferencia en condiciones de igualdad: Tres películas cubanas." *Contracorriente: A Journal of Social History and Literature in Latin America* 12.2 (2015): 271–306.
Begin, Paul. "Regarding the Pain of Others: The Art of Realism in Icíar Bollaín's *Te doy mis ojos*." *Studies in Hispanic Cinemas* 6.1 (2010): 31–44.
Behar, Ruth. "Queer Times in Cuba." *Bridges to Cuba/Puentes a Cuba*. Ed. Ruth Behar. Ann Arbor: University of Michigan Press, 1995. 394–415.
Bejel, Emilio. "*Strawberry and Chocolate*: Coming out of the Cuban Closet?" *South Atlantic Quarterly* 96.1 (Winter 1997): 65–82.
Belle epoque. Dir. Fernando Trueba. Perf. Fernando Fernán Gómez, Jorge Sanz, Maribel Verdú, Penélope Cruz, Ariadna Gil, and Miriam Díaz-Aroca. Animatógrafo, Euriages, Fernando Trueba Producciones, Lolafilms, and Sogepaq, 1992.
Beltrán Brotons, María Jesús. "Universos pictóricos y el arte cinematográfico de Icíar Bollaín en *Te doy mis ojos* (2003)." *Miradas glocales. Cine español en el cambio de milenio*. Eds. Burkhard Pohl & Jörg Türschmann. Madrid/Frankfurt: Iberoamericana/Veruert, 2007. 323–336.
Bemberg, María-Luisa, dir. *Camila*. Perf. Susú Pecoraro and Imanol Arias. GEA Cinematográfica S.R.I. e Impala S.A., 1984. Re-release, Cinemateca-Condor Media, 2002. DVD.
Benjamin, Walter. "The Work of Art in the Age of Mechanical Reproduction." *Illuminations. Essays and Reflections*. New York: Harcourt, Brace & World, 1968. 217–252.
Berenschot, Denis Jorge. *Performing Cuba: (Re)Writing Gender Identity and Exile Across Genres*. New York: Peter Lang, 2005.
Berthet, Catherine. "Sociocritique de la musique de film, II: Carmen." *Co-Textes* 25, (1993): 7–136.
Berthier, Nancy. "Fraise et chocolat." *Cinquante couples insolites*. Ed. Gérard Langlois. Condé-sur-Noireau: Corlet, 2005. 231–235.
Berthier, Nancy. "Cine y nacionalidad.: El caso del remake." *Miradas glocales: Cine español en el cambio del milenio*. Madrid/Fankfurt: Iberoamericana/Vervuert, 2007. 337–346.
_____. "Voyage au pays d'Alejandro Amenábar." *Le Cinéma d´Alejandro Amenábar*. Ed. Nancy Berthier. Toulouse: PY Mirail, 2007. 13–26.
Besas, Peter, *Behind the Spanish Lens*. Denver: Arden, 1985.
Blackwelder, Rob. "*El Crimen Del Padre Amaro* Movie Review." ContactMusic.com. n/d. Accessed 10 November 2013 at http://www.contactmusic.com/movie-review/padreamaro
Blackwood Collier, Mary. *La Carmen essentielle et sa réalisation au epectacle*. New York: Peter Lang, 1994.
Blanco García, Ana Isabel. "Violencia doméstica y nuevos modelos de mujer. *Te doy mis ojos* o la importancia de la mirada femenina." *Cuestiones de género: de la igualdad y la diferencia* 0 (2005): 9–32.
Blommers, Thomas. "Social and Cultural Circularity in *La historia oficial*." *Ciberletras* 6 (2002). n/p.

Boero, Paulo. "Uncanny Oscar Winners: Memory, Affect, and Oppositional Cinema in Postdictatorial Argentina." *Hispanet Journal* 6 (2013): 1–26.
Bollaín, Icíar. "Escribe Icíar Bollaín: Respuestas a la violencia en pareja." *Noticias del guión.* Accessed 2 Nov 2015 at http://www.abcguionistas.com/noticias/articulos/11111111/escribe-iciar-bollain-respuestas-a-la-violencia-en-pareja.html.
_____. "Historia de amor y maltrato," *El País Semanal* 5 octubre 2003: 24–27.
Bollaín, Icíar, dir. *Te doy mis ojos.* 2003. Perf. Laia Marull and Luis Tovar. La Iguana y Alto Producción, 2003. New Yorker Films, 2006.
Bordwell, David, and Kristin Thompson. *Film Art. An Introduction.* 7th ed. Boston: McGraw-Hill, 2004.
Brescia, Pablo. *"El crimen del Padre Amaro." Chasqui* 32.2 (Nov. 2003): 184–186.
Brussat, Frederic, and Mary Ann. "Film Review: *El Crimen del Padre Amaro.*" *Spirituality and Practice* n/d. Accessed 1 October 2014 at: http://www.spiritualityandpractice.com/films/films.php?id=5343.
Bueno, Fernanda Vitor. *The Myth of Camila O'Gorman in the Works of Juana Manuela Gorriti, Maria Luisa Bemberg, and Enrique Molina.* Dissertation Abstracts International, Section A: The Humanities and Social Sciences (DAIA) 2008 June; 68 (12): 5080. University of Texas, Austin, 2007. Abstract no.: DA3290816.
Cantero, Mónica. "Visions and Voices of the Self in *Take My Eyes.*" *Visions of Struggle in Women's Filmmaking in the Mediterranean.* Ed. Flavia Laviosa. New York: Palgrave Macmillan, 2010. 45–60.
Carbonetti, María de los Ángeles, Rita de Grandis, Mónica Escudero, and Omar Rodríguez. "Representation of Women in the Films of María Luisa Bemberg. *Women Filmmakers: Refocusing.* Eds. Jacqueline Levitin, Judith Plessis and Valérie Raoul. Vancouver: University of British Columbia Press, 2002. 239–249.
Carmen. Dir. Carlos Saura. Perf. Antonio Gades, Laura del Sol, and Cristina Hoyos. Emiliano Piedra, and TVE, 1983.
Carrera, Carlos, dir. *El crimen del padre Amaro.* Perf. Gael García Bernal, Ana Claudia Talancón & Sancho García. Alameda Films, et al. 2002.
Casamayor, Odette. "Tomás Gutiérrez Alea: Au-delà de *Fraise et chocolat*/Beyond *Strawberry and Chocolate.*" *Ecrans d'Afrique* 23 (1998): 84.
Castro de Paz, José Luis. "Raíces profundas (mito, guerra e infancia en el cine español)." In Pérez Perucha, Julio, Ed. (2005). 359–388.
Català, Josep María. "Una habitación sin vistas. Formas del tiempo complejo." In Pérez Perucha, Julio, Ed. (2005). 335–357.
Chanan, Michael. *Cuban Cinema.* Minneapolis: University of Minnesota Press, 2004.
Cibreiro, Estrella. "Recapturing a Lost Time: The Artist's Depiction of Postwar Spain." *Interfaces: Image Texte Language,* 19–20.1(2001–2002): 205–224.
Colmeiro, José F. "La doble revolución: Masculinidades transgresoras en el cine cubano." *Cine-Lit: Essays on Hispanic Film and Fiction* 6 (2008): 25–35.
_____. "Rehispanicizing Carmen: Cultural Reappropriations in Spanish Cinema." *Carmen: From Silent Film to MTV.* Eds. Chris Perriam and Ann Davies. Amsterdam, Netherlands: Rodopi; 2005. 91–105.
Cortázar, Julio. *Hopscotch.* (Gregory Rabassa, Trans.). New York: Random House, 1966.
Costello, Judith A.M. "Politics and Popularity: The Current Mexican Cinema." *Review: Literature and Arts of the Americas* 38.1 (2005): 31–38.
Craig, Herbert E. "La directora María Luisa Bemberg y las protagonistas de sus películas *Camila* y *De eso no se habla.*" *Asterión: Literatura, Arte, Cine* 6.24 (1999): 29–33.
Cros, Edmond. "Lecture sociocritique du film *La historia oficial.*" Luis Puenzo, *La historia oficial.* Montpellier: Institut international de sociocritique: Cettre d'études e de recherches sociocrituqes (*Co-Textes* 23), 1992. 91–106.

Cruz, Jacqueline. "Amores que matan: Dulce Chacón, Icíar Bollaín y la violencia de género." *Letras hispanas*, 2.1 (2005): 67–81.

Cruz, Maximiliano. "Los curas van al cine. (El cierre ciclónico)." *Nexos* 24.297 (2002): 89.

Cruz-Malavé, Arnaldo. "Lecciones de cubanía: Identidad nacional y errancia sexual en Senel Paz, Martí y Lezama Lima." *Cuban Studies* 29 (1 Jan 1999): 129–154.

_____. Lecciones de cubanía: Identidad nacional y errancia sexual en Senel Paz, Martí y Lezama Lima." *Revista de Crítica Cultural* 17 (Nov. 1998): 58–67.

Curry, Richard K. "Clarifying the Enigma: 'Reading' Víctor Erice's *El espíritu de la colmena*." *Bulletin of Hispanic Studies*, LXXIII.3 (July 1996): 269–275.

_____. "La estructuración del discurso fílmico en *Camila* de María Luisa Bemberg: filtros." *Letras femeninas* 18,1–2 (Spring–Fall 1992): 11–23.

_____. "La deixis en *Te doy mis ojos*: una invitación a la empatía." *Revista Lingüística y Literatura*. 63 (2013). 339–352.

_____. "Representations of Violence in Icíar Bollaín's *Te doy mis ojos*." *Hispanic Journal* 34.1 (Spring 2013): 131–145.

Cusato, Domenico Antonio. "*Fresa y chocolate* de Senel Paz: Régimen y homosexualidad." *Inti: Revista de Literatura Hispánica* 59–60 (Spring–Fall 2004): 123–132.

Cuya Gavilano, Lorena. "Ser para otro: *Máscaras, Fresa y chocolate* y la retórica de la metáfora homosexual." *Bulletin of Hispanic Studies* 88.7 (2011): 811–828.

Darke, Chris. "'Les Enfants et les Cinéphiles': The Moment of Epiphany in *The Spirit of the Beehive*." *Cinema Journal* 49.2 (Winter 2010): 152–158.

Davies, Ann. "The Male Body and the Female Gaze in Carmen Films." *The Trouble with Men: Masculinities in European and Hollywood Cinema*. Eds. Phil Powrie, Ann Davies & Bruce Babington. London: Wallflower; 2004. 187–95.

_____. "The Spanish femme fatale and the Cinematic Negotiation of Spanishness." *Studies in Hispanic Cinemas* 1.1 (2004): 5–16.

Davies, Catherine. "Recent Cuban Films: Identification, Interpretation, Disorder." *Bulletin of Latin American Research* 15.2 (1996): 177–192.

Deleuze, Gilles. *Cinema 1. The Movement-Image*. Trans. Hugh Tomlinson & Barbara Habberjam. Minneapolis: University of Minnesota Press, 1986.

_____. *Cinema 2. The Time-Image*. Hugh Tomlinson & Robert Galeta, Trans. Minneapolis: University of Minnesota Press, 1989.

Deleyto, Celestino. "Women and Other Monsters: Frankenstein and the Role of the Mother in *El espíritu de la colmena*." *Bulletin of Hispanic Studies*, LXXVI (1999): 39–51.

Deveny, Thomas. "Alejandro Amenábar, Composer." *Bulletin of Spanish Studies* 87.2 (March 2010): 194–224.

_____. *Cain on Screen: Contemporary Spanish Cinema*. Metuchen & London: Scarecrow, 1993.

Díaz, Roberto Ignacio. "The Spirit of Cuba and the Ghost of Opera." *Symposium: A Quarterly Journal in Modern Literatures* 61.1 (Spring 2007): 57–74.

D'Lugo, Marvin. "Historical Reflexivity: Saura's Anti-Carmen." *Wide Angle: A Film Quarterly of Theory, Criticism, and Practice*, 9.3 (1987): 52–61.

_____. *The Films of Carlos Saura. The Practice of Seeing*. Princeton: Princeton University Press, 1991.

Edwards, Gwynne. "*Carmen*." *Catholic Tastes and Times*. Eds. Margaret A. Rees & Mary Hallaway. Leeds: Trinity and All Saints' College, 1987. 127–155.

_____. *Indecent Exposures. Buñuel, Saura, Erice & Almodóvar*. London: Marion Boyars, 1995.

_____. "Saura's *Bodas de sangre*: Play into Film." *Hispanic Studies in Honour of Geoffrey*

Ribbans. Eds. Ann Mackenzie & Dorothy S. Severin. Liverpool: Liverpool University Press, 1991. 275–282.
Egea, Juan. "El monstruo metafórico en *El espíritu de la colmena*." *Revista de Estudios Hispánicos* 36 (2002): 523–543.
Ehrlich, Linda C., ed. *The Cinema of Víctor Erice. An Open Window*. Lanhan, MD: Scarecrow, 2007.
Ehrlich, Linda C., and Celia Martínez García. "Las canciones de Erice: La naturaleza como música/la música como naturaleza." *Secuencias* (Instituto Universitario de Ciencias de la Educación, Universidad Autónoma de Madrid) 31 (primer semestre 2010): 7–31; Translated and reprinted as "Erice's Songs: Nature as Music/Music as Nature." *Framework: Journal of Cinema and Media*, 52 (Spring 2012): np. Accessible at: http://www.frameworkonline.com/Issue52/521lceandcmg.html
Ellis Neyra, Rachel. "From '¡Patria o muerte!' to 'El rincón de la paciencia': Reading the Cuban Nation in Time in *Memorias del subdesarrollo*, *Fresa y chocolate*, and *Suite Habana*." *Habana elegante* 52 (Fall–Winter 2012): np.
Erausquín, Estela. "María Luisa Bemberg's Revolt." *Revista Canadiense de Estudios Hispánicos* 27.1 (Fall 2002):45–57.
Erice, Víctor. "Pardo alla carriere—Conversation with Víctor Erice," 67⁰ Festival del Film 6-16 August 2014 Locarno. Locarno, Switzerland. 13 August 2014. Accessed at: "Conversation with Victor Erice at Locarno." www.youtube.com/watch?v=Vr9 HDt4xhCU
Erice, Víctor, dir. *El espíritu de la colmena*. Prod. Elías Querejeta. Perf. Fernando Fernán Gómez, Teresa Gimperra, Ana Torrent. 1972. The Criterion Collection, 2006.
Escudero, Isabel. "Apuntes acerca de *El espíritu de la colmena*." In Pérez Perucha, Julio, Ed. (2005). 469–480.
El espíritu de la colmena. Dir. Víctor Erice. Perf. Fernando Fernán Gómez, Teresa Gimpera, Ana Torrent, and Isabel Tellería. Elías Querejeta Producciones, 1973.
Evans, Peter William. "The Monster, the Place of the Father, and Growing up in the Dictatorship." *Vida hispánica* 31.3 (1982): 13–17.
Falicov, Tamara L. "Film Production in Argentina under Democracy: 1983-1989. *The Official Story* (*La historia oficial*) as an International Mind." *Southern Quarterly: A Journal of the Arts in the South* 39.4 (Summer 2001): 123–34.
_____. *The Cinematic Tango. Contemporary Argentine Film*. London: Wallflower, 2007.
Fernández Romero, Diana. "Ecos de *Te doy mis ojos*: voces y silencios de algunas receptoras del filme." *Nueva Literatura Hispánica* 8–9 (2004–2005): 267–296.
Fiddian, Robin. "*El espíritu de la colmena/The Spirit of the Beehive* (Víctor Erice, 1973: *To Kill a Mockingbird* as Neglected Intertext." *Spanish Cinema 1973-2010. Auteurism, Politics, Landscape and Memory*. Eds. María M. Delgado & Robin Fiddian. Manchester: Manchester Up, 2013. 21–34.
_____, and Peter W. Evans. *Challenges to Authority: Fiction and Film in Contemporary Spain*. London: Tamesis, 1988.
Figueiredo, Monica. "Do Livro ao Filme. Un 'Crime' que Atravessou Séculos." *Letras de Hoje: Estudos e Debates de Assuntos de Lingüística* 40.4 (Dec. 2005): 127–137.
_____. "*El crimen del padre Amaro*: Du livre au film, un 'crime' qui a traversé les siècles." (Teresa Cristina Cerdeira da Silva, Trans.). *Excavatio: Emile Zola and Naturalism* 21.1–2 (2006): 273–83.
Firpo, Arturo. "Glosario de *La historia oficial*." *Luis Puenzo, La historia oficial*. Montpellier: Institut international de sociocritique : Cettre d'études e de recherches sociocrituqes (*Co-Textes* 23), 1992. 49–57.
Forcinito, Ana. "De la plaza al mercado: La memoria, el olvido y los cuerpos femeninos

en Puenzo, Solanas y Aristarain." *Chasqui: Revista de Literatura Latinoamericana* 29.2 (Nov. 2000): 122–34.
Foster, David William. "*Camila*: Beauty and Bestiality." *Contemporary Argentine Cinema*. Colombia: University of Missouri Press, 1992. 14–26.
_____. "Documenting Queer, Queer Documentary." *Revista Canadiense de Estudios Hispánicos* 35.1 (2010): 105–119.
_____. "Negociaciones queer en *Fresa y chocolate*: Ideología y homoerotismo." *Revista Iberoamericana* 69.205 (Oct–Dec 2003): 985–999.
_____. "*The Official Story* (*La historia oficial*): Truth and Consequences." *Contemporary Argentine Cinema*. Colombia: University of Missouri Press, 1992. 38–53.
Frechilla, Emilio. "Entre la realidad y la ficción: La narrativa cinematográfica de Alejandro Amenábar." *Interface: Bradford Studies in Language, Culture and Society* 7 (Summer 2004): 83–94.
Freisen, Maria. "Sauras Carmen: KörpergewordenSchrift." Eds. Claudia Gronemann, Christiane Maass, Sabine A. Peters & Sabine Schrader. *Körper und Schrift*. Bonn, Germany: Romanistischer; 2001. 109–115.
Fresa y chocolate. Dirs. Tomás Guitérrez Alea, and Juan Carlos Tabío. Perf. Jorge Perrugorría, Vladimir Cruz, and Mirta Ibarra. ICAIC, Instituto Mejicano de Cinematografía, and Telemadrid, 1993. Mr. Bongo Films, n.d. DVD.
Freud, Sigmund. *The Interpretation of Dreams*. (James Strachey, Trans.). New York: First Discus, 1965.
Gabara, Esther. "La ciudad loca: An Epistemological Plan." *Journal of Latin American Cultural Studies* 9.2 (Aug 2000): 119–135.
Galasso, Norberto. *Los malditos: hombres y mujeres excluídos de la historia oficial de los argentinos*. Buenos Aires: Ediciones Madres de Plaza de Mayo, 2005.
Gallo, Marta. "La imagen de Camila." *Mujer y sociedad en América: IV Simposio Internacional:* Vol 1. Ed. Juana Alcira Arancibia. Westminster, CA; Mexicali: Instituto Literario y Cultural Hispánico; Univ. Autónoma de Baja California, 1988. 209–22.
_____. "La voz de Camila O'Gorman." *Paunch* 65–66 (1991). 63–86.
García, Carlos Javier. "Documentalismo y lectura alegórica." *Letras peninsulares*, 8, 3 (Winter 1995–1996): 439–51.
_____. "Duplicación interior en *La ley del deseo* y *Carmen*." *Cine-Lit: Essays on Peninsular Film and Fiction*. Eds. George Cabello-Castellet, Jaume Martí-Olivella & Guy H. Wood, Guy H. Corvallis: Portland State University, Oregon State University & Reed College, 1992. 219–26.
_____. "Horizontes discursivos y desconcierto en la película *Abre los ojos*." *Estudios Humanísticos: Filología* 30 (2008): 371–378.
García de la Rasilla, Carmen. "Teaching Golden Age Theater through Filmic Adaptations." *Approaches to Teaching Early Modern Spanish Drama*. Eds. Laura R. Bass & Margaret Greer. New York: MLA, 2006. 69–75.
García Orso, Luis. "Observer of Everyday Life: Carlos Carrera and *El Crimen del Padre Amaro* (The Crime of Father Amaro)." *Through a Catholic Lens: Religious Perspectives of Nineteen Film Directors from around the World*. Ed. and intro. Peter Malone. Lanham, MD; Rowman & Littlefield; 2007: 97–102.
García Santamaría, José Vicente. "*El espíritu de la colmena* en el proyecto Querejeta." In Pérez Perucha, Julio, Ed. (2005). 53–78.
García Santillán, Florencio Oscar. *Temas culturales e históricos de la obra fílmica de María Lusia Bemberg*. Dissertation Abstracts International, Section A: The Humanities and Social Sciences (DAIA) 1998 April; 58 (10): 3762. University of New Mexico, 1997. Abstract no.: DA9813137.
García-Soza, Gladis, and Anne M. White. "Spellbound: Resisting the Power of Popular

Myth in Erice's *El espíritu de la colmena.*" *Cultura popular: Studies in Spanish and Latin American Popular Culture.* Eds. Shelley Godsland & Anne M. White. Bern: Peter Lang, 2002. 163–174.

Gatto, Katherine Gyekenyesi. "Women, Madness, and Confinement in María Luisa Bemberg's *Camila* (1984)." *JAISA: The Journal of the Association for the Interdisiciplinary Study of the Arts* 7.1–2 (Autumn 2001–Spring 2002): 103–110.

_____. "Women, Madness, and Confinement in María Luisa Bemberg's *Camila.*" *Cuadernos de Aldeeu* 17.1 (2001): 161–166.

Gavela Ramos, Yvonne. "El acto colectivo de recordar: Historia y fantasía en *El espíritu de la colmena* y *El laberinto del fauno.*" *Bulletin of Hispanic Studies* 88.2 (2011): 176–192.

Genette, Gerard. *Narrative Discourse.* 1972. (Jane E. Lewin, Trans.). Oxford: Basil Blackwell, 1980.

Giannetti, Louis. *Understanding Movies.* 13th ed. Boston: Pearson, 2014.

Gimeno Ugalde, Esther. "Cuadros en movimiento: La pintura en el cine: Relaciones intermediales en *La hora de los valientes* (Mercero 1998) y *Te doy mis ojos* (Bollaín)." *Revista de Literatura y Cultura Españolas* 12.16 (2011): 215–240.

_____. "La pintura en el cine: Relaciones intermediales en *La hora de los valientes* (Mercero 1998) y *Te doy mis ojos* (Bollaín 2003)." *Revista de Literatura y Cultura Españolas* 12.16 (2011): 215–240.

Gómez, María Asunción, and Santiago Juan-Navarro. *Alejandro Amenábar.* (Emmanuel Vincenot & Elisabeth Navarro, Trans.). Montreuil: Cinéastes, 2002.

González, Eduardo. "La rama dorada y el árbol deshojado: Reflexiones sobre *Fresa y chocolate* y sus antecedentes." *Foro Hispánico: Revista Hispánica de los Países Bajos* 10 (May 1996): 65–78.

González del Pozo, Jorge. "La liberación a través del arte en *Te doy mis ojos* de Icíar Bollaín." *Ciberletras* 19 (julio 2008): np. 12 Dec. 2011.

González Lara, Gerardo Salvador. "*El crimen del padre Amaro*: De la obra literaria del siglo XIX al lenguaje cinematográfico del siglo XXI." *Actas de Congreso XV de la Asociación Internacional de Hispanistas* III. 19–24 julio 2004. Monterrey, México. 641–649. Accessed 2 September 2015 at: cvc.cervantes.es/ literaura/aih/pdf/15/aih_15_3_050.pdf

González Vidal, Juan Carlos. "La problemática de la identidad en *La historia oficial*, de Luis Puenzo." *La problemática de la identidad en la producción discursiva de América Latina.* Eds. Phillippe Schaffhauser & Blanca Cárdenas Fernández. Perpignan: CRILAUP, 2005. 93–104.

Gorostiza, Jorge. "El punto de fuga en el exágono. La influencia del espacio." In Pérez Perucha, Julio, Ed. (2005). 173–192.

Goss, Brian Michael. "*Te doy mis ojos* (2003) and *Hable con ella* (2002): Gender in Context in Two Recent Spanish Films." *Studies in European Cinema* 5.1 (2008): 31–44.

Gover de Natasky, Miryam E. "La ficción como testimonio en el espacio textual de *La historia oficial*, guión cinematográfico correspondiente a Aída Bortnik y Luis Puenzo." *Alba de América: Revista Literaria* 25.47–48 (July 2006): 349–56.

Graham-Jones, Jean. "*Camila* y una pasión sudamericana: Bemberg, Monti y un paraíso perdido argentino." *Segundas Jornadas Internacionales de Literatura Argentina/Comparatística: Actas.* Ed. Daniel Altamiranda. Buenos Aires: Universidad de Buenos Aires, 1997.102–110.

Grandis, Rita de. "Introducción: María Luisa Bemberg o las trampas de la clase." *Revista Canadiense de Estudios Hispánicos* 27.1 (Fall 2002): 3–14.

Grullón, Diana. "Tres representaciones fílmicas de la carencia femenina como espacio liminal en Buñuel, Bemberg y Biraben." *Hispanet Journal* 3 (2010): 1–16.

Guillot Carvajal, Mario L. "*Fresa y chocolate*: ¿Una película racista?" *Revista Hispano Cubana* 9 (Winter 2001): 195–198.
Gutiérrez Carbajo, Francisco. "Icíar Bollaín." *Seis manifestaciones artísticas. Seis creadoras actuales*. Madrid: Universidad Nacional de Educación a Distancia, 2006. 57–78.
———. "Relato breve y cine: De Senel Paz a Gutiérrez Alea." *Actas del XIV Congreso de la Asociación Internacional de Hispanistas, IV: Literatura hispanoamericana*. Eds. Isías Lerner, Robert Nival & Alejandro Alonso. Newark, DE: Cuesta, 2004. 239–44.
Hagen, Kirsten von. "À la recherche de Carmen." *AlteMythen-NeueMedien*. Eds. Yasmin, Hoffmann, Walburga Hülk & Volker Roloff. Heidelberg: Universitätsverlag, 2006. 193–216.
Hamdorf, Wolfgang M. "We ha die Macht?: Gespräch mit Icíar Bollaín über 'Öffne meine Augen.'" *Film Dienst* 58.16 (2005): 14.
Hart, Stephen M. "Bemberg's Winks and Camila'a Sighs: Melodramatic Encryption in *Camila*." *Revista Canadiense de Estudios Hispánicos* 27.1 (Fall 2002): 75–85.
———. *A Companion to Latin American Film*. Rochester, NY: Boydell & Brewer; 2004.
Herbert, Daniel. "Sky's the Limit: Transnationality and Identity in *Abre los ojos* and *Vanilla Sky*." *Film Quarterly* 60.1 (Fall 2006): 28–38.
Heredia, Aída. "La Carmen de Saura dentro del género 'romance': tradición y ruptura." *Explicacion de Textos Literarios*, 20.1 (1991–1992): 79–87.
Hermoso Gómez, Bettina. "¡Una de cine! El cine como acercamiento a los problemas sociales: *Te doy mis ojos*." *Revista Electrónica de Didáctica del Español como Lengua Extranjera* 4 (junio 2005): np.
Hernández-Rodríguez, R. *Splendors of Latin Cinema*. Santa Barbara: ABC-CLIO, 2010.
Hess, John. "*Strawberry and Chocolate*: Melodrama, Sex, and the Cuban Revolution." *Jump Cut: A Review of Contemporary Media* 41 (May 1997): 119–125.
Higginbotham, Virginia. *Spanish Film under Franco*. Austin: University of Texas Press, 1988.
———. *The Spirit of the Beehive/El espíritu de la colmena*. Trowbridge: Flicks Books, 1998.
Hill, Deborah J. "From Dictatorship to Democracy: Carlos Saura's *Carmen*." *The Kingdom of Dreams in Literature and Film*. Ed. Douglas Fowler. Tallahassee: Florida State University Press; 1986. 92–103.
Hind, Emily. "Provincia in Recent Mexican Cinema, 1989–2004." *Discourse* 26.1&2 (Spring 2004): 26–45.
La historia oficial. Dir. Luis Puenzo. Perf. Héctor Alterio, and Norma Aleandro. Historias Cinematográfica Cinemania, 1985.
Holden, Stephen. "A Priest Who Makes the Women Swoon." *New York Times* 15 November 2002. Accessed 1 October 2014 at http://www.nytimes.com/movie/review?res=9404E1DC1730F936A25752C1A9649C8B63
Hopewell, John. *Out of the Past. Spanish Cinema after Franco*. London: BFI, 1986.
Jablonska, Aleksandra. "Las perspectivas de los narradores en 'El lobo, el bosque y el hombre nuevo' de Senel Paz y su adaptación fílmica." *Cuento en Red: Estudios Sobre la Ficción Breve* 12 (Fall 2005): 121–130.
Jaehne, Karen. "Love as a Revolutionary Act: An Interview with María Luisa Bemberg." *Cineaste: America's Leading Magazine on the Art and Politics of the Cinema* 14.3 (1986). 22–24.
La jaula de oro. Dir. Diego Quemada-Díez. Perf. Brandon López, Rodolfo Domínguez, and Karen Martínez. Animal de Luz Films, Kinemascope Films, and Machete Producciones, 2013.
Jeffries, Lesley. "The Role of Style in Reader-Involvement: Deictic Shifting in Contemporary Poems." *Journal of Literary Semantics* 37 (1) (2008): 69–85.

Jenckes, Katharine. "Identity, Image, and Sound in Three Films by María Luisa Bemberg." *Cine-Lit III: Essays on Hispanic Film and Fiction*. Eds. George Cabello-Castellet, Jaume Martí-Olivella & Guy H. Wood. Corvallis: Oregon State University, 1998. 61–67.
Jordan, Barry. *Alejandro Amenábar*. Manchester: Manchester University Press, 2012.
Kemp, Phillip. "*Fresa y chocolate/Strawberry and Chocolate*." *Sight and Sound* 4(1998): 48.
Kepner, Christine Goring. "Three Films of María Luisa Bemberg: A Female Gaze." *Journal of Christianity and Foreign Languages: Journal of the North American Christian Foreign Language Association* 4 (Spring 2003): 40–61.
Kinder, Marsha. *Blood Cinema. The Reconstruction of National Identity in Spain*. Berkeley: University of California Press, 1993.
_____. *Refiguring Spain: Cinema/Media Representation*. Durham: Duke University Press, 1997.
_____. "The Children of Franco in the New Spanish Cinema." *Quarterly Review of Film Studies*, ed. Katherine Kovács, 8.2 (Spring 1983): 57–76.
King, John. *Argentine Cinema*. Plymouth: Plymouth Arts Centre, 1986.
_____, Sheila Whitaker, and Rosa Bosch, eds. *An Argentine Passion. María Luisa Bemberg and her Films*. London: Verso: 2000.
Knollmueller, Marit. "Death Is a Dream: Placing *Abre los ojos* in a Spanish Tradition." *Studies in European Cinema* 6.2–3 (2009): 203–214.
Kriger, Clara. "*La historia oficial/The Official Story*: Luis Puenzo, Argentina, 1984." *The Cinema of Latin America*. Eds. Alberto Elena & Marina Díaz López. London: Wallflower, 2003: 177–183.
Labanyi, Jo. "Memory and Modernity in Democratic Spain: The Difficulty of Coming to Terms with the Spanish Civil War." *Poetics Today* 28.1 (Spring 2007): 89–116.
Laraway, David. "Alejandro Amenábar and the Embodiment of Skepticism in *Abre los ojos*." *Hispanófila* 153 (May 2008): 65–77.
Lauer, Jean. "When a Woman Thinks Alone: Rethinking Mexican History through Women and Faith." *Iowa Journal of Cultural Studies* 7 (Fall 2005): 81–105.
Ledoux, Aurélie. "Le Syndrome d'Ackroyd dans *Ouvre les yeux* et *Les Autres*." *Le Cinéma d'Alejandro Amenábar*. Ed. Nancy Berthier. Toulouse: PY Mirail, 2007. 101–112.
Lema-Hincapié, Andrés. "Carlos Saura's *Carmen*: Hybridity and the Inescapable Cliché." *Carmen: From Silent Film to MTV*. Eds. Chris Perriam & Ann Davies. Amsterdam: Rodopi; 2005. 151–65.
Levine, Linda Gould. *Feminismo ante el franquismo: entrevistas con feministas de España*. Miami: Ediciones Universal, 1980.
_____. "Saved by Art: Entrapment and Freedom in Icíar Bollaín's *Te doy mis ojos* (2003)." *Generation X Rocks: Contemporary Peninsular Fiction, Film and Rock Culture*. Eds. Christine Henseler & Randolph D. Pope. Nashville: Vanderbilt University Press, 2007. 216–234.
Lomillos, Miguel-Ángel. "El discurso familiar en *El espíritu de la colmena*: La separación de los padres." *Banda Aparte* 9–10 (1998): 57–89.
López, Ana M. "An 'Other' History: The New Latin American Cinema." *New Latin American Cinema*. Ed. Michael T. Martin. Vol. 1. Detroit: Wayne State University Press, 1992. 135–56.
López, Pablo. "Las mejores películas de la historia del cine: *El espíritu de la colmena*." *Fotogramas*, núm. 1689 (sept. 1983): 45–52.
López, Tania Cepero. "Deconstructing Cuban Identity: Senel Paz's *The Wolf, the Woods and the New Man*: And Its Film Adaptation *Strawberry and Chocolate* by Tomás Gutiérrez Alea." *Caribbean without Borders: Literature, Language and Culture*. Eds.

Dorsia Smith, Raquel Puig, & Ileana Cortés Santiago. Newcastle upon Tyne: Cambridge Scholars, 2009. 175-193.
Majfud, Jorge. "*El crimen del padre Amaro*: El triunfo ético de la derrota." *Escritos Críticos* 12 abril 2012. 15 June 2015. http://majfud.org/2012/04/12/el-crime-del-padre-amaro/.
Manrupe, Raúl y Portela, María Alejandra, eds. *Un diccionario de films argentinos (1930-1995)*. Buenos Aires: Corregidor, 2001.
Maqua, Javier. "Miradas y silencios." In Pérez Perucha, Julio, Ed. (2005). 151-172.
Marrero, Miguel. "Cinematic Grand Narratives: Spectatorship and Identity Politics." *Atenea* 24.2 (Dec 2004): 135-145.
Martín, Juan Carlos. "Representations of Humans and Technology: The Construction of Identity in Miguel Bardem, Pedro Almodóvar, and Alejandro Amenábar." *Science, Literature, and Film in the Hispanic World*. Eds. Jerry Hoeg & Kevin S. Larsen. New York: Palgrave Macmillan, 2006. 221-243.
Martín, Marina. "Amenábar." *Film Historia* (2002). Accessed at: www.publicacions.ub.es/bibliotecadigital/cinema/filmhistoria/2002/amanabar.htm.
_____. "Entre lo real y lo soñado en el cine de Alejandro Amenábar. Bifurcaciones de *Abre los ojos*." *Literatura y otras artes en America Latina*. Eds. Daniel Balderson, Oscar Torres Duque, Laura Gutiérrez, Brian Gollnick & Eileen Willingham. Iowa City: University of Iowa Press, 2004. 91-102.
Martín-Márquez, Susan L. "Monstrous Identity: Female Socialization in *El espíritu de la colmena*." *New Orleans Review* 19.2 (Summer 1992): 52-58.
Marzal Felici, Javier. "Una poética del silencio: Relato mítico y aprendizaje del tiempo." In Pérez Perucha, Julio, Ed. (2005). 35-52
Maule, Rosanna. "Cultural Specificity and Transnational Address in the New Generation of Spanish Film Authors: The Case of Alejandro Amenábar." *Spanishness in the Spanish Novel and Cinema of the 20th-21st Century*. Ed. Cristina Sánchez-Conejero. Newcastle upon Tyne: Cambridge Scholars, 2007. 107-120.
McClary, Susan. "Carmen as Perennial Fusion: From Habanera to Hip-Hop." *Carmen: From Silent Film to MTV*. Eds. Chris Perriam & Ann Davies. Amsterdam: Rodopi; 2005. 205-216.
Menne, Jeff. "A Mexican Nouvelle Vague: The Logic of New Waves under Globalization" *Cinema Journal* 47.1 (Fall 2007): 70-92.
Mérimée, Prosper. *Carmen*. Paris: Encre, 1984.
Metz, Christian. *Film Language. A Semiotics of the Cinema*. (Michael Taylor, Trans.). New York: Oxford University Press, 1974.
Miles, Robert J. "'Entre dos fuegos': The Function of Teresa and the Possible Subplot in *El espíritu de la colmena*." *Journal of Romance Studies* 7.2 (Summer 2007): 99-122.
_____. "Out of Order: "Spanishness" as Process in *El espíritu de la colmena*." *Spanishness in the Spanish Novel and Cinema of the 20th-21st Century*. Ed. Cristina Sánchez-Conejero. Newcastle upon Tyne: Cambridge Scholars, 2007. 157-167.
_____. "Reclaiming Revelation: *Pan's Labyrinth* and *The Spirit of the Beehive*." *Quarterly Review of Film and Video* 28 (2011): 195-203.
_____. "The Shadow of Maeterlinck's *La Vie des abeilles* and *El espíritu de la colmena*." *Bulletin of Hispanic Studies* 87.8: 961-976.
_____. "Victor Erice as Fugitive." *Bulletin of Spanish Studies* 84.1 (2007): 57-78.
Miller, Paul. "I Hear, Therefore I Know: Post-Dictatorial Traumatic Expression and Death and the Maiden." *Studies in American Jewish Literature* 32.2 (2013): 121-140.
_____. "'Tú no eres revolucionario': Notas sobre transiciones ideológicas en dos películas de Gutiérrez Alea." *Cifra Nueva: Revista de Cultura* 9-10 (Jan-Dec 1999): 95-99.
Mistral, Gabriela. *Desolación*. Santiago: Editorial del Pacífico, 1957.

Mitjaville, Alain. "Sur L'esprit de la ruche." *Les Cahiers de la Cinémathèque* 38/39 (Winter 1984): 181–184.
Molina Foix, Vicente. "La guerra detrás de la ventana. Notas de lectura de *El espíritu de la colmena*." *Revista de Occidente* 53 (1985): 112–118.
_____. "The War Behind the Window: Notes on *The Spirit of the Beehive*." (Guy H. Wood & Julie H. Croy, Trans.). *The Cinema of Víctor Erice: An Open Window*. Ed. Linda C. Erhlich. Lanham: Scarecrow, 2007. 107–111.
Monaco, James. *How to Read a Film. Movies, Media, Multimedia*. 3rd ed. New York: Oxford University Press, 2000.
Monterde, José Enrique. "Metáforas del conocimiento." In Pérez Perucha, Julio, Ed. (2005). 217–140.
Montiel, Alejandro. "Verme morir entre memorias tristes. Entonaciones de un melodrama escueto." In Pérez Perucha, Julio, Ed. (2005). 285–306.
Mora, Carl J. *Mexican Cinema: Reflections of a Society, 1896–2004*. Jefferson, NC: McFarland, 2005.
Mora, Sergio de la. *Cinemachismo. Masculinities and Sexuality in Mexican Film*. Austin: University of Texas Press, 2006.
Moral, Javier *et alia*. "*El espíritu de la colmena*: Segundo debate." In Pérez Perucha, Julio, Ed. (2005). 427–447.
Moraña, Mabel, Enrique Dussel, and Carlos Jaúregüi. "Colonialism and Its Replicants." *Coloniality at Large: Latin America and the Postcolonial Debate*. Durham: Duke University Press, 2008. 1–20.
Morris, Barbara. "La mujer vista por la mujer: El discurso fílmico de María Luisa Bemberg." *Discurso femenino actual*. Ed. Adelaida López de Martínez. Puerto Rico: Universidad de Puerto Rico, 1995. 253–267.
Mujeres al borde de un ataque de nervios. Dir. Pedro Almodóvar. Perf. Carmen Maura, Antonio Banderas, Julieta Serrano, and Rosy Palma. El Deseo, 1988.
Mukařovský, Jan. "Intentionality in Art," *Aesthetic Function, Norm and Value as Social Facts*. (Mark E. Suino, Trans.). Ann Arbor: University of Michigan Press, 1970. 89–128.
Mulvey, Laura. "Visual Pleasure and Narrative Cinema." *Screen: The Journal of the Society for Education in Film and Television*. 16.3 (1975): 6–18.
Muñoz, Willy Oscar. "*The Official Story*: A Documentary Discourse." *Transformations: From Literature to Film*. Ed. Douglas Radcliff-Umstead. Kent: Romance Langs. Dept, Kent State University; 1987: 205–13.
Nelson, Anitra. "Tomás Gutiérrez Alea (1928–1996)." *Journal of Iberian and Latin American Studies* 3.2 (Dec. 1997): 99–107.
Noble, Andrea. *Mexican National Cinema*. New York: Routledge, 2005.
Oropesa, Salvador. "El nacionalismo democrático español en Carlos Saura: *Carmen* (1983) y *Goya en Burdeos* (1999)." *Letras peninsulares* 16.1 (Spring 2003): 129–45.
Ortigão, Ramalho. "Literatura de observación: *El crimen del padre Amaro*." (Raquel R. Aguilera, Trans.) *Revista de Occidente* 264 (May 2003): 118–134.
Palao, José Antonio. "Realmente, ella no duerme." In Pérez Perucha, Julio, Ed. (2005). 267–284.
Pardo, García, Pedro Javier. "La metaficción de la literatura al cine: La anagnórisis metaficcional de *Niebla* a *Abre los ojos*." *Celehis: Revista del Centro de Letras Hispanoamericanas* 22 (2011): 151–174.
Parrondo, Eva. *et alia*. "*El espíritu de la colmena*: Primer debate." In Pérez Perucha, Julio, Ed. (2005). 403–426.
_____. "Madre, hijas y espíritu..." "*El espíritu de la colmena*: Segundo debate." In Pérez Perucha, Julio, Ed. (2005). 241–266.

Parsons, Deborah. "Nationalism or Continentalism? Representing Heritage Culture for a New Europe." *Beyond Boundaries: Textual Representations of European Identity.* Ed. Andy Hollis. Amsterdam: Rodopi; 2000. 1–22.
Paz, Carlos. "Jerga y sexo en *Fresa y chocolate.*" *Cuadrivium* 1.1 (Spring 1998): 37–44.
Pena Pérez, Jaime. "Nocturno 34." In Pérez Perucha, Julio, Ed. (2005). 389–402.
____. *Víctor Erice. El espíritu de la colmena.* Barcelona: Paidós, 2004.
Pérez Perucha, Julio, ed. *El espíritu de la colmena ... 31 años después.* Valencia: Instituto Valencià de Cinematografía Ricardo Muñoz Suay, 2005.
Perri, Dennis "Amenábar's *Abre los ojos*: The Posthuman Subject." *Hispanófila* 154 (Sept. 2008): 89–98.
Perriam, Chris. "Alejandro Amenábar's *Abre los ojos / Open Your Eyes* (1997)." *Spanish Popular Cinema.* Eds. Antonio Lázaro Reboll & Andrew Willis. Manchester: Manchester University Press, 2004. 209–221.
____. "*El espíritu de la colmena.* Memory, Nostalgia, Trauma (Víctor Erice, 1973)." *Burning Darkness: A Half Century of Spanish Cinema.* Ed. Joan Ramón Resina. Albany: SUNY Press, 2008. 61–81.
Perrin, Annie. "Sur les traces d'Œdipe." *Luis Puenzo, La historia oficial.* Montpellier: Institut international de sociocritique : Cettre d'études e de recherches sociocrituqes (*Co-Textes* 23), 1992. 6–36.
Phillipon, Alain. "Victor Erice. Le détour par l'enfance." *Cahiers du cinéma* 81 (mars 1988): vi–vii.
Pinet, Carolyn. "Retrieving the Disappeared Text: Women, Chaos and Change in Argentina and Chile after the Dirty Wars." *Hispanic Journal* 18.1 (Spring 1997): 89–108.
Podalsky, Laura. *The Politics of Affect and Emotion in Contemporary Latin American Cinema: Argentina, Brazil, Cuba, and Mexico.* New York: Palgrave MacMillan, 2011.
Poirier, Agnes. "Review of *El crimen del padre Amaro.*" *Screen Daily* 16 September 2002. Accessed 10 November 2013 at: http://screendaily.com/the-crime-of-father-amaro-el-crimen-del-padre-amaro/4010511.article
Poirson-Dechonne, Marion. "L'horreur et ses masques dans les films d'Alejandro Amenabar." *Les Cinémas de l'horreur: Les Maliques.* Ed. AnneMarie Paquet-Deyris. Condé-sur-Noireau: Corlet, 2010. 167–173.
Powrie, Phil, et al. *Carmen on Film: A Cultural History.* Bloomington: Indiana University Press; 2007.
La prima Angélica. Dir. Carlos Saura. Perf. José Luis López Vázquez, Fernando Delgado, and Lina Canalejas. Elias Querejeta Producciones, 1974.
Prince, Stephen R. *Movies and Meaning. An Introduction to Film.* 6th ed. Boston: Pearson, 2013.
Puenzo, Luis, Dir. *La historia oficial.* Perf. Héctor Alterio and Norma Aleandro. Almi Pictures. 1985. Koch Lorber, DVD, 2004.
Puenzo, Luis, et al. *La historia oficial.* Montpellier: Institut international de sociocritique: Cettre d'études e de recherches sociocrituqes (*Co-Textes* 23), 1992.
Pujante Segura, Carmen. "La metaficción e intertextualidad en *Prénom: Carmen* de Jean-Luc Godard/ Metafiction and Intertextuality in *Prénom: Carmen* by Jean-Luc Godard/Metaficcióiintertextualitat a *Prénom: Carmen* de Jean-Luc Godard/ Metafikzioa eta testuartekotasuna Jean Luc Godard *Prénom: Carmen* filmean" *452°F Journal of Literary Theory and Comparative Literature* 1 (2009): 77–88.
Quiroga, José. "Homosexualities in the Tropic of Revolution." *Sex and Sexuality in Latin America.* Eds. Daniel Balderson and Donna J. Guy. New York: New York University Press, 1997. 133–151.

Ralph, Wendy L. "Lorca/Gades: Modes of Adaptation in *Bodas de sangre*." *Anales de la Literatura Española Contemporánea* 11.1-2 (1986): 193-204.
Ramblado Minero, María de la Cinat. "La isla revolucionaria: El dilema de la identidad cubana en *Fresa y chocolate* y *La nada cotidiana*." *Letras Hispanas: Revista de Literatura y Cultura* 3.2 (Fall 2006): 86-94.
Ramírez-Pimienta, Juan Carlos. "El narcocorrido religioso: usos y abusos de un género." *Studies in Latin American Popular Culture* 29.1 (2011): 184 -201.
Ramsey, Cynthia. "*The Official Story*: Feminist Re-Visioning as Spectator Response." *Studies in Latin American Popular Culture* 11 (1992): 157-69.
Rasmussen, Ole Wehner. "Carmen, Carmen og Carmen: I anleidning af Carlos Sauras film." *(Pre)Publications*, 84 (Feb 1984): 35-47.
Rear Window. Dir. Alfred Hitchcock. Perf. James Stewart, and Grace Kelly. Paramount Pictures, 1954.
Requena, Jesús González. "Escrituras que apuntan al mito." *Escritos sobre el cine español 1973-1987*. Valencia: Filmoteca de la Generalitat Valenciana, 1989: 89-100.
Ricci, Cristián H. "Vigilar y castigar como modelo social en *El crimen del padre Amaro* de Eça de Queirós." *Espéculo: Revista de Estudios Literarios* 22 (Nov. 2002-Feb. 2003): np.
Richardson, Nathan E. "Youth Culture, Visual Spain, and the Limits of History in Alejandro Amenábar's *Abre los ojos*." *Revista Canadiense de Estudios Hispánicos* 27.2 (Winter 2003): 327-346.
Riley, E.C. "The Story of Ana in *El espíritu de la colmena*." *Bulletin of Hispanic Studies* 61.4 (1984): 491-497.
Rivero-Moreno, Yosálida C. "Neobarroco postmoderno en dos películas del cine español: *Éxtasis* y *Abre los ojos*." *Hispanic Journal* 23.2 (Fall 2002): 133-142.
Rodríguez Marchante, Oti. *Amenábar, vocación de intriga*. Madrid: Espuma, 2002.
Rogers, C.R. *On Becoming a Person: A Therapist's View of Psychotherapy*. London: Constable, 1961.
_____. "A Theory of Therapy, Personality and Interpersonal Relationships, as Developed in the Client-centered Framework." *Psychology: A Study of Science*, Vol. 3. Ed. S. Koch. New York: McGraw-Hill, 1959. 210-211; 184-256.
_____. *A Way of Being*. Boston: Houghton Mifflin, 1980.
Romano, Mia. "Voces y cuerpos abusados: Representaciones de la identidad en *Nada* y *Te doy mis ojos*." *El Cid* 20 (Spring 2008): 47-67.
Ros, Xon de. "Innocence Lost: Sound and Silence in *El espíritu de la colmena*." *Bulletin of Hispanic Studies* 76.1 (Jan 1999): 27-37.
_____. "Víctor Erice's 'voluntad de estilo' in *El espíritu de la colmena*." *Forum for Modern Languages* 31.1 (Jan 1995): 74-83.
Ruffinelli, Jorge. "De una Camila a otra: Historia, literatura y cine." *Foro Hispánico: Revista Hispánica de los Países Bajos* 10 (May 1996): 11-25.
_____. "María Luisa Bemberg y el principio de la transgresión." *Revista Canadiense de Estudios Hispánicos* 27.1 (Fall 2002): 15-44.
Russell, Dominique. "Monstrous Ambiguities: Víctor Erice's *El espíritu de la colmena*." *Anales de la literatura española contemporánea* 32.1 (2007): 179-203.
Saborit, José. "La pintura en la mirada. Notas sobre la presencia de la pintura en *El espíritu de la colmena*." In Pérez Perucha, Julio, Ed. (2005). 93-106.
Salas, Hugo. "Some Girls Are Bigger Than Others: María Luisa Bemberg." *Senses of Cinema: An Online Journal Dedicated to the Serious and Eclectic Discussion of Cinema* 22 (Oct 2002): np.
Santí, Enrico Mario. "*Fresa y chocolate*: The Rhetoric of Cuban Reconciliation." *MLN* 113.2 (Mar 1998): 407-425.

Los santos inocentes. Dir. Mario Camus. Perf. Alfredo Landa, Francisco Rabal. Ganesh Producciones Cinematográficas, andTVE, 1984.
Sartingen, Kathrin, and Esther Gimeno Ugalde. "Icíar Bollaín: *Te doy mis ojos* (2003)." *Spanische Filme des 20. Jahrhunderts in Einzeldarstellungen*. Berlin: Schmidt, 2012. 345–262.
Saura, Carlos, dir. *Bodas de sangre*. Prod. Emiliano Piedra. Perf. Antonio Gades & Cristina Hoyos. 1981.
――――. *Carmen*. Prod. Emiliano Piedra. Perf. Antonio Gades & Laura del Sol. Emiliano Piedra & TVE, 1983.
――――. *El amor brujo*. Prod. Emiliano Piedra. Perf. Antonio Gades, Cristina Hoyos & Laura del Sol. 1986.
Schickel, Richard. "Movies: His Collar Is Too Tight." *Time* 22.160 (2002): 88.
Schupp, Patrick. "The Flamenco Trilogy." *Carlos Saura: Interviews*. Ed. Linda M. Willem. Jackson: University Press of Mississippi; 2003. 88–95.
Schwartz, Ronald. *Great Spanish Films since 1950*. Lanham, MD: Scarecrow, 2008.
――――. *Spanish Film Directors, 1950–1985*. Metuchen & London: Scarecrow, 1986.
Seguin, Jean-Claude. "*Fresa y chocolate* (Tomás Gutiérrez Alea, 1993): Nobody's perfect." *Cuba: Cinéma et révolution*. Eds. Julie Amiot-Guillouet & Nancy Berthier. Lyon: Grimh: 2006. 213–220.
Serna Servín, Juan Antonio. "An Ideological Study of the Film *Strawberry and Chocolate*." *Anuario de Cine y Literatura en Español: An International Journal on Film and Literature* 3 (1997): 159–166.
Shields, Ronald E. "Acting Prima Donna Politics in Tomás Gutiérrez Alea's *Strawberry and Chocolate*." *More Than a Method: Trends and Traditions in Contemporary Film Performance*. Eds. Cynthia Baron, Diane Carson & Frank P. Tomasulo. Detroit: Wayne State University Press, 2004. 219–246.
Simerka, Barbara, and Christopher Welmer. "Tom Cruise and the Seven Dwarves: Cinematic Postmodernisms in *Abre los ojos* and *Vanilla Sky*." *American Drama* 14.2 (Summer 2005): 1–15.
Simonari, Rosella. "Bringing Carmen Back to Spain: Antonio Gades's Flamenco Dance in Carlos Saura's Choreofilm." *Dance Research: Journal of the Society for Dance Research* 26.2 (Winter 2008): 189–203.
Smith, Jennifer. "Violence and Hegemonic Masculinity in *Historias de Kronen*, *El Bola* and *Te doy mis ojos*." *Prisma Social* 13 (Dec–May 2014): 219–256.
Smith, Paul Julian. "Abre los ojos." *Sight and Sound* 10.3 (March 200): 50.
――――. "Between Metaphysics and Scientism Rhetoricizing Víctor Erice." *The Moderns: Times, Space, and Subjectivity in Contemporary Spanish Culture*. Oxford: Oxford University Press, 2000. 89–107.
――――. "High Anxiety: *Abre los Ojos/Vanilla Sky*." *Journal of Romance Studies* 4, 1 (2004): 91–102.
――――. "The Language of Strawberry." *Sight and Sound* 4 (1994): 30–32.
――――. *Vision Machines: Cinema, Literature and Sexuality in Spain and Cuba, 1982–1993*. London: Verso, 1996.
――――. "Whispers and Rapture." *Sight and Sound* 11.11 (1993): 28–29.
Sobral, Filomena Antunes. "Configuração televisual da metrópole: Lisboa em *O Crime do Padre Amaro* do século XXI." *Revista Comunicação Midiática* 7.1 (2012): 58–76.
Soles, Diane. "Administración de la crítica: Tácticas de censores y cineastas cubanos en los noventa." *Cultura y letras cubanas en el siglo XXI*. Ed. Araceli Tinajero. Madrid: Iberoamericana Vervuert, 2010. 77–94.
Soliño, María Elena. "Escaping Toledo's History of Repression. Painting as Therapy in

Icíar Bollaín's *Te doy mis ojos.*" *Letras peninsulares* Special issue: *Representations of the City in Peninsular Literature and Film.* 21.1 (2008): 33–52.
Solórzano, Fernanda. "Secreto a voces." *Letras libres* 4.44 (agosto 2002): 97.
Soriano, Michèle. "La esfinge argentina. Nationalisme et invstissements spéculaires dans *La historia oficial* de Luis Puenzo." *Luis Puenzo, La historia oficial.* Montpellier: Institut international de sociocritique : Cettre d'études e de recherches sociocrituqes (*Co-Textes* 23), 1992. 59–89.
Sotelo, Susan Baker. "Father Amaro's Crime: From the Portuguese Novel to the Mexican Film." *Studies in Honor of Lanin A. Gyurko.* Eds. Ken Hall & Ruth Muñoz-Hjelm. Newark, DE; Juan de la Cuesta; 2009: 247–261.
Stanley, Robert Henry. *Making Sense of Movies. Filmmaking in the Hollywood Style.* Boston: McGraw-Hill, 2003.
Stephanis, Rebecca M. "La construcción del 'Hombre nuevo': El intelectual y el revolucionario en *Memorias del subdesarrollo, Fresa y chocolate* y *Guantanamera.*" *Brújula: Revista Interdisciplinaria Sobre Estudios Latino-americanos* 1.1 (Dec 2002): 30–36.
Stone, Rob. "Breaking the Spell: Carlos Saura's *El amor brujo* and *El desencanto.*" *Bulletin of Spanish Studies: Hispanic Studies and Researches of Spain, Portugal, and Latin America* 80.5 (2003): 573–592.
_____. *Spanish Cinema.* Harlow: Longman, 2002.
Sztrum, Marcelo. "Nota sobre el voseo para evitar malentendidos en *La historia oficial.*" *Luis Puenzo, La historia oficial.* Montpellier: Institut international de sociocritique : Cettre d'études e de recherches sociocrituqes (*Co-Textes* 23), 1992. 37–47.
Szuchman, Mark D. "Depicting the Past in Argentine Films: Family Drama and Historical Debate in *Miss Mary* and *The Official Story.*" *Based on a True Story: Latin American History at the Movies.* Ed. Donald F. Stevens. Wilmington: Scholarly Resources, 1997. 173–200.
Tal, Tzvi. "Viejos republicanos españoles y joven democratización latinoamericana: Imagen de exilados en películas de Argentina y Chile: 'La historia oficial' y 'La frontera.'" *Espéculo: Revista de Estudios Literarios* 15 (July–Oct 2000): n/p.
Tandeciarz, Silvia R. "Citizens of Memory: Refiguring the Past in Postdictatorhsip Argentina. *PMLA* 122.1 (2001): 151–69.
Taylor, Claire. "María Luisa Bemberg Winks at the Audience: Performativity and Citation in *Camila* and *Yo la peor de todas.*" Eds. Lisa Shaw & Stepanie Dennison. *Essays on Modernity, Gender, and National Identity.* Jefferson, NC: McFarland, 2005. 110–124.
Taylor, Low. "Image and Irony in *The Official Story.*" *Literature Film Quarterly* 17.3 (1989): 207–209.
Terrasa, Jacques. "Les écrans noirs d'Alejandro Amenábar." *Le Cinéma d´Alejandro Amenábar.* Ed. Nancy Berthier. Toulouse: PY Mirail, 2007. 27–42.
Thakkar, Amit. "Cine de choque: Image Culture, the Absence of the Patriarch and Violence in Alejandro Amenábar's *Abre los ojos.*" *New Cinemas: Journal of Contemporary Film* 9.11 (2011): 19–34.
Thibaudeau, Pascale. "El cine de la denuncia social en España: el caso de *Te doy mis ojos* de Icíar Bollaín." *Foro hispánico: Revista hispánica de Flandes y Holanda.* 32 (2008): 231–249.
_____. "Réalités virtuelles et destins manipulés à travers *Ouvre les yeux* d'Alejandro Amenábar." *Le Cinéma d´Alejandro Amenábar.* Ed. Nancy Berthier. Toulouse: Presses Universitaires du Mirail, 2007. 79–99.
Thomas, Sarah. "Ghostly Affinities: Child Subjectivity and Spectral Presences in *El espíritu de la colmena* and *El espinazo del diablo.*" *Hispanet Journal* 4 (December 2011): 1–23.
Tierney, Dolores. "Transnational Political Horror in *Cronos* (1993), *El espinazo del diablo*

(2001), and *El laberinto del fauno* (2006)." *The Transnational Fantasies of Guillermo del Toro*. Eds. Ann Davies, Deborah Shaw & Dolores Tierney. New York: Palgrave Macmillan, 2014. 161–82.
Los Tigres del Norte. *Jaula de Oro*. Fonovisa Records, 1984.
Tobin Stanley, Maureen. "Liberating Mythography: the Intertextual Discourse between Mythological Banishment and Domestic Violence as Exile in *Take my Eyes* (*Te doy mis ojos*)." *Exile through a Gendered Lens: Women's Displacement in Recent European History, Literature, and Cinema*. Eds. Gesa Zinn & Maureen Tobin Stanley. New York: Palgrave Macmillan, 2012. 99–117.
Tomlinson, Emily. "Mapping the Land of 'I don't remember': For a Re-evaluation of *La historia oficial*." *Bulletin of Hispanic Studies* 81.2 (Apr 2004): 215–28.
Torrecilla, Jesús. "La modernización de la imagen exótica de España en *Carmen*, de Saura." *Anales de la Literatura Española Contemporánea* 26.2 (2001): 337–56.
Triquell, Ximena. "*Fresa y chocolate* o el peso de la diferencia." *IV Congreso de Postgraduados en Estudios Hispánicos/4th Hispanic Studies Postgraduate Conference*. Eds. Isidoro Pisonero del Amo, José Gámez Fuentes, Greg Hainge & José M. Martín. London: Consejería de Educación y Ciencia, 1995. 181–185.
Ulland, Rebecca Jean. *Post-Dictatorship Historical Fiction in Argentina: A Dialogue between Past and Present*. Dissertation Abstracts International, Section A: The Humanities and Social Sciences (DAIA) 2007 Feb.; 67 (8): 3000. University of Minnesota, 2006. Abstract no.: DA3227593.
La vaquilla. Dir. Luis García Berlanga. Perf. Alfredo Landa, Guillermo Montesinos, Santiago Ramos, and José Sacristán. In-Cine Compañía, and Jet-Films, 1985.
Velasco, Juan. "Loss, History and Melancholia in Contemporary Latin American Cinema." *Pacific Costal Philology* 39 (2004): 42–51.
Vieira, Estela. "National Cinema and Intertextuality in Alejandro Amenábar: From Hollywood to Julio Cortázar." *Bulletin of Spanish Studies: Hispanic Studies and Researches on Spain, Portugal, and Latin America* 91.8 (Oct. 2014) 1229–1244.
Viridiana. Dir. Luis Buñuel. Perf. Silvia Pinal, Fernando Rey, and Francisco Rabal. UNICI and Gustavo Alatriste P.C., 1961.
Vossen, Ursula. "Víctor Erice: *El espíritu de la colmena* (1972)." *Spanische Filme des 20. Jahrhunderts in Einzeldarstellungen*. Ed. Ralf Junkerjürgen. Berlin: Schmidt, 2012. 180–192.
Ward, Scott. "A Postmodern Offspring of Don Juan Tenorio: *Abre los ojos*." *Letras Hispanas. Revista de Literatura y Cultura* 9.1 (Spring 2013): 36–47.
West, Dennis. "*Strawberry and Chocolate*, Ice Cream and Tolerance: Interviews with Tomás Gutiérrez Alea and Juan Carlos Tabío." *Cineaste: America's Leading Magazine on the Art and Politics of the Cinema* 21.1–2 (1995): 16–20.
Wheeler, Duncan. "The Representations of Domestic Violence in Spanish Cinema." *Modern Language Review* 107.2 (April 2012): 438–500.
Whitaker, Sheila. "Pride and Prejudice: María Luisa Bemberg." *The Garden of Forking Paths: Argentine Cinema*. Eds John King & Nissa Torrents. London: British Film Institute, 1988. 115–121.
White, Anne M. "Seeing Double? The Remaking of Alejandro Amenábar's *Abre los ojos* as Cameron Crowe's *Vanilla Sky*." *International Journal of Iberian Studies* 15.3 (2002): 187–197.
Wilkinson, Stephen. "Behind the Screen and into the Closet: Reading Homosexuality in the Cuban Revolution through *Conducta impropia, Antes que anochezca* and *Fresa y chocolate*." *Identity and Discursive Practices: Spain and Latin America*. Ed. Francisco Domínguez. Bern: Peter Lang, 2000. 283–305.
_____. "Critiques of Sexual and Political Intolerance in Leonardo Padura's Novel *Más-*

caras and the film *Fresa y chocolate*." *The Detective Fiction of Leonardo Padura Fuentes*. Ed. Carlos Uxó. Manchester: Manchester University Press, 2006. 132–159.

Willem, Linda M. "Metafictional Mise en Abyme in Saura's *Carmen*." *Literature Film Quarterly* 24.3 (1996): 267–73.

_____. "Text and Intertext: James Whale's *Frankenstein* in Víctor Erice's *El espíritu de la colmena*." *RLA: Romance Language Annual* 9 (1997): 722–725.

Williams, Bruce. "De la puerta de Ibsen a la Plaza de Mayo: La historización transtextual de lo femenino." *El testimonio femenino como escritura contestataria*. Eds. Emma Sepúlveda Pulvirenti, Emma & Joy Logan. Santiago: Asterión, 1995: 85–100.

_____. "In the Realm of the Feminine: María Luisa Bemberg's *Camila* at the Edge of the Gaze." *Chasqui. Revista de Literatura Latinoamericana* 25.1 (May 1996): 62–71.

_____. "The Reflection of a Blinded Gaze: María Luisa Bemberg, Filmmaker." Ed. Marjorie Agosí. *A Woman's Gaze: Latin American Women Artists*. Fredonia, NY: White Pine, 1998. 171–190.

Wood, Jason. The *Faber Book of Mexican Cinema*. London, England; Faber & Faber; 2006.

Zecchi, Barbara. "Women Filming Male Bodies: Subversions, Inversions and Identifications." *Studies in Hispanic Cinemas* 6.1 (2006): 187–204.

Zunzunegui, Santos. "Between History and Dream: Víctor Erice's *El espíritu de la colmena*." (Tom Conley, Trans.). *Modes of Representation in Spanish Cinema*. Eds. Jenaro Talens & Santos Zunzunegui. Minneaplolis: University of Minnesota Press, 1998. 128–154.

_____. "El estado de las cosas: Imágenes, sensaciones y afectos en *El espíritu de la colmena*." In Pérez Perucha, Julio, Ed. (2005). 21–34.

Index

Numbers in **_bold italics_** refer to pages with photographs.

Adamson, Sylvia 161, 203n1
Aldama, Frederick Luis 206
Aleandro, Norma 83, **_86_**, 99, 187, 213, 217
Aleixandre, Vicente 159
Almendros, Néstor 119
Almodóvar, Pedro 16, 209, 216
Alterio, Héctor 83, **_86_**, 185, 187, 213, 217
Alvaray, Luisela 203n1, 206
Alvear, Marta 200n5
Amenábar, Alejandro vii, 120, 128, 129, 131, 133, 135, 136, 137, 138, 150, 164, 189, 201n2, 201n3 201n6, 202n13, 202n14, 202n17, 203n19, 206, 201, 209, 211, 212, 214, 215, 217, 218, 220, 221
Ana y los lobos 44
Apocalypse Now 78
Aranoa, León de 164
Argaman, Einav 203n1
Arocena, Carmen 196n17, 206
¡Ay, Carmela! 44

Babel 20, 206
Bach, Caleb 67, 206
Balaguer, Javier 162
Barnard, Timothy 100, 206, 207
La Barraca 54, 181
La batalla de Chile 91
Bazin, André 195n7, 207
Begin, Paul 204n11, 207
Bejel, Emilio 118, 207
Belle epoque 22, 200n2
Beltrán, Lola 15, 16
Bemberg, María Luisa vii, 64, 66, 69, 70, 71, 78, 81, 101, 185, 198n1, 199n9, 206, 207, 208, 209, 210, 211, 212, 213, 214, 218, 220, 221, 222
Benjamin, Walter 13, 207

Besas, Peter 196, 207
Bizet, Georges 45, 46, 48, 49, 50, 51, 53, 183, 197–198n18
Blackwelder, Rob 157, 207
Blanco García, Ana Isabel 170, 207
Blood Wedding see *Bodas de sangre*
Bloomers, Thomas 99
Bodas de sangre 42, 44, 45, 53, 54, **_55_**, 56, 57, 180, 181, 209, 218, 219
Bollaín, Icíar viii, 159, 161, 164, 169, 172, 175, 177, 178, 192, 203n2, 204n6, 204n7, 207, 208, 209, 212, 213, 214, 219, 220
Bordwell, David 195n7, 206
Bortnik, Aida 90, 186, 212
Brotons, Beltrán 204n14, 207
Buñuel, Luis 24, 44, 45, 69, 203n19, 209, 212
Buñuel y la mesa del rey Salomón 44
Burton, Julianne 200n5

cainismo 22, 24, 195n11, 195n6, 209
Caprichos 43
Los Cardenales 157
Carrera, Carlos 139, 140, 190, 203n6, 208, 211
Castelli, Juan José 89
La caza 44
CDR [Comités para la defensa de la Revolución] (also vigilancia) 105, 106, 107, 108, 118
Cervantes 4, 31, 203n19
Chanan, Michael 103, 208
Cidade de Deus 103
Colmeiro, José 62, 197n11, 208
Conducta impropia (also *Mauvaise conduite*) 119, 221
Conversaciones Cinematográficas de Salamanca 163

Coppelia 109, 114
Coppola, Francis Ford 78
"Corrido del padre Amaro" 157
Cortázar, Julio 3, 194n1, 208, 221
Cría cuervos 44
Cruz, Jacqueline 177, 204n9, 209
Cruz-Malavé, Arnaldo 104, 209
cryonization 128, 129, 130, 132, 190, 202n17
Cuba: Cinéma et Révolution 103

Davies, Ann 42, 62, 197n11, 208, 209, 214
day residue 130, 131, 132, 133, 134, 137, 138
De Falla, Manuel 45, 57, 58, 59, 184, 197n13
deixis/deictics 138, 140 159, 160, 161, 162, 164, 167, 170, 171, 172, 175, 176, 177, 204n9, 206, 209, 213
De la Barca, Calderón 128, 130, 203
Deleuze, Gilles 195n7, 209
Deleyto, Celestino 195n3, 196n11, 209
Del Sol, Laura **47**, 57, 183, 184, 208, 219
De Quieró, Eça 140, 190, 218
desaparecidos [disappeard] 83, 89, 90, 91, 92, 94, 97, 99, 100, 101
Descartes 120, 200
de-subjectivisation 161, 206
Deveny, Thomas 194n4, 195n11, 209
Dirty War [guerra sucia] 87, 90, 92, 93, 94, 95, 97, 98, 99, 101, 198n8, 217
D'Lugo, Marvin 62, 209
Don Quijote 4, 31
Doré, Gustave 43, 62
Dussel, Enrique 26, 216

Echevarría, Esteban 72, 73
Edwards, Gwynne 60, 197n11, 209
Egea, Juan F. 195n5, 196n12, 210
Eisenstein, Sergei 103
El Greco 164
Elisa, vida mía 44
empathy 37, 160, 170, 171, 172, 173, 175, 176, 177, 178, 204n9, 204n15
El entierro del Conde Orgaz 164
Erice, Víctor vii, 7, 8, 27, 30, 31, 32, 34, 38, 39, 40, 41, 179, 196n9, 196n10, 206, 210, 211, 215, 216, 217, 218, 219, 221, 222
Escudero, Vicente 56, 181
establishing shot 12, 13, 14, 54, 195n8
estética franquista 44, 53

fabula y sujet 123, 195n5
Fados 44
Falicov, Tamara 100, 210
Fernán Gómez, Fernando 30, 37, 179, 207, 210
Filipelli, Raú 99

Flamenco 44
Flamenco, flamenco 44, 197n13
Flemming, Harry 54–55, 181
Flores, Pepa 43, 49
Flores de otro mundo 204n7, 204n8
Foster, David William 67, 107, 211
Foucault, Michel 139
Fraga Iribarne, Manuel 163
Franco, Francisco (Francoism) 21, 24,25, 27, 31, 33, 44, 45, 53, 62, 153, 196n16, 197n17
Frankenstein 28, 29, 31, 38, 39, 40, 180,181, 218
Frechilla, Emilio 136, 211
Freud, Sigmund 131, 136, 137, 201n4, 224n15, 202n16, 211
Friere, Paolo 199n4

Gades, Antonio 43, 45, 46, **47**, 48, 49, 52, 53, 54, 56, 57, 58, 60, 61, 62, 180, 182, 183, 184, 208, 218, 219
García Berlanga, Luis 21, 24, 221
García Landa, José Ángel 201n5
García Lorca 45, 53, 54, 56, 57, 180, 181, 218
García Orso, Luis 203n6
Gatto, Katherine 198n7, 212
Genette, Gérard 123, 201n9, 212
Giannetti, Louis 197n7, 221
Gimperra, Teresa 179, 210
Los golfos 44
González del Pozo, Jorge 204n6, 212
González Iñárritu, Alejandro 20, 209
Goss, Brian 204n11, 212
Goya, Francisco de 43
Goya en Burdeos 44, 216
Guevarra, Che 102, 118, 200n1
Gutiérrez, Eduardo 89
Gutiérrez Alea, Tomás 102, 104, 106, 116, 117, 118, 140, 188, 207, 208, 211, 213, 214, 215, 216, 217, 219, 221
Guzmán, Patricio 91

Handel, George Frideric 24
Hart, Stephen 67, 87, 103, 198n8, 200n8, 213
Higginbotham, Virginia 196n15, 213
histoire/récit 123, 124, 125, 126, 128, 138, 201n10
historical film 70, 78, 79, 80,88, 90, 1, 92, 101,118, 198n9, 199n9, 199n10
Hitchcock, Alfred 14, 218
Hola, ¿estás sola? 204n7, 204n8
Hopewell, John 41, 62, 197n17, 213
Hoyos, Cristina 43, 57, **61**, 181, 183, 184, 208, 219

Iberia 44, 197*n*14
ICAIC 102, 103, 118, 188, 211
Intentionality 7, 33, 194*n*1, 216

El jardín de las delicias 44
"La jaula de oro" (corrido) 9, 10, 195–196*n*6
La jaula de oro (film) 9, 10, 213
Jaúregüi, Carlos 26, 216
Jeffries, Lesley 160, 213
Jiménez Leal, Orlando 119
Jordan & Allison 197*n*17
Juan Moreira 89, 90
Jurado, Rocío 58, 59

Katmandú, un espejo en el cielo 204*n*8
Kepner, Christine 198*n*3, 214
Kill Bill 162
Kinder, Marsha 196*n*15, 214
Knollmueller, Marit 136,137, 202*n*14, 214

Laraway, David 136, 202*n*15, 214
Levine, Gould 204*n*14, 214
Levinson, Stephen C. 203*n*1
Lezama Lima, José 104, 113, 114, 118, 189, 209
liberation theology 145, 155
El lobo, el bosque y el hombre nuevo 102, 188, 213
Lomillos, Miguel Ángel 195*n*2, 214
López, Pablo 195*n*6, 214
López Vázquez, José Luis 18, 217
Lucía, Paco de 43, 49,182, 183, 197*n*18
Los lunes al sol 164
Lyons, John 203*n*1

Madres de la Plaza de Mayo [Mothers of the Plaza de Mayo] 90, 91, 94, 95, 99, 211
Manrupe, Raúl 99, 215
maquis 36, 37, 196*n*14
Mar adentro 164, 202*n*13
Marisol 43, 197*n*18
Martí, José 114
Martín, Juan Carlos 136
Martín, Mariana 136, 215
Martín-Cabrera, Luis 198*n*1, 200*n*2
Marull, Laia **165**, 166, 168, 169, 192, 203*n*2, 208
Máscaras 116, 209
Mataharis 204*n*8
Mauvaise conduite 119
McVey-Gil, Mary 200*n*2
Memorias del subdesarrollo 118, 210, 220
Mérimée, Prosper 42, 45, 46, 49, 50, 51, 53, 182, 197*n*5, 215

Metz, Christian 11, 195*n*7, 215
Migration in Contemporary Hispanic Cinema 194*n*4
Miles, Robert J. 196*n*11, 215
Miss Mary 101, 220
Mistral, Gabriela 64, 77, 78, 215
Mitjaville, Alain 196*n*15, 215
Molina Foix, Vicente 195*n*2, 216
Monaco, James 197*n*7, 216
Moraña, Mabel 26, 216
Moreno, Mariano 89
Mujeres al borde de un ataque de nervios 15, 16, 17, 40, 200*n*2, 216
Mukařovský, Jan 6, 7, 50, 194*n*3, 216
Muñoz, Willy Oscar 199*n*4, 216

New Mexican Cinema 10
La nuit de Varennes 78
Nunca más 83

Padura Fuentes, Leonardo 116, 221
"El país de Nomeacuerdo" 95, 96
Paz, María 200*n*2
Paz, Senel 102, 188, 209, 213, 214
Pena, Jaime 196*n*10
Perri, Dennis 136, 217
Perriam, Chris 136, 195*n*2, 195*n*3, 208, 214, 215, 216
Pessoa, Silvia 198*n*1, 200*n*2
Phillippon, Alain 27
Podalsky, Laura 101, 217
Poirier, Agnes 157, 217
La prima Angélica 19, 44, 217
Prince, Stephen 195*n*7, 217
Proceso de Reorganización Nacional 87, 96, 97, 200*n*10
Puenzo, Luis 23, 70, 83, 85, 90, 100, 101, 186, 199*n*4, 208, 210, 212, 213, 214, 217, 220

¡Que viva México! 103
Quemada-Díez, Diego 9, 10, 213

Rayuela [Hopscotch] 3, 194*n*1, 208
Rear Window 14
Le retour de Martin Guerre 78
Richardson, Nathan 201*n*3, 203*n*19, 218
Riley, E.C. 196*n*9, 196*n*15, 218
Rodríguez Marchante, Oti 128, 218
Rosas, Juan Manuel 76, 77, 78, 80, 81, 185, 186, 199*n*12
Ruffinelli, Jorge 67, 198*n*9, 199*n*13, 218

Sábato, Ernesto 183
Sacchi, Fabiana 198*n*1, 200*n*2
Salomé 197*n*14

Index

Santí, Enrico 107, 200*n*3, 218
Los santos inocentes 23, 219
Saura, Carlos 3, 19, 42, 44, 45, 46, 47, 48, 50, 51, 52, 53, 54, 57, 60, 61, 62, 138, 182, 183, 196*n*1, 197*n*10, 208, 209, 211, 213, 214, 216, 217, 218, 219, 220, 221, 222
Schwartz, Ronald 196*n*9, 197*n*17, 219
Scola, Ettore 78
Seguin, Jean-Claude 200*n*3, 219
El séptimo día 44
Sevillanas 197*n*14
Shields, Ronald 114, 219
Simonari, Rosella 61, 197*n*11, 219
Smalley, Deana 200*n*2
Smith, Paul Julian 116, 117, 118, 196*n*10, 202*n*12, 204*n*14, 219
Solás, Humberto 118, 200*n*5
Soliño, Maraía Elena 170, 204*n*12, 219
Solo mía 162
Sommer, Doris 67
Somoza, Anastasio 200*n*4
"Soy infeliz" 15, 16
Stanley, Tobin 195*n*7, 204*n*12, 219
Stone, Rob 196*n*7, 220
Szuchman, Mark 101, 204*n*10, 220

Tabío, Juan Carlos 102, 106, 188, 207, 211, 221
Tango 44
Taranovsky, Kiril 50, 197*n*7
Tarantino, Quentin 162
Taylor, Claire 69, 220
Tellería, Isabel 39, 179, 210
Terrasa, Jacques 201*n*6, 220

Thakkar, Amit 136, 137, 203*n*19, 220
Thibaudeau, Pascale 170, 204*n*12, 220
Thomas, Sarah 39, 220
Tierney, Dolores 196*n*14, 220, 221
Los Tigres del Norte 9, 195*n*5, 221
Torrecilla, Jesús 197*n*12, 221
Torrent, Ana **28**, 30, 179, 210, 221
Trueba, Fernando 22, 207

Ugalde, Gimeno 204*n*14, 212, 219
La vaquilla 22, 24, 221
La vida es sueño 128, 129

Vigne, David 78
Viridiana 24, 25, 221
Volek, Emil 2, 201*n*5

Walsh, María Elena 95
West, Dennis 107, 221
Whale, James 29, 196*n*14, 222
Wheeler, Duncan 178, 204*n*14, 221
Wilkinson, Stephen 116, 117, 221
Willem, Linda 60, 219, 222
Williams, Bruce 198*n*3, 222
Women on the Verge of a Nervous Breakdown see *Mujeres al borde de un ataque de nervios]*
"word" 71, 72, 73, 77, 78
"The Work of Art in the Age of Mechanical Reproduction" 13, 207

Zecchi, Barbara 204*n*13, 222
Zito Lema, Vicente 99

www.ingramcontent.com/pod-product-compliance
Lightning Source LLC
Chambersburg PA
CBHW032050300426
44116CB00007B/682